DATE DUE

DEMCO 38-296

OF

MAKING

MANY BOOKS

. .
.

PENN STATE REPRINTS
IN BOOK HISTORY

Edited by
James L. W. West III
and
Samuel S. Vaughan

This reprint series, which operates in conjunction with the Penn State Series in the History of the Book, aims to give second life to classic works in the field of publishing history. The series will include publishers' memoirs, house histories, and studies of particular developments in the book trade—the advent of the paperback, for example, or the rise of the literary agent, or the history of the best-seller, or the coming of the book club. Titles are to be divided in roughly equal proportions between American and British/Continental subjects. Each reprinted title will include a new introduction by a book historian or by a person from the world of trade publishing.

OF MAKING

MANY BOOKS

A Hundred Years of Reading, Writing and Publishing

by

ROGER BURLINGAME

The Pennsylvania State University Press
University Park, Pennsylvania

The original version of the introduction, by Charles Scribner, Jr., appeared in the *ALA Bulletin,* March 1957. The expanded version, by Charles Scribner III, was published first in a limited edition by the Rowfant Club, Cleveland, Ohio, in 1985; it has appeared also in volume 13 of the Documentary Series of the *Dictionary of Literary Biography.*

Typographical errors in the original edition at xi.25, 111.1, and 318.31 have been corrected for this reprinting.

Burlingame, Roger, 1889–1967.
    Of making many books : a hundred years of reading, writing, and
publishing / by Roger Burlingame.

          p.   cm. — (Penn State series in the history of the book)
    Includes index.
    ISBN 0-271-01619-1 (cloth : alk. paper)
    ISBN 0-271-01611-6 (paper : alk. paper)
    1. Charles Scribner's Sons—History.   2. Publishers and
publishing—United States—History—19th century.   3. Publishers and
publishing—United States—History—20th century.   I. Title.
II. Series.
    Z473.C46B87   1997
    070.5—dc20   96-14230
                                                                CIP

Reprinted, with a new introduction, in 1996
by The Pennsylvania State University Press, Suite C,
820 N. University Drive, University Park, PA 16802,
by arrangement with Scribner, An Imprint of
Simon & Schuster Inc.

CONTENTS

INTRODUCTION

This history of Charles Scribner's Sons begins in 1846 with the publishing partnership of Isaac Baker and Charles Scribner. The younger partner, Scribner, was a New Yorker of twenty-five, who had graduated from Princeton in the class of 1840. He had first planned a career in the law, but because of his frail health he was told to give that up for something less strenuous; he turned to publishing as a more congenial profession. I wonder if the relative hardship of the two occupations would still be appraised in quite the same way. Would any doctor dare prescribe a career in publishing today?

The location selected for the new firm was an unused chapel in the old Brick Church (then called the Brick Meeting House) on the corner of Nassau Street and Park Row in downtown Manhattan. In those days the area was a kind of headquarters of the book trade; no doubt it was also comforting to set up shop within such hallowed walls. At that time, to start an independent publishing company—that is, a company devoted solely to book *publishing*—was something of an innovation. Most of the established houses had either grown out of printing plants, following the noble tradition of the sixteenth-century Plantin Press in Antwerp, or were offshoots of retail bookshops. On the one hand, a printer might venture into publishing to provide work for his presses; on the other, a bookseller might become a part-time publisher to supply extra books to sell in his store.

There were, however, practical advantages to Scribner's decision to be more specialized. Since the firm was able to start business without having to worry about the costs of keeping a manufacturing plant busy, it was possible to focus on the work of new authors, particularly American authors, without having to compete with others in publishing reprints of the best-selling writers from England—Sir Walter Scott, Macaulay, and the Victorian poets. In short, the firm set out to originate works, to discover fresh talent. It's still a good policy. I might add that in the nineteenth century the more lucrative occupation of American publishers was to issue unauthorized reprints of English writers. American publishers were consequently viewed by their English counterparts as just slightly worse than pirates on the high seas. (In those days there was no such thing as international copyright protection.)

According to modern tastes, not all of the first titles of Baker and Scribner would be candidates for the best-seller list. There were lots of theological treatises, most of them almost impenetrable today. I believe that the first work we published was an austere tome entitled *The Puritans and Their Principles* by Edwin Hall. How uncomfortably would that book stand on a shelf today nestled between some of our current best-sellers. Of course, nothing does more for a fledgling publishing house than its first best-seller, and I might not be here today were it not for the big sale, at the very beginning of our history, of a book entitled *Napoleon and His Marshals* by the Rev. J. T. Headley. By all accounts it was far from being a model of historical accuracy—but then how many best-sellers are?

There were also the familiar and more trying cases in which the first book or books of an author were disappointments. For instance, there was Donald G. Mitchell, who wrote under the pen-name "Ik Marvel" and who came to the firm after one decidedly non-bestseller at another house.

Scribner decided to invest in Mitchell's future, but the second book, *Battle Summer*, about the author's travels in Europe during the revolutions of 1848, was equally disappointing. His next book, however, *Reveries of a Bachelor*, published in 1850, caught on immediately and the hoped-for success was won in spades. I think the title might have helped. From then on Ik Marvel was, as we say, a name author—if a name we've since forgotten. A hundred years later, you might be interested to know, while my father was clearing out our printing plant in New York City, he came upon an antique box containing the original printing plates of *Reveries of a Bachelor*. It is difficult to explain why for so many decades these had escaped melting: perhaps through a series of oversights, but perhaps equally as a result of the irrational respect publishers have for a best-seller, even last century's.

Isaac Baker died in 1850 and that left Charles Scribner alone. It was a period of growth, and there were several new projects that did much to put the new firm on the map. Over the years Scribner had been building up a fine list of books on religion. This program reached a high point around the time of the Civil War when he set out to publish an American version of the mammoth work of German biblical scholarship, Lange's *Commentary on the Holy Scriptures*. Eventually completed in twenty-six large volumes—financed at enormous cost—the set was both a commercial and critical success. It was co-published in Britain by Clark of Edinburgh—something of a feather in the cap of the American firm, for Clark had already begun his own translation of Lange, which he then dropped in favor of Scribner's edition. Publishing ties are often very old, and here we have a good case in point since Scribners and T. and T. Clark of Edinburgh again collaborated on a revision of Hastings' *Dictionary of the Bible* almost a hundred years later.

In 1865 Charles Scribner and Company took its first step
into magazine publishing with the somewhat staid (that's an
understatement) *Hours at Home*. It was presented as a quasi-
religious magazine, one that would bring into every home
the virtues by which Americans were supposed to live. The
first issue included, as I recall, two short biographies of early
Christian saints, an article on the rivers of Palestine and, in
a similar vein, an article about the unsuccessful attempt by
missionaries to get the king of the Hawaiis to give up
drinking. The magazine, unlike the missionaries, was successful, and plans were soon made to transform it into
something far more ambitious.

In 1870 a new imprint, Scribner & Company, was formed
to publish a successor magazine entitled *Scribner's Monthly*,
"an illustrated magazine for the people." (The first twelve
issues were collected and reprinted a few years ago to mark
our 125th anniversary, so you may actually find some copies
of *Scribner's Monthly* still around.) The magazine thrived and
was soon strong enough to attract young American writers.
But the founder did not live to see its success, for Charles
Scribner died of typhoid the next year, 1871, on a trip
abroad. Behind him in the firm he left his eldest son, John
Blair, and on this young man—he was only twenty at the
time—fell the whole job of carrying on the family interests
in the business.

It was, however, hardly a period of marking time. In two
years Scribner & Company launched a famous children's
periodical, *St. Nicholas*, under the editorship of Mary Mapes
Dodge, with the prolific Frank R. Stockton as assistant editor. Stockton is perhaps best remembered today for his short
story "The Lady or the Tiger?" The magazine brought many
now-classic books to the publishing firm and established it
permanently in the field of children's literature. Mary Mapes

Dodge's own novel, *Hans Brinker, or the Silver Skates,* first published under the Scribner imprint in 1876 and still enjoyed by new generations of readers, is an example of one such offspring of *St. Nicholas* magazine. In a somewhat different vein was the *American Boy's Handy Book,* published in 1882 by the truly immortal Dan Beard. I say "truly immortal" because we still get letters addressed to him. In this connection I have to tell a story on myself: when I first took over our Scribner paperback program in 1976, we had a "new" paperback on the list entitled *Shelters, Shacks, and Shanties* by D. C. Beard and I tried (very hard) to locate its countercultural, "back-to-nature" author before discovering that he was long since dead and that the book had originally been published in 1914!

A second important development at that time was the coming of age of the subscription book department, which began to undertake some very big things. In association with Messrs. Black of Edinburgh, Scribners brought out the first American edition of the *Encyclopaedia Britannica* (ninth edition); it sold some seventy thousand sets, *four times* as many as were sold in Britain. In those days publishers liked to play up the size of sales figures by various imaginary calculations, and thus Scribners advertised that if all those volumes of the encyclopaedia were laid end to end they would reach "from New York to beyond Omaha"—an inspiring thought. Perhaps this explains "Scribner, Nebraska" (look it up on the map).

In later years the subscription department published library sets of the works of such well-known authors as Kipling, Stevenson, Henry James, and J. M. Barrie—to name just a few. Its successor, the reference book department, is today, more than a century later, the foremost American publisher of reference works such as the *Dictionary of Ameri-*

can Biography, the *Dictionary of American History*, and several other series which we'll get to later. It is no exaggeration to say it's our crown jewel.

But let's return to the 1870s, for that was a critical decade. In 1875, Charles Scribner II had graduated from Princeton and at once joined his brother John Blair in the firm. There were two other partners at the time, Edward Seymour and Andrew Armstrong. But Seymour died in 1877, and the next year Armstrong sold the Scribners his share, intending to start up his own concern (foolish man). That left the book publishing company wholly owned and controlled by the Scribner family. The name was now changed to Charles Scribner's Sons. The very next year, in 1879, John Blair died, leaving Charles II, who was then only twenty-five, to manage the business alone. At first he was to have his hands full. For one thing, there were rumblings in the magazine subsidiary, Scribner & Company; the other owners, it seemed, chafed at being in any way beholden to Charles Scribner's Sons (perhaps they chafed at being beholden to a twenty-five-year-old). In any event, they talked of publishing books themselves; each side soon regarded the other as the tail trying to wag the dog. When in 1881 one of the outside partners, Roswell Smith, bought up enough stock to acquire individual control, the equilibrium was disturbed. Since C.S. II refused to retain a minority interest in his business, he sold to Smith all of Scribner's share in the magazine company. Thus *Scribner's Monthly* and the children's magazine *St. Nicholas* passed entirely out of the hands of the Scribner family. The remaining owners were reincorporated as the Century Company; *Scribner's Monthly* was by agreement renamed the *Century Magazine*, and the rest, as they say, is history. Under the terms of the sale, Charles Scribner's Sons agreed to stay out of the magazine business for five years. To judge from what happened later, it seems that Scribner kept his eye on the clock.

The next decisive step taken by C.S. II had to do with the textbook business. Beginning in the 1850s the firm had built up a solid and celebrated list of school books, but this area of publishing was becoming increasingly specialized, perhaps too much so for what was then primarily a trade house. In any case, in 1883 Scribner announced the sale of his entire list of school books to Ivison, Blakeman, Taylor & Company, one of the largest educational houses in the United States.

Within four years of taking over, Charles II had pruned the firm down drastically. But he was by nature a builder, and we can be sure that while part of the business was being dismantled he'd already begun to think of something much bigger and better to set up in its place. The new educational department that he started ten years after the sale of the old one is a good case in point. In 1884 his younger brother, Arthur Hawley Scribner, having graduated from Princeton, came into the firm to help him. (This is an admittedly familiar refrain, one that recurs at regular intervals through-out our family history.) The two brothers formed a partner-ship that lasted almost fifty years. The firm soon benefited from the initial pruning, for the remaining branches flow-ered as never before. Many of the American authors it introduced are still famous. There was H. C. Bunner, whose first book of poems, *Airs from Arcady and Elsewhere*, came out in 1884 in an edition of fifteen hundred copies. Even a century ago the market for new poets was rather special—now, regrettably, it is virtually nonexistent. George Washing-ton Cable first appeared in print in *Scribner's Monthly* with a short story, " 'Sieur George," in 1873. Six years later several of his stories were collected and published as the beloved

Old Creole Days. Another cherished Southern connection was Thomas Nelson Page, whose book *In Ole Virginia* was the first of many about the South.

Now, lest it be thought that the firm was the literary heir of the Confederacy alone, I hasten to add some names from other parts of the country. There was Henry Adams, whose *History of the United States* was published in 1889–91 in nine volumes and whose ironical letters to the firm offer a model for any difficult author to follow. Henry Van Dyke, "Poet, preacher, author, university teacher, diplomat" (to quote our *Dictionary of American Biography*; a Princeton colleague described him as the only man able to strut while sitting down), started out on the Scribner list with a pamphlet entitled *The National Sin of Literary Piracy* in 1888; how his publisher must have loved that one. Van Dyke wrote another book several years later that caused a rather awkward situation: the book was entitled *Fisherman's Luck* and, to its publisher's bad luck, the title contained a prominent and equally regrettable single-letter misprint that almost put Scribners instantly out of business and the author into an early grave.

Three famous children's books of that period were Edward Eggleston's *Hoosier Schoolboy* in 1883; Howard Pyle's *The Merry Adventures of Robin Hood*, also in 1883, and Frances Hodgson Burnett's *Little Lord Fauntleroy* in 1886. Robert Louis Stevenson first appeared on the list in 1885 with *A Child's Garden of Verses*. A later edition of this book, with pictures by Jessie Willcox Smith, was one of the original titles in the "Scribner Illustrated Classics," still in print today. These classics later became famous for their illustrations by Howard Pyle, N. C. Wyeth, and other members of the Brandywine school.

During the 1880s, ideas for a new magazine were being thought out as Charles Scribner waited out the five-year moratorium on magazine publishing. It was virtually inconceivable that he could have been content without a magazine. As a boy of fifteen he had started up a little comic monthly called *Merry Moments* and soon had to give it up, not because it proved unsuccessful but because to his father's way of thinking it was far *too* successful for a full-time schoolboy. Few could have been surprised, then, in December 1886 when the clock struck twelve, so to speak, and the firm announced the new *Scribner's Magazine*. Its original editor, from 1887 to 1914, was Edward L. Burlingame, son of the American diplomat Anson Burlingame and literary adviser to Scribners since 1879. Under him the magazine grew into something finer and more successful than the most hopeful would have dared to foresee. But to tell the story of the magazine, to cover its contribution to American literature and American life for more than half a century, is beyond the scope of this introduction. Yet its history would include the very writers whose books helped to build the reputation of the publishing firm, for the magazine was really a double asset to Charles Scribner's Sons: not only in itself, as a profitable magazine, but also as a net for new talent, authors like Edith Wharton who would follow their magazine debuts with many successful books.

In 1894 the firm capped the climax of fifteen years under C.S. II by moving into a stately, six-story building on Fifth Avenue and 21st Street designed by the renowned American Beaux-Arts architect Ernest Flagg. Flagg happened to be Scribner's brother-in-law—nepotism was also a family tradition. On the ground floor was a magnificent bookstore, the prototype for the more famous store on 48th Street and Fifth Avenue. (Incidentally, the Scribner building and bookstore on 21st Street later was sold and became a toy warehouse; I hope that's not in some way prophetic.) Scribners was to remain at 21st and Fifth for nineteen years, until 1913, during which time a cornucopia of new authors was added to the house. This was truly a "golden age" of American book publishing, and I don't think there can be any doubt that at the turn of the century Scribners had virtually cornered the market on American literature.

Among our native authors was Theodore Roosevelt, whose *Rough Riders* in 1899 was the first of many successful books for Scribners. The editors tended to get a little carried overboard after the author moved to the White House. On the jacket of one of his books the copy-writer hailed him as the "American Homer," which provoked a spate of scornful letters from readers protesting the hyperbole. The embarrassed President asked his editor, "Why at least couldn't you have said *Herodotus*?" Another lasting association was begun in 1896 with the publication of a book on aesthetics, *The Sense of Beauty*, by a young philosophy teacher at Harvard, George Santayana. Almost forty years later Santayana produced a best-selling novel, *The Last Puritan*, published in 1935. It would be hard to think of another philosopher equally versatile in letters. Edith Wharton's first book, written in collaboration with Ogden Codman, Jr., *The Decoration of Houses*, started a now famous career (though not in decorating); not long ago the book was reissued in paperback, which says something about the cycles of taste.

Not long after, two other distinguished authors made their debuts, Ernest Seton-Thompson (who later, to the confusion of librarians and card cataloguers, reversed his surnames), with *Wild Animals I Have Known*, published in 1898, and James Huneker, whose *Mezzotints in Modern Music* followed a year later. The turn of the century brought another cluster of famous first editions. John Fox, Jr.'s *Blue Grass and Rhododendron* appeared in 1901; two years later

Scribners published his novel *The Little Shepherd of Kingdom Come*, which is probably the most successful best-seller the house has ever had. A different sort of novelist, Henry James, appeared on the list with *The Sacred Fount* in 1901. Sadly, his greatest fame was to come long after his death, but James did live to see the great New York Edition of his novels and stories, which was published by the firm beginning in 1907 and was reissued by us in its entirety in the 1950s.

The year 1913 marked a new chapter in the history of the house. In that year another move was made up Fifth Avenue to the new and even larger Ernest Flagg building at 48th Street. (Charles Scribner believed in keeping his brother-in-law busy.) This was the third headquarters since Charles II's presidency and the scene of the last of the two almost equal periods in his fifty years with the firm. Scribner had been fielding a whole new team of young editors, the most famous of whom was Maxwell Perkins, whose correspondence with Ernest Hemingway will be published in time for our 150th anniversary. I think it is probably one of the clearest windows into the world of editor-author relations. Lest I sound too worshipful of Perkins, let me tell you two stories that you won't find in Scott Berg's near-definitive biography. On one occasion Thomas Wolfe was not too happy with the major surgery that Perkins performed on his manuscripts, which had arrived—literally—in crates. His ego bruised, Wolfe came into Perkins's office and saw on the desk an ashtray given to the editor by the Western writer Will James and fashioned in the shape of a coiled rattlesnake. Wolfe pointed to it and ceremoniously announced: "Portrait of an editor."

Another story, about a best-selling and still-living novelist, reveals the "passive" side of Perkins's editorial technique.

One day this writer came in with her manuscript. She was agonizing and going through the torments of the damned: how was she ever going to get the book written and how was she going to develop her characters and so forth? Perkins sat attentively "taking notes"—doodling pictures of Napoleon, as was his habit. With his hearing aid turned off he was almost stone deaf: he heard nothing of the author's impassioned monologue. He just sat there the whole time nodding and making appropriate social noises and doodling until finally, after about an hour, his troubled author stood up, heaved a great sigh of relief, and said: "Max, I can't tell you how helpful you've been: your advice is infallible." The legend endures.

Another well-known Scribner editor, and a distinguished poet in his own right, was John Hall Wheelock. These two men, Perkins and Wheelock, were both young Harvard graduates who invaded a then predominantly Princeton company and brought it great many new successes by their editorial intuition and skill.

In 1913 Charles Scribner's only son, another Charles (III), graduated from Princeton and began his own career in publishing. He was a contemporary of Perkins and Wheelock, and his age gave him a ready grasp of the importance of the new writers who were beginning to appear on the scene. Another era in American literature was dawning, and the firm's enthusiasm for the new authors was to yield it a rich harvest. There was Alan Seeger, whose *Poems* came out in 1916, best remembered for his "rendezvous with death." Four years later, F. Scott Fitzgerald heralded the jazz age with his first novel, *This Side of Paradise*. Stark Young's *The Flower in Drama* appeared in 1923 and, in the following years, Ring Lardner's *How to Write Short Stories* (1924), James Boyd's *Drums* (1925, a year best remembered for *The Great*

Gatsby), and John W. Thomason, Jr.'s *Fix Bayonets* (also in 1925). In 1926 Ernest Hemingway's *The Torrents of Spring* and *The Sun Also Rises* were both published. In view of Hemingway's later achievements and his equally enduring loyalty to the firm, we shall always think of that as a year set apart. Thomas Wolfe, at the end of this glorious decade, made his debut with *Look Homeward, Angel* in 1929—a year otherwise remembered less favorably.

Around this time, the long career of Charles Scribner II was drawing to a close; "Old C.S.," they now called him, *sotto voce*. In 1928, he turned over the presidency to his younger brother Arthur and continued only as chairman of the board. (Well, "only" is perhaps not quite the right word; I gather he interfered in everything: older brothers never change their spots.) Happily, he lived to see the first published volumes of the *Dictionary of American Biography*, a project which extended from 1928 to 1937 and a work to which he had given his utmost support: it was probably the most important project the firm had ever undertaken and was developed with the American Council of Learned Societies, which has subsequently collaborated with Scribners on other reference projects. In 1930 Charles II died and was followed two years later by the loyal and patient Arthur, leaving Charles III (my grandfather) to preside alone. He was only forty-two at the time.

It would be hard to think of a more difficult time in which to take over the management of a large publishing house. The Great Depression was in its worst stage, and the future must have appeared most uncertain for books. Yet the firm continued to look for fresh talent and take chances on new authors in a way that marks this as one of the most enterprising periods in all our history—an achievement that testifies to the aims and courage of C.S. III and to the devoted support that his associates, Max Perkins in particular, gave him. In the following years many important new works appeared, not only by already established authors such as Fitzgerald, Hemingway, and Wolfe, but also the first books of many then relatively unknown writers who were later to become famous. Among these firsts by new authors were Marcia Davenport's great biography of Mozart, published in 1932 and still in print; Nancy Hale's *The Young Die Good* (a title I always get wrong), also in 1932; Marjorie Kinnan Rawlings's *South Moon Under*, in 1933—followed by her most famous novel, *The Yearling*, five years later; Hamilton Basso's *Beauregard*, in 1933; Taylor Caldwell's *Dynasty of Death*, in 1938, and Christine Weston's *Be Thou the Bride*, in 1940. An extraordinary decade of debuts.

The years preceding World War II also saw the growth of a new children's book department under the gifted editorial direction of Alice Dalgliesh. Until this time there was no formal distinction at Scribners between children's books and adult books: children's books were simply considered part of general adult book publishing, a potentially dangerous situation when it came to making publishing decisions. When *The Wind in the Willows*, still one of our juvenile bestsellers, was originally submitted to my great-grandfather, there was no way he was going to publish it; he thought it was a lot of nonsense and foolishness, "something only a child would want to read." Fortunately, President Theodore Roosevelt, on whose recommendation the book had been submitted, persuaded him otherwise. So in the 1930s a separate children's department was finally established and soon became one of the more flourishing branches of the firm. It was founded by Alice Dalgliesh, who in 1934 was already an experienced editor and, indeed, author in her own right. She proceeded to build one of the most distinguished lists of children's books in American publishing. I might note that, having joined the firm as the first female editor, she had been there already three or four days before she went to see my grandfather, who liked her very much and wanted to know how she was getting on. "Oh, just fine, Mr. Scribner, but there is one thing I'd like." "Of course," he said, "What is it?" "Do you think I might have a desk?" And he replied, "Well, yes, I don't see why not. Of course you can. It just never occurred to us you'd need one." And so with Miss Dalgliesh the women's movement dawned at 597 Fifth Avenue.

At the same time the 1930s also saw some sad losses. Thomas Wolfe was the most visible, a loss due primarily to his own self-proclaimed dependence on his editor, Max Perkins, which not surprisingly led to his desire to sever that editorial umbilical cord. Then, in 1937, *Scribner's Magazine* folded after fifty glorious years of publication, a casualty of newer and slicker magazines and, I suppose, of the radio.

Right after the war, yet another Charles Scribner (IV or Jr.: my father, out of Princeton and back from service) joined the firm. It was to be the last year of Max Perkins's life, but he left behind two budding novelists, James Jones and Alan Paton. Now the manner of Alan Paton's arrival at Scribners is an unusual one. His manuscript came in "over the transom," for it hadn't got farther than the post office when its box broke open and the manuscript fell into complete disarray. Somebody was called from Scribners and actually went and pieced it together. Fortunately, he also brought it back to Scribners and gave it to Perkins to read. And so *Cry, the Beloved Country* came to be published in 1948. It had a first printing of five thousand copies, and within a year after publication there were one hundred and twenty-five thousand copies in print, a fitting debut for that courageous South African writer.

In 1952 Charles III died very suddenly; he had just finished reading the manuscript of Hemingway's short classic, *The Old Man and the Sea*, which was dedicated to him and Perkins, Papa's two closest friends and mentors at Scribners. Although Perkins had always been Hemingway's official editor and had corresponded with him extensively, the only "editor" from whom Hemingway ever accepted suggestions was my grandfather. Nobody else could get Hemingway to change a word.

After his father's death, Charles Scribner, Jr., moved back from Washington, where he'd been sent as a cryptanalyst during the Korean War, and took the helm at the ripe age of thirty-one. Now you'll recall his grandfather had had to do the same at twenty-five, one tradition we can live without. One of his first moves was to close the Scribner printing and warehousing plant, which had operated since 1908. It was a few blocks down the street and had been designed, again by Ernest Flagg, as a complete manufacturing unit. But new economic realities indicated that even a relatively large firm could not profitably support its own printing plant.

Publishing in general had entered a new era. Shortly after C.S., Jr. took over, he got a phone call from a Hollywood producer who wanted to know the title of the most recent Philo Vance mystery. (The Philo Vance mysteries—the *Canary Murder Case*, the *Benson*, the *Greene*, the *Bishop*, and so forth—were written by S. S. Van Dine in the 1920s and 1930s, and were very successful; all of them had been made into movies.) Well, Scribner thought a moment and said the last one was the *Gracie Allen Murder Case*. The producer replied, "Oh, no, no, no, I know the *Gracie Allen*; that's not the one I want; that was written ten years ago. I want the most recent, the last one." Scribner responded, "Well, that *is* the last one." The producer exclaimed, "It can't be. What happened?" "What happened is simple. The author died." To which the producer replied with utter incredulity, "Well, you didn't have to let the *series* die, did you?" Indeed, book publishing had entered a new era.

Now in a different spirit Scribner set out to recapture some of our past—our backlist, you might say our literary capital, most of which had by this time been licensed to paperback and cheap-hardcover reprinters. He wanted to bring these books back under the Scribner imprint. This move was soon to prove invaluable. Admittedly, he had no intention at the time of putting them into paperback himself—in fact, one of the reasons he was taking them back was that he didn't *like* paperbacks. He didn't believe in them and compared having your own in-house paperback line to keeping you own pet cobra in your living room. But he soon changed his mind—albeit reluctantly—and invented the Scribner Library, our own line of quality paperbacks, at which point he now had at his disposal a cornucopia of classics to convert into paperbacks, beginning with *The Great Gatsby, Tender Is the Night, The Sun Also Rises, Ethan Frome*, and so on. His industry colleagues credited him with uncanny foresight and patience in reverting all those licenses in preparation for the new Scribners paperback line. In publishing it's the result, not the motive, that counts.

I think it's fair to say that by the 1950s the star-studded Perkins years had left an unfortunate legacy. The editors were on the perpetual lookout for the new Hemingway or Wolfe to arrive—like Godot. Their attention was fixed on the fiction front, to the exclusion of other areas of publishing. To restore some balance to the list—and a balanced list is essential to a publisher's survival—Scribner set out to develop fields of nonfiction: history, biography, how-to books. He hired a most gifted editor, Elinor Parker, who invented a new category in practical arts, the needlepoint book, the first of which was Erica Wilson's *Crewel Embroidery*. But Charles Scribner, Jr.'s own true love was for reference works, and these years saw the birth of works that have become the staple of every major school, college, and public library. He completed the *Album of American History* and began the *Dictionary of Scientific Biography*, a fifteen-year project sponsored by the American Council of Learned Societies with a grant from the National Science Foundation. It has since become the model for multivolume reference works of original scholarship. There followed the *Dictionary of the History of Ideas*, the *Dictionary of Foreign Policy*, and, again with the American Council of Learned Societies, the magisterial *Dictionary of the Middle Ages*. These series are especially important today when libraries are increasingly short of funds for purchasing monographs. By the 1970s the reference department had become the new creative center of publishing at Scribners.

During the 1970s the sales force was greatly enlarged, ensuring national distribution for all Scribner books as well as for other publishers distributed by Scribners. During the sixties and seventies Scribners also became far more active in acquiring books from British firms and publishing the works of British authors, both established and new. One example is Anthony Burgess's literary biography of Hemingway. Another is the crime novelist P. D. James; now hailed as the reigning successor to Agatha Christie and Dorothy Sayers, she finally broke into bestsellerdom after *seven* books written during the course of two decades.

In the context of my thumbnail history of Scribners very little of recent times is truly new; we were doing much the same a century ago. In effect, the postwar decades may be viewed as a recapitulation of earlier themes; that is to say, striking a balanced list, recognizing the importance of non-fiction, maintaining a backlist, bringing out series of books such as reference sets, and co-publishing with British firms. Soon after I joined Scribners in 1975, my first editorial project was to revive, edit, and write an introduction to the one, and long-forgotten, play of F. Scott Fitzgerald, *The Vegetable, or from President to Postman.* That was my way of taking a gentle step from the halls of academia to the realities of Fifth Avenue, involving as it did many glorious hours spent within our publishing archives, which had been donated to Princeton a decade earlier. It was also a good introductory lesson that old books can become new books. Since then there have been many exciting developments at the firm. Our list is always expanding, and several new talents have been launched, of which P. D. James, now the Baroness James, is an outstanding example as well as a personal favorite. I think it is fair to say that a very special place in our collective hearts will always belong to the newly launched novelist, and that's as it should be.

In 1984 we took the most important step since our founding when we accepted the offer to merge into Macmillan and become part of its thriving and extended publishing family. A more promising home could not have been imagined for our reference, juvenile, college, and trade departments and authors. Macmillan books were originally introduced and distributed in America by Charles Scribner in 1859. A hundred and twenty-five years later we had come full circle—which is what history is all about.

In the fall of 1988 Macmillan, our parent company, was the subject of a hostile takeover by Robert Maxwell. For the next four years it continued to sail under Maxwell's flag until, after that tycoon's mysterious death and the debacle of his debt-ridden empire, it was sold to Simon and Schuster just prior to the latter's acquisition by Viacom. Today the invigorated Scribner imprint—both in adult trade books and library reference works—continues to flourish within Simon and Schuster as it celebrates its sesquicentennial in 1996.

A few years ago my father expressed his concern about the future of that antiquated object, the book, to General Sarnoff of RCA. They were having lunch together, and Scribner got up the courage to ask whether Sarnoff thought the book would survive the present revolution of technology and mass communication: that is to say, films, cassettes, video, and others yet undreamed of. "No need to worry," assured the General. "Just remember there are more candles sold annually in the United States today than a hundred years ago." A consoling thought.

In a very special way, books themselves provide illumination. Once removed from the shelf, the best give off a steady, glowing light—hardly strobe or flash, and certainly not neon; the light they radiate is mellower and warmer. So unless IBM or RCA or Xerox has a surprise in store for us all, I don't imagine you'll see the Scribner lamp imprinted on a box of candles for some time to come.

Charles Scribner III
New York, 1996

PUBLISHER'S NOTE
TO THE FIRST EDITION

This book marks the hundredth anniversary of a publishing house. As the year 1946 approached, it seemed to those directing the house that the publication of a book was the most natural way of signalizing the event. It was felt, however, that a merely formal history could interest only those engaged in publishing and bookselling. Furthermore, such a history could not rightly present the essential truth about a publishing house: that whatever honor or glory it may have is reflected from the writers associated with it. The story of bookmaking is most accurately recorded in the interchange of letters between author and publisher, and fortunately the letters of this house are practically complete since its earliest days.

The value of this mass of correspondence, as far as this book is concerned, could be realized only if it were placed in the hands of a writer equipped to select what was most relevant and to interpret its meaning. Roger Burlingame proved to be a happy choice for this undertaking, as the circumstances of his life had made him intimate with the history of the house. He has had complete freedom of access to all files, and those directing the house have sought to avoid any interference with this book by injecting personal suggestions. This is his book, based on his personal knowledge and on material gleaned from the files. Since this was to be a picture of the past, it was agreed that the use of letters should be limited to those of authors who were no longer living. In the few cases where living authors are mentioned or quoted, the subject under discussion would have been inadequately treated without their inclusion. Permission has been obtained from the heirs for the use of the letters quoted, wherever that was possible.

[xxvii]

The Scribner Building at 597 Fifth Avenue.
Scribner Papers, Princeton University Library.

PREFACE
TO THE FIRST EDITION

To the outsider, correspondence with authors is surely the most appealing part of a publisher's record. Specialists in other businesses are, of course, fascinated by the publisher's peculiar problems such as the narrowness of profit margins, the fantastic elusiveness of sales, the breakdown of normal advertising formulas — to the point where it seems incredible that a publisher can survive at all — let alone for a full century of spectacularly changing American time. But even these other merchants, sellers of soap or land, bonds or service or mere "good will," must, as they ponder the publisher, finally focus on the mystic factor which makes his business differ from all others — which almost stops his business from being a business at all — his author. For here is an outside factor, an independent being, a human, changeable, unpredictable, sometimes disordered and often ornery critter on whom a publisher is ultimately wholly dependent and who, in turn, is helpless without him.

Where, indeed, is there anything like it in business history? Does the inventor force a manufacturer of machines into a similar uncertainty? No, for an inventor is vulnerable; there are statutes and lawyers and a dozen evasions in the manufacturer's bag of tricks against him. Even an actor, singer or acrobat in the showman's business is there in the shop — he can be dealt with, discreetly, yes, but at close range. He is not in Tibet, Samoa or the Hebrides while his employer, with all his precarious plant, is in New York. So the student of business, unless, as many do, he either sets publishing aside as over his depth or condemns it beyond the pale of economic law, must study first of all this extremely substantial ghost outside the gate.

But most of all the general public, to whom this book is presented, is interested in the author and in how his inner thinking becomes print and paper which can be bought, sold, hired, borrowed; which can be consumed a thousand times and remain always ready for new consumption; which, indeed, can be burnt to a crisp and survive. All this is engrossing mystery to ordinary folk to whom other business is usual and understood.

It is true that part of the public is curiously informed on certain aspects. There are those who think of books as produced by a staff working along an assembly line from typewriter to dust-jacket. There are readers who seldom read or remember an author's name and never a publisher's. There are others who think only of the author; who regard the publisher as his employee or service man through whom, however, he acquires a fabulous fortune. And in still other quarters, there is a persistent legend that the author is a poor, exploited creature whom the publisher browbeats, conceals and turns, eventually, into a prostitute for his own enrichment. And many who have walked around the lunatic periphery of literature, suppose a classic conflict between author and publisher in which even a moment's armistice would be unthinkable.

Having served in both camps, I am in a peculiar spot at the threshold of this book. It is a delicate position because I have seen both truth and fallacy in some of these estimates. I grew up in the nomansland between the publishing tradition and my own violent wish to write. My father was the editor of *Scribner's Magazine*. He was committed two ways, yet friendly to authors. He was committed, first, to his own understanding of literature which had set high levels. But he was committed, too, to a business which must live. He knew that art might please even when it failed, in its entirety, to please him but he refused to let it degrade, whatever the pleasure. He was fortunate in working under a captain who never accepted the dictatorship of business over taste or truth.

Yet there was tension and I felt it. There was long patience with the author on one side, whose part this editor must sometimes take, and with the publisher on the other, whose part he must sometimes oppose. There was the breathless struggle for space, for my father wanted what was good printed, and the moments of saying no were bitter. Yet the publisher's back could not be broken. There was the struggle with the public which said its yes and no often with violent ignorance. To give this public education without giving it indigestion was one of the hardest jobs he and his great colleague William Crary Brownell had to meet.

The tension did not break my father but it determined him to keep me out of both Houses. He had seen authors bend and crack under their art and he had seen publishers dismal over their ledgers. He told me: Be an engineer. Be a lawyer, he said with less conviction.

When, in engineering, calculus stopped me, my father saw that the curse was on me. He read some of my writing and told me with agony that it was good. Finally, when Mr. Scribner offered me a job, he was almost happy, and I knew then that he was sure it was the lesser evil. At worst it would delay me from the desperate author's trade.

It delayed me ten years. Work in a publishing house is not inspiriting to a young author's ambitions. Soon after I began, a friend asked me what I did. "I am an office boy," I said. "On a good day, I can lick a thousand stamps." I think some word of my bitterness got to Mr. Brownell, for one day he said to me, taking me in, in his charming way, on his own level: "Isn't it true, Roger, that ninety-nine per cent of the time, we are doing work that any office boy could do as well?" Then he looked a long time out the window across Fifth Avenue and turned suddenly. "But once a month," he said, "or once every six months, there comes a moment which no one but you could cope with. Into that single moment of work goes all your education, all your background, all the thinking of your life." So was written the first entry of my inestimable debt to one of the greatest men I have had the fortune to know.

In the ten years, I learned the worst of authors and the best of publishers. I had to tease, cajole, humor, placate and scold angry and brooding men and women who had found a superfluous semicolon or refused to believe a royalty report or searched the *Times* in vain for an advertisement or been unable to buy a copy of their precious books in Brentano's or received a long-suffering bill for corrections, after illegibly rewriting a book on the page-proof; and others who believed that the entire House of Scribner had been erected and maintained for the exclusive delight of printing their books. Against this I saw on the inside the persistent struggle to reconcile cost with beauty of manufacture, the generous adjustment of royalty to "plant," the failure of advertising and the inexplicable moments when expected best-sellers stopped in the midst of their first editions.

Yet youth is a curious thing. I was still young when I left Scribners to beat my path as a so-called free-lance author. I forgot my lessons as quickly as I had learned them. When my first dubious literary conceptions attained the flesh of print, I too haunted the bookstores, complained about advertising, royalty, semicolons and jackets with the worst of them and referred to the unhappy gentlemen who had tried to break even on my efforts as "confidential publishers." Yet there were grievances too that I think will still stand scrutiny. So today I can read an author's lament to his publisher with more understanding than if I had never written one to mine, and I can see a deal of background behind the patient, irritated or evasive lines of the publisher's reply.

So, in my maturity, when forgotten things are suddenly remembered and balance one another with a surprising symmetry, I face the task of this book with sympathetic eagerness, for in its material is a macrocosm, gigantic in its magnification, of my own life. And the tradition of this House, vast, legendary and mysterious, seasoned my earliest nourishment. To have opened to me now the total truth; to be able to discern fact from myth and find the result even finer in quality and pattern than my fancy, is an experience which is more than satisfying in the fullness of its circle.

From all these personal currents combined with a hopeful sense of what the reader will want to read, has evolved a book which is in no usual sense a history. I have attempted no chronological narrative, nor are the letters and other records arranged in any scheme of time. The basic truths of the story are, indeed, timeless. Thus we will find in a letter of the 1840's the same mood, the same ambition, the same perplexity that we will find in one written a century later. The phrasing is altered by manners, but the subject is the important thing. So I have grouped the letters by subject. I have juxtaposed, for example, letters of Thomas Wolfe and Henry James on the loneliness of their art. I have shown identical complaints from Harold Frederic and Scott Fitzgerald. Letters from the first Charles Scribner and from his grandson expose the eternity of publishing problems.

With this arrangement, full focus is possible on the author-publisher relationship which is the only aspect of the business in which a layman can have any deep concern. Lest any author might feel a sense of injury from omission, I have adopted a single rule. I have included no letter from a living author. There is no similar restriction on letters by living publishers or editors (presumably immune to such feelings) even if they are written to living authors. In occasional instances where an editor is also an author I have quoted only letters written in his editorial capacity. The letters form, in their full collection, a pattern of the period as well as of the subject as complete, I believe, as any that could be garnered from a publisher's files. With a very few exceptions, none of them has ever before been published. Many reflect with sharpness the politics and morals of their time. There are letters written from the bottom of depression and from pinnacles of exaltation; letters from war, from jungles, from lazy south-sea isles.

So from the whole, history does at last emerge, not in dull chronicle, but in a continuity which, when the whole is read, is very definite. The movement of the trends of literature is as obvious as the movement from horse-car to airplane. If, from it all, the House of Scribner stands out as hero, it is because, with the most candid allusions to its villainy which I have ruthlessly included, the record was overwhelming. And it is the record, apart from all design by me or any other, which must be the arch of triumph through which the hero enters upon his second hundred years.

OF

MAKING

MANY BOOKS

• •
•

I

THE LONELY ART

Through the files of a publisher's correspondence with his creative authors runs a conflict of themes echoing the torment of the writing art. One is a cry for immediate help; the other is resignation to the conviction that direct help is forever impossible. Out of this conflict come despondency and exaltation. Out of it, too, in time, comes manuscript.

But writing is a lonely business. All through the record we feel the author reaching for something outside the blank sheet in his machine or on his table; for aid beyond the circle of his mind. For him there is no school but the library in which the technique of the masters is deeply hidden. There is no framework but of his own designing, no spectrum of colors, no floodlight, backdrop or proscenium arch. There are no "rules of speech" which may not be put aside, as Havelock Ellis once said, "if a writer is thereby enabled to follow more closely and lucidly the form and process of his thought."

So even the technique by which his created image is molded into words must be the product of the writer's solitary effort.

Tom Wolfe, standing on the outer threshold of his adolescence, discovered this truth and met it squarely.

"Alone in my mind," he wrote to John Hall Wheelock in the summer of 1929, "I know that I am now a man in years and as I face my work alone I am pretty close to naked terror, naked nothing. I know that no one can help me or guide me or put me right. . . ."

Yet once he had confessed the fear and recognized the re-solving truth, he found release.

"I am far from being melancholy," he went on. "I am more full of strength and power and hope than I have been in years. I have in me at the present time several books, all of which are full of life and variety, and rich detail. . . . I feel packed to the lips with rich ore . . . all America stretches below me like a vast plain, the million forms that repeat themselves in the city, and that torture us so by their con-fusion and number, have been fused into a calmer temper. . . . I want to tear myself open and show my friends all that I think I have. I am so anxious to lay all my wares out on the table — when one thing that I have done is praised to say, 'You have not seen 1/10 or 1/20 of what is in me. Just wait.'"

Wolfe lapsed at times into "the old child's belief — that there are older people who are wiser and stronger and who can help me." And they did help him to cut and arrange the immense mass of material which came out of his hermitage. Yet they never altered his thought or supplied his substance. They did not teach him to write. He learned alone and in his "Anatomy of Loneliness" he expressed what was almost a religion of soli-tude.

Many years before, Henry James had met "the terrible law of the artist" which forced him away from society and to the conclusion that without the companionship of his art, "for me, the world would be, indeed, a howling desert." Yet James, like Wolfe, found his power in lonely reflection. "When I practice it," he wrote in a notebook lately revealed by F. O. Matthies-sen,* "the whole field is lighted up — I feel again the multi-

*Henry James: The Major Phase, by F. O. Matthiessen. New York: Oxford University Press, 1944.

[2]

tudinous pressure of all human situations and pictures, the surge and pressure of life. All passions, all combinations are there."

This same sense of overwhelming potential — if only he could reach it — often drove F. Scott Fitzgerald into an agony of frustration. Fitzgerald loved people and the battle of ideas but he knew the dangers of his weakness. In a letter to Maxwell Perkins in 1924, he wrote:

> "I feel I have an enormous power in me now, more than I've ever had in a way but it works so fitfully and with so many bogeys because I've talked so much and not lived enough within myself to develop the necessary self reliance. Also I don't know anyone who has used up so much personal experience as I have at 27."

This passage from a long confession is singularly lucid in its analysis and packed with warning. The generations of authors who used the alibi of the search for "copy" as an excuse for social experience — and Fitzgerald was never one of them — came happily to an end as the curtain dropped on the romantic era; but those who have not yet learned what talk does to writing are more than ever with us. So in the world of 1946 with its tempting machinery for quick articulation, Fitzgerald's underscored words are more pertinent than when he wrote them.

Robert Louis Stevenson, who, more than most authors, was able to detach himself and watch his own intimate performance from a hill-top, wrote in his "Letter to a Young Gentleman who Proposes to Embrace the Career of Art," of the public's indifference to a writer's lonely labor.

> "The artist," he wrote, "works entirely upon honour. The public knows little or nothing of those merits in the quest

[3]

of which you are condemned to spend the bulk of your en-
deavors. Merits of design, the merit of first-hand energy,
the merit of certain cheap accomplishment which a man of
the artistic temper easily aquires — these they can recognize,
and these they value. But to those more exquisite refinements
of proficiency and finish, which the artist so ardently desires
and so keenly feels, for which (in the vigorous words of
Balzac) he must toil 'like a miner buried in a landslip,' for
which, day after day, he recasts and revises and rejects — the
gross mass of the public must be forever blind. To those lost
pains, suppose you attain the highest pitch of merit, pos-
terity may possibly do justice; suppose as is so probable, you
fail by even a hair's breadth, rest certain they shall never
be observed. Under the shadow of this cold thought, alone
in his studio, the artist must preserve from day to day his
constancy to the ideal."

So the record shows that authors who take their work seriously find no salvation outside themselves. This does not mean,
however, that they don't look for it. They do, and in the intervals between these stern confessions, probably always will.
From their dark waters they are forever sending out cries for
life-savers to be thrown them from the editorial ship. But
the editor on the bridge knows well enough that his author will likely swim directly away from the buoy into new
depths and save himself at last on some far shore of his own
choosing.

To his publisher, in thwarted moments, the author is humble.
There is, after all, no one else to whom he can turn. Most
of his friends are no good to him. If they are writers they
have their separate concerns, and even jealousies are not unknown among them. Husbands and wives — with occasional
impressive exceptions — inject emotional cross-currents into

their advice. But the interest of author and publisher is the same, however much each may fail in meeting it.

"I speak to my publisher," wrote Richard Harding Davis to Charles Scribner in 1892, "as I speak to my family physician." In this mood, an author will confess the same dismal reflections which torture the patient who suspects a cancer, and the same exultant relief when the doctor gives a happy diagnosis. So John Fox, Jr., sending in a manuscript, had been racked by doubt until the good word came.

"If you had jumped on me with both feet," he wrote to Charles Scribner, "and told me that the work was rotten all through — I'd have believed you and had not a word to say. Your second note was like a temporary stay to a toothache which Mr. Burlingame's letter cured completely today. You've no idea of the worry I've had with that story . . . and I've been writing in an unbroken nervous fit that has nearly driven me crazy. But the tension has snapped now. . . ."

And to Edward L. Burlingame, he replied to the letter which had accomplished such a feat of editorial dentistry, "it brought me the peace that passes understanding."

The same rise and fall of spirit were felt by Harold Frederic during the gestation of his impressive historical novel *In the Valley*, which still stands as a landmark in American regional literature. In October, 1886, he wrote Burlingame that he had begun it. "You will know," he said, "how to discount my statement of faith that it is to be the best thing of the kind ever done by an American." Three months later he sent in the first half which he had entitled *Douw Mauverenson* and not receiving an immediate acceptance, began discounting on his own account.

"I have been very nervous," he wrote, "and at times despondent, about 'Douw' since I sent the first half of it to you.

[5]

No doubt it was silly, but I could not help construing your silence to mean that it was no good. The result is that I have only done three additional chapters and these very badly. . . . You will let me know . . . as soon as possible, won't you?"

This periodic sinking is a prevailing symptom of the hypochondria of authorship. The most professional, the most successful writers are rarely immune to it.

"I am quite worked out," Stevenson wrote from the south Pacific, "and this cursed end of the Master [of Ballantrae] hangs over me like the arm of the gallows; but it is always darkest before dawn, and no doubt the clouds will soon rise; but it is a difficult thing to write, . . . and I cannot yet see my way clear. If I pull this off, the Master will be a pretty good novel or I am the more deceived. . . ."

"I am heartily glad," wrote J. M. Barrie about Tommy and Grizel, *"that you like the story. Often I was most depressed and my spirits went down like a bucket in a well when re-reading in the morning what I had written overnight but I suppose we are all like that."*

Some of the later authors, while perhaps no more harassed by these emotions, articulated them more violently. Thus Scott Fitzgerald in 1920 wrote to Maxwell Perkins that he had "decided to quit work and become an ash man." In April, 1924, he wrote:

"It is only in the last four months that I've realized how much I have — well, almost deteriorated *in the three years since I finished* The Beautiful and Damned."

Yet at this moment of self-accusation, he was in mid-career on *The Great Gatsby,* an incomparably better book as he realized in a sudden upswing four months later.

"I think my novel," he wrote about it in this restored mood, "is about the best American novel ever written."

And Thomas Wolfe, from a retreat in Switzerland, where his loneliness had been invaded by chattering people, wrote his publishers that "I have stopped writing and do not want ever to write again." Yet this was after the publication and immense literary success of *Look Homeward, Angel.* "There is no life in this world worth living," he added, "there is no air worth breathing. . . ."

Long experience teaches editors to appraise these moods and to treat them hardily. They have learned that despair must often hang in the gulf between the luminous image in an artist's mind and its flat reproduction on his paper. They know, however, that his view across will settle into a perspective if, in the interval, he can rest his eyes by some diversion. It is the peculiar genius of Maxwell Perkins, for example, to change the subject at the crisis of an author's self-complaint. He talks of other authors and other books or, provokingly, of politics until the writer, in his locked circle, becomes aware of a diverse and industrious world outside.

Once, when an author stood in Perkins's office pouring out his unhappiness, Perkins went to the window as if overcome by the burden of his sympathy. After a while, however, he said, without turning:

"You know I can't understand why all these busy people move so slowly. The only ones who move fast are the boys on roller skates who have nothing to do. Why don't we — why doesn't everybody — wear skates?"

William C. Brownell, when you met him face to face, seemed so intimate with all the great mass sorrows of the world, that an author felt shame for having added the featherweight of his own. Slowly, reluctantly, Brownell would come out of his cosmic communion into your presence and smiling suddenly

—but only with his eyes—he would make a wise, comic or sometimes even ribald comment on your tangle which would at least give a cathartic to your mind so that you could start afresh. But one had to work at Brownell's editorial treatment, especially if it were written. His criticism was so subtle in its suggestion that an author found health in the very effort of extracting its meaning. He was wise enough only to suggest, never to explain, leaving the author to work out for himself how to correct his writing.

"I think," he wrote to Olive Tilford Dargan about certain of her poems, "if you were to force yourself to take a thoroughly detached, objective view of them you would yourself see where & how you could give them more edge, make them more effective, organize them a little more crisply, give them more play, more focal points, group your iron filings around more nodes—I don't know what, exactly. Shoot them at a philistine mark would be perhaps in brief my counsel!"

Brownell's "I don't know what, exactly" pointed his belief that nothing must ever be forced upon the author—as if he said, "We will work this out together; I am as puzzled about it as you."

Burlingame's way (as it was his personal habit when he was troubled) was to fall back on the masters. The astonishing mechanics of his memory made the vast background of his reading useful to him and to his authors.

"Read Jessica's love scene," he would say to a distracted novelist, "in 'The Merchant of Venice.' Then I think this chapter of yours will come clear to you."

His use of books as tools was not, however, confined to accepted classics. Once when Edith Wharton was struggling with a paragraph of *The Fruit of the Tree* he referred her to a passage in *Guy Livingstone,* suggesting that "it might be worth while to glance at the perfervid old book and see how it reads."

With Mrs. Wharton, however, the problem of morale was not one with which her publisher had often to deal. She applied her own cures.

"After doing over 40,000 words of 'The Valley' without a break," she wrote Brownell in 1900, "I suddenly found the tank empty. I turned back to my short stories, and the change of air at once renewed my activity."

Once she showed as clearly as any author could, the effect of the long loneliness her work had forced upon her, and the suggestive help her publishers had given. In a letter to Burlingame which is strikingly reminiscent of Balzac's "miner buried in a landslip," she wrote:

> *"Your answer puts a finger on the two points that were troubling me . . . I shall restudy it* [The Fruit of the Tree] *in the helpful light of your comments, & I think it will come out as I want it to. Outer daylight does so much for me when I have been down in the mine too long."*

But the pathology of authors is, on the whole, less interesting than the picture which the record shows of writers healthily at work. Its chief value is in heartening apprentices; in proving to the earnest beginner that disease is a sporadic by-product of his work — that it is curable and that its after-effects are generally useful to him. For his normal progress, he may find some solider substance in the more dynamic moments of work and life.

It is probable that people of a later generation will shy away from any precept of James Barrie lest, perish the thought, it should make them "write like he did." He held one principle, however, which might prove useful to the most hard-boiled "realist" of our bright new world. He showed no one a job until it was finished.

"I seem to write very slowly nowadays," he wrote of Sentimental Tommy, *"the story is evidently to be longer than I fancied. It wd be fatal to it to send you a part to go on with, as all my work develops on new lines as I go on that necessitates changes at the beginning, and in rewriting I condense enormously, striking out the 'brilliant things.' I wish this had been otherwise for my sake as well as yours. For mine because it is no doubt true as you say, that I have been silent long enough, for yours because you want it. You have been very considerate, and I hope at least that Tommy will eventually do a good turn for both of us. He is only a boy as yet, rather afraid of becoming a man as if he knew I had designs on him."*

Here is the novelist who puts his plot in the hands of his characters. As his book grows and they develop into independent and wayward folk, he knows they will write his story for him. If he shows a part to his editor now, the editor will either demand a synopsis of the rest or, which is worse, he will write his own end in his mind and be disappointed when the author's story is finished.

Sherwood Anderson, of a very different temper, felt this strongly and had a superstition, as he wrote Maxwell Perkins in 1935, even against "talking about a novel while I am in it."

In later days, however, when authors are badgered by agents and publishers into selling their books before they are begun, or induced to talk over the radio or at cocktail parties in the literary lunatic fringe about half-finished scripts, such wisdom is difficult. Stout indeed is the character which can withstand these temptations, especially when money is attached or the threat that the busy public will "forget" unless steadily fed with such half-baked reminders.

Yet the honest artist is often still restrained by his reluctance to let an imperfect job into the press. A writer will sometimes become so engrossed in his eternal polishing that he will drive his publisher crazy with the delay and damage his script besides. There are stories of editors forcing their way into an author's house, diverting him with some bright object and snatching the paper from his hands. In such cases, the publisher must use a delicately balanced judgment, knowing as he does that an impatient move may either destroy or save a work of art. If he knows his author well he is unlikely to go wrong.

There are exceptions, of course — whole types of exceptions — who are outside any and all of these circles. There are many highly profitable workers in the writing trade who are not hurt by radio or movie or the tempo of the times or by any pressure a publisher may put upon them. But these do not strictly belong in a chapter labeled "The Lonely Art."

They are less lonely and their trade is not art in quite the same sense. This does not mean that they are not of high importance. These romancers, adventure and mystery writers who openly and frankly follow a formula beloved by a huge public are as essential to a publisher as his historians or his economists, his writers on salmon-fishing or metaphysics. Their work furnishes the elements of certainty in his ledgers and he can take a moral satisfaction in the knowledge that it refreshes millions of people in a tired world.

But these artisans have aids which are denied the subtler craftsmen. They still have to learn to write by writing, but there are rules in the construction of plot, the arrangement of incident; certain do's and don'ts which may be taught and remembered. They make, therefore, less complex demands upon their editor.

So it is a paradox of publishing that the literary department must give most of its time and worry to those who bring in the least sensational profit.

A publisher may explain that "success of esteem" is important enough in giving prestige (now called *kudos*) to his house to justify all the labor it may involve. He may explain that a classic brings substance to a publisher long after its author's death. He may say that he interests himself in a new author whose book he knows won't sell because that same author may one day write one which will. (And even the best books often do.) But whatever he may say, he does these things partly — however singular the thought may appear to an observer of ordinary business — because he loves it.

"And when can we see the novel?" a Scribner editor once wrote to his favorite author. "It gives me a great lift to hear that it is nearly finished; has not the month of my silence given time for it to be altogether done? I am decidedly hungry to get at it, for I know that it will be good and refresh eyes strained by scanning the horizon for something of the greater sort. Except for some half dozen of the elect, among whom I have learned to count you, I should very often have to come down like another Sister Anne and report that I couldn't see anything coming."

Yet while this editor was watching in his tower, the mill below was grinding full speed at the run of its stuff and the editor might easily have stayed below and watched the good money flow in.

II

TOOLS OF THE TRADE

"A man will turn over half a library," said Doctor Johnson, "to make one book."

It is easy to imagine Samuel Johnson engaged in this exercise. Those who divide literature into rigid categories for students who haven't time to read it, usually file Johnson away in the critical rather than the creative drawer and everyone knows that the material of a critic, historian, biographer or cyclopedist is ranged on shelves. The poet and novelist, on the other hand, are more usually seen by the public communing with nature or society and interpreting life direct.

But the record shows that the best creative writers read hungrily and constantly; that they can no more work without books in reach than a carpenter can work without his square. Books, indeed, seem to be the one compensation for the author's loneliness. They are permissible companions but, more important, they are silent teachers and the only ones he can find. Without them, craftsmanship, technique, cannot be learned, whatever the writer's gifts of observation and reflection. Obviously they build his vocabulary and the patterns of his composition, but more subtly they are stimulants of his thinking. They prick ideas into his consciousness. How this happens is mysterious, for often a problem can be resolved by reading a piece of writing which seems wholly unrelated.

Why, for instance, did Sherwood Anderson, in the same letter in which he wrote his publisher, "I have gone hog-wild on a long novel"— a wholly American novel — send out a cry for "the letters of Vincent Van Gogh . . . in two or three volumes"?

[13]

Sidney Howard, a master craftsman in the modern theatre, whose plays were mostly American and contemporary, had as broad and deep a background of reading as any writer of his time. When he struck a snag in his work, he would spend a day or two rereading Buckle's *History of Civilization in England*, or *Arabia Deserta*, and these books would bring him clear. On the title page of Scribner's edition of *Lucky Sam McCarver*, a play of late New York, he recognized his debt to Gibbon's Rome.

Stevenson, methodically industrious in his self-teaching, said that frank imitation of the great authors was the best exercise for a beginner. In his essay, "A College Magazine," he tells of his own experience.

> *"Whenever I read a book or a passage that particularly pleased me, in which a thing was said or an effect rendered with propriety, in which there was either some conspicuous force or some happy distinction in the style, I must sit down at once and set myself to ape that quality. I was unsuccessful, and I knew it; and I tried again, and was again unsuccessful; but at least in these vain bouts, I got some practice in rhythm, in harmony, in construction and the co-ordination of parts. I have thus played the sedulous ape to Hazlitt, to Lamb, to Wordsworth, to Sir Thomas Browne, to Defoe, to Hawthorne, to Montaigne, to Baudelaire and to Obermann. . . .*
>
> *"That, like it or not, is the way to learn to write, whether I have profited or not, that is the way."*

Later authors who quarrel with all this emphasis on style dispute Stevenson's method, but their clamor for books to read goes on. A publisher is peculiarly aware of this because he is, after all, the great source of books; the one to whom a writer naturally appeals for such tools. So the files are full of wonderings "if, perhaps, you can get it for me wholesale," or "if you could charge it, somehow, against my royalties," or even, "if you have an old copy lying around. . . ." A wise publisher knows how often these hints are hungry demands, thinly veiled; that they are "musts" and that a writer may wither in mid-career unless they are met.

Sometimes, too, an editor will anticipate an author's asking and guess at a book to fit his unspoken need. Thus Maxwell Perkins wrote to Ernest Hemingway in 1926:

> "*I'm sending you a book I believe you'll like — Trelawney's* Adventures of a Younger Son. *It's alive with grand material . . . and, though its manner and method of expression has some of the defects of its period, it is direct, vigorous and honest. It just seemed to me it might suit you. I'd wanted it for years (having seen excerpts) and just now found it again in print."*

In later times, when the authors of a house have become more intimate with the editors and with one another, publishers have been generous with their products within the family. This has brought not only stimulus but healthy criticism and discussion. It has let light from the outside world into the hermit's cell in those dangerous moments when he believed himself the sole producer of honest work. But it has given encouragement too, for writers are often more deeply moved by the word of other writers than by the comment of the professional critics. "They write for one another," Sidney Howard used to say, "not for the public and least of all for the critics."

In the decade of the 1920's (which later became a "literary epoch") the family of younger Scribner authors was a close and genial group and the editors took care that they kept abreast of one another's work. Their comments were impulsive, often naïve, always honest — sometimes to the brutal point.

To his editor who had sent him Wolfe's *Look Homeward, Angel* fresh from its first printing, James Boyd wrote, in 1929:

"It strikes me, strikes me hard not as a novel, hardly as a book but as a great inchoate bellow of the human soul. I don't know where he'll end but I have an uneasy feeling that the little fellows had better move over for this bird. But whether I mean the little fellows on Parnassus or on Blackwell's Island I don't yet know. I only know somebody's got to move. And on personal grounds there's no writer I'd rather move over or down for myself. Although there will be no question of volunteering. It will be a case of the brewers' big horses."

Scott Fitzgerald, restless, impatient, drew strength and relief from reading. Even after the late, warm evenings with the people of his group — with Ring Lardner, with Sid Howard and Tom Boyd and Bob Sherwood, Scott would often go home to read through the night. If the books he read were those of his friends, friendship never prejudiced his comment. His affection for Tom Boyd, for instance, and his admiration for Boyd's *Through the Wheat* did not prevent him from writing at another time of Boyd's "ignorance, his presumptuous intolerance and his careless grossness which he cultivates for vitality as a man might nurse along a dandelion with the hope that it would turn out to be an onion. . . ." Even Ring Lardner, to whom he dedicated *All the Sad Young Men* and whom he grouped with "the very greatest artists" did not escape Scott's judgment when Lardner's famous story, "Haircut," struck him as "mediocre."

He was deeply concerned over his friend Ernest Hemingway, who he was afraid had been hurt by early editorial advice. Of *The Sun Also Rises* he wrote after reading it in galley proof:

"I liked it but with certain qualifications. The fiesta, the fishing trip, the minor characters were fine. The lady I didn't like, perhaps because I don't like the original. . . . Do ask him for the absolute minimum of necessary changes, Max — he's so discouraged about the previous reception of his work by publishers and magazine editors."

But Fitzgerald was more deeply influenced by poetry, especially Shelley —"what a good man he was compared to that colossal egotist Browning!"— by Samuel Butler, Stendhal, Conrad, Hardy and Edith Wharton — a surprising background for this pioneer of the American jazz age. Perkins, of course, fed him *War and Peace,* principal item in his diet for all young authors, and urged upon him such critical books as Eastman's *Enjoyment of Poetry* and Robinson's *The Mind in the Making.* Robinson, Fitzgerald thought, "states the entire case for modernity's hope of progress."

It was said carelessly, in the twenties, that these boys, some of whom have risen to grand stature in maturity, were more influenced by contemporaries than by the masters proved by time. This belief, held by a despairing elder generation in a fantastic era of prohibition, rampant crime and the lapse of moral standards in high places is not sustained — by one publisher's records at least. The letters of his young men show indeed less awe of the old — because it was old — and more tolerance of the new. But almost without exception, their deeper roots were in the literature of the Bible ("I am soaking in it," wrote Tom Wolfe), Shakespeare, Tolstoi, Fielding or the English poets or, as with Sherwood, Howard and John Marquand (who began in the Scribner family), in the historical and critical classics.

On the other hand, James Barrie, of an older school, admitted his greatest influence to have come from a contemporary.

Again and again, in letters as well as in his essays, he speaks of Stevenson as "the Master." "I feel," he wrote after receiving Charles Scribner's cable confirming the news of Stevenson's death, "as if a great incentive to work had been taken from us. . . . I question if I have written a chapter of 'Sentimental Tommy' without thinking how this or that wd strike him."

Stevenson's demands on his publisher for book-tools were incessant and of wide variety. He was, of course, isolated much of the time from the world, in the Adirondacks or in South Seas Samoa where books must come slowly, by mail.

> "I wish you could send . . . on loan:
>
> (1) *The volume of Napier's Peninsular War, which contains Salamanca; for a guess it is the fourth.*
> (2) *Xenophon in English*
> (3) *Amadale by Wilkie Collins*
>
> "And if you would purchase for me:
>
> 1. *Smith's smaller Latin-English Dictionary, or a cheaper one if as good.*
> 2. *Cicero's Epistles (with good notes)*
> 3. *The Æneid (with notes, if not dear — if dear, in the good old honest German paper sides.)*
>
> "I fancy these could come by post; any other way here is most expensive."

Again:

> "Could you order also *The Figaro* for me, say for three months, beginning with the next arrival? And — Heavens, what a troubler I am — the following books to borrow:
>
> 1. *Thiers for 1813–14 and 15.*

[18]

2. *The memoirs of the princess Caroline, wife of Jerome Buonaparte, King of Westphalia.*
3. *A good life of Fouché, duc d'Otranto and* to buy

"Shubert's songs, if they cannot be got cheaper, say, in Peter's edition, where they make 4 parts; but if they can be got cheaper in some (perhaps) pirated form, why then so, and to the devil with shame!"

When these letters arrived at the Broadway office, Charles Scribner would abandon his busy desk and devote days to research. In the middle eighties this was not a matter of picking up a telephone.

"I send to you today," he wrote Stevenson in 1887, *"the articles by Dr. Eggleston which have appeared in the* Century Magazine . . . *the earlier ones will probably be of no special service, but the later ones on social life in the colonies will interest you. I also send today two numbers of the* New York Nation *which give an account of the* Memoirs of Queen Katherine, *a copy of which you want, and which I hope to secure for you.*

"I have made a number of inquiries from those who should know and have looked into the best books of reference, and I am convinced that Marshal McDonald did not leave any memoirs; nor can I find that any book has recently been published on the campaign of 1814, and enclosed you will find extracts from the letters of Mr. John C. Ropes and General de Peyster from whom I made inquiries and who are well informed on the history of the period. . . ."

Not telephone inquiries, these, of the secretaries of the distinguished authorities; nor rapidly dictated notes. Distinguished persons in the eighties were offended by the new, vulgar typewriting. They were not pleased by obviously dictated letters. So Charles Scribner wrote laboriously in his own longhand to Mr. Ropes and the celebrated general and historian, John Watts de Peyster, and these gentlemen answered with the same courtesy to provide tools for a writer of fiction.

Stevenson was quite desperate when the answers to his requests did not arrive promptly far out in the Pacific.

"Man of Little Faith," he wrote Burlingame from Honolulu, "do you remember our last meeting in New York? And how you promised — ay and made hieroglyphics in a note book — to send me the Saturday and the Weekly St. James's; and lo! — not one! Please send them from now till I let you hear of a further movement, and I will try to forgive this awful blow. We had all so Built *upon these papers!"*

Many of these books, articles and letters were certainly direct tools. Xenophon in English, Cicero and the Æneid may have been indirect or mere pleasurable exercises for a relaxed mood. The need for direct tools was, of course, especially overwhelming for historical novelists, authors of detective or mystery stories who are as meticulous as lawyers in research and accurate documentation and, finally, the writers of what publishers' salesmen still call "serious books" to distinguish them from fiction.

Once the author of a two-volume history of the United States became obsessed with the need of possessing a set of the formidable *Dictionary of American Biography* in twenty volumes. To buy such a thing was out of the question, for this author had failed to meet Henry Adams's requirement (expressed to Charles Scribner in 1888) that a man must be rich to indulge in the "luxury" of history. So he stopped one rainy day on the way to his Connecticut farm where he lived and worked, and parked his car on Fifth Avenue at Forty-eighth Street.

"It is a Scribner book, isn't it?" he said to his astonished editor.

"Why, yes — but twenty volumes . . ."

"But I must have it. I work in the lonely country. I don't ask you to give it to me. But if you could lend me a set — for six months — I'll finish your book in half the time!"

It ended by the head of the Subscription Department helping him load the heavy octavo volumes in the back of his car while the rain poured down. The record shows that he drove the books back to Forty-eighth Street — a year and a half later. But this same author, whose shamelessness enforces anonymity, at another time borrowed from the Scribner file library, two rare volumes to assist him in an interim book written for another publisher!

A singular story of the catalytic effect of books is that of Willard Huntington Wright who was converted, during his thirties, from "serious" writing to one of the most disciplined kinds of fiction. Wright began as a critic, not only of literature and the fine arts but of drama and music as well. In these fields and others he often produced two books a year with such titles as *What Nietzsche Taught, Modern Painting — Its Tendency and Meaning, The Future of Painting* and *Modern Literature.* At the same time he held critical editorships on newspapers and magazines.

Suddenly in mid-career, he was threatened with serious nervous breakdown from overwork. His doctor forbade him to read — a dangerous prescription for such a man. "You mean no books at all?" said Wright, feeling the reason for continued existence ebbing away from him. "None," said the doctor, weakening a little as he watched his patient's face, "unless we except detective stories, mysteries. . . ."

So Wright, like an alcoholic who, during a cure, will gorge himself with sweets, covered his bed with volumes: he demanded every novel ever written even remotely concerned with crime and detection. Having got these he did not merely read them. He made a profound study of them. He emerged from the hospital as "S. S. Van Dine" and with elaborate synopses of three novels whose hero, Philo Vance, would one day be known to readers in a dozen languages.

The books of Wright's cure were catylists in that they altered his life without becoming actual ingredients of "Van Dine's" material—for the detective, Philo Vance, was truly an original and the Van Dine formula was new. But they were tools, too, in that they shaped the whole pattern of the author's new technique. Later he demanded other tools, direct tools, to give him the facts he needed to make credible and convincing, the intricate details of his scenes and incidents: "Dear Max," he telegraphed in the midst of the *Kennel Murder Case,* "will you be good enough to send me to Los Angeles immediately *The Early Ceramic Wares of China* by Hetherington and *The Later Ceramic Wares of China* by Hobson stop I need both of these books for data."

Wright's stories, wrought with such tools, carried strong conviction. Once a physician reader wrote their publisher:

> *"Other than texts on medicine these are the most interesting books I have ever found.*
>
> *"The Benson murder appeals most strongly to me. I am very desirous of obtaining newspapers that were printed shortly after the tragedy and read the speculations, theories, etc., concerning the possible murderer. . . . For this reason will you answer the following question. 'What was the exact date or the approximate date on which Alvin Benson was murdered?' "*

To which Maxwell Perkins replied:

"The author seems . . . to have been so successful in giving the impression of reality that you have mistaken this case for a record of facts, whereas in truth it is fiction. There are therefore no newspaper or other records which would have any bearing upon it, nor did Alvin Benson ever exist."

But Perkins made one slip in his guessing when he sent Willard Huntington Wright, for his comment, the advance copy of a Fitzgerald volume.

"You ask me," wrote the creator of Philo Vance, "what I thought of the 'Jazz Age' stories — I think they are cheap, silly, and amateurish."

III

THE FLESH OF PRINT

"Unfortunately," wrote Charles Scribner in 1906 to his author F. Hopkinson Smith, "publishing is not an exact science."

He might have added, with the agreement of many of his associates, that it is not an exact business, either; which is, perhaps, why many of his friends who thought of business in terms of delegated authority, mimeographed memos, blanket orders and clean desks used to say that "C.S." was not a good executive.

C.S. did not press buttons. Secretaries did not rush in and out of his office. He did not entrust precious, immediate papers to the filing and finding of clerks. His desk was cluttered with old books which had some special trick of beauty for comparison, with catalogs of type and cloth, with complex authors' letters, with contracts containing special clauses; with a dozen things which would be needed at some instant of the day's work and C.S. knew where to put his hand when each was needed. Outside his office eternally hovered a little group of men. They had not made appointments. They could not, for in the normal course of their day, problems arose one hour, which must be solved in the next. They were proud and sensitive men, specialists, and each held in his hand some delicate curiosity different from all others and the only thing that could co-ordinate them was the long, detailed experience in every specialty of C.S. himself.

It was true that some of these experts — editors, art directors, typographers, pressmen and salesmen, each a kind of artist in his way—often squirmed under C.S.'s insistence on knowing the whole score at any given moment. They called him a dictator—"the Czar"; they called him unreasonable and finicky, capricious and captious. And outsiders, unable to reconcile the fact that a "bad businessman" had successfully conducted a good business for fifty-two years—and held all the strings in his hand—called him, at last, a "genius."

Perhaps he was. Perhaps all successful publishers are geniuses, more or less. Perhaps all of the Alices who move in this strange Wonderland where, day by day, everything grows "curiouser and curiouser" must have a touch of genius and be, at times, bad businessmen as well, in order to survive at all.

It is the job of a publisher to make thoughts into print and paper, multiply them into thousands, dress them in tangible cloth and sell them for tangible dollars to creatures whose moody minds must translate the whole thing back into thought before they get their money's worth. The publisher must deal, intimately, with this elusive material from the time it exists only in a vague author's dream until it becomes the property of the world. Sometimes these little slippery eels of thought grow into serpents which return, long after, to bite the publisher with the venom of libel suits or attacks upon his morality. In any case, throughout the process, he faces an imponderable at every turn. The jumps which may be made by author, critic, bookseller and public at any stage of the game are usually unpredictable and must be guessed at with an intuition bred of long and constant watching which cannot ignore the pettiest detail. Yet while these mystic processes are going on, the publisher is subject to inexorable, material demands. The rhythm of the presses must not be interrupted. Paper must be bought. Authors, office boys and linotypers must be paid. And the red and black marks upon the ledger must be studiously followed, for the margins between them, in the publishing business, are dangerously small.

Charles Scribner, with his eye on all these things at once, appeared unreasonable. Some of his workers, facing him in his old-world office were terrified. The benign expression of his bearded father looking down from the wall behind the desk, did not balance C.S.'s challenging face and forbidding eyes. The creaking of his ancient chair, the faded and slightly torn shade at the window, the beam of old-book-dusty sunlight filtering through the tear and the rows of dark old leather volumes against the wall did little to soften the vivid presence of the Chief. So, sometimes, a younger or newer man, hovering by the threshold, would lose his nerve and slink back to his desk reporting along the way that the boss was in no mood . . .

The trembling of these weakhearts was enhanced by the characteristic geography of the offices. C.S. did not surround himself by genial salesmen as any good businessman would do. He surrounded himself by editors who, unless you know their weaknesses, are cool, cynical and generally formidable persons. The editors were, also, in inscrutable communion with the authors who are, of course, inimical to the ordinary procedure of any department. So a salesman, pressman, typographer or art man, approaching his chief, must first run the gauntlet of the editors' eyes.

But those who had lived long in this upside-down world, understood the temper of the man who ran it. They knew that C.S. loved and demanded fight. He could not tolerate yes-men because they did not give him the information his restless, probing mind was forever seeking. If you agreed with him, he employed devices to make you disagree. In the midst of a discussion he would reverse his position. And for a man whose peculiar genius was predicated on an infallible memory he had a capacity for "forgetting" which bewildered his people.

"You men keep me in the dark," he would say. "For months you tell me nothing. Then, when it is too late, you present me with an accomplished fact."

"But, Mr. Scribner, we discussed this . . ."

"Whom do you mean by 'we'?"

"But, Mr. Scribner, you said . . . Only last week, you said . . ."

"Don't tell me what I said. This comes to me today for the first time."

More level heads remembered then that their early arguments had been full of holes. They remembered that what they had said had not been worth remembering. Next time they were more careful marshaling their facts.

There were those, to be sure, who never reconciled these devices with the way they thought a boss should behave. Other men, they said, got results through a gentler, kindlier, less bedeviling process. Other men left their employees alone, gave them authority, kept hands off a job which only a specialist could do. They said these things, forgetting that even a specialist's job must be co-ordinated with the job of another specialist — that a book's cover, for instance, must satisfy author, salesman, bookseller, treasurer, public and the House's tradition all at once.

Yet men rarely left the Scribners. On the very threshold of departure a curious charm drew them back to C.S. His smile, unexpectedly following his frown, reduced men to sweat and almost tears of relief. Sometimes his smile was induced by a humorous sidelight which had flashed upon his mind. Often it came from the sense that he had gone too far or that his worries were small fish in the world's sea of miseries. For C.S. was hounded by a relentless personal conscience. His conscience loathed injustice and, if he believed that he had hurt someone unjustly, he stopped at nothing until he had put his hand on the man's shoulder with a friendliness that was more eloquent than any apology.

And C.S. almost never fired anyone. Once he fired a cashier and the next morning the cashier came back to his desk as usual. "He can't fire me," the cashier said, "I've been here twenty years." It was true. In a House where business was so personal and loyalties so intertwined with all its detail, a man's very heartstrings, if there are such things, were twisted, after twenty years, around his chair. So the man kept coming back with his old nine-to-five fidelity until, ten years later, he died, comfortably, with his boots on. And C.S. just "forgot" that he had fired him.

Once an editor left to become an author on his own account. After a year of trying to serve God, so to speak, and Mammon, he decided that the worst place in the world for an author to be was a publishing house — both for the author and the publisher. C.S. called him in to say good-by. He wished him fortune and then hesitated. "Your work here has always been —" he began, and the editor saw his struggle between truthfulness and cordiality —"has always been . . . has always been . . . competent."

Authors would leave, occasionally. They are restless folk and are accustomed to appreciate their own work in high terms. When it doesn't sell, the public may be at fault, but the publisher is easier to blame. Advertising is an obvious target. A publisher's advertising is rightly subject to criticism on the grounds of quality. The wrong thing said about a book in one advertisement may do it serious harm. Book advertising is carefully read by the comparatively small group of people who buy books — compared, that is, with the large group which reads them. But the common author's complaint on advertising is not with its attractiveness but with its quantity. They crave display in mediums of whose millions of readers every one buys clothes and food and only a few thousand ever buy books. So authors who leave a publisher because he underadvertises them often come back when they find his problem is common to the entire business.

And is there an author in the world so professional or so busy that he does not prowl in the bookstores, the week of publication? Not always does he write, as Edwin Arnold did, in 1892, "Wherever I have wandered I have seen the bookstores full of the handsome volume." And if his book is not there, front and center of all others, who is blamed? The bookstore?

Authors left Scribner's for various reasons. Kipling was charmed by Frank Doubleday when Doubleday was on *Scribner's Magazine* and took his books to Doubleday's new house when he started it. This was a case of personal friendship which a publisher would be foolish to combat. Kipling kept up warm relations with the House which had introduced him through its magazine to literary America and took an eager interest in its production of his subscription edition, called "Outward Bound," illustrated by his father. John Marquand left, and readers of his later books agree that he might naturally be happiest in a Boston house.

Authors worry about "getting in a rut." Publishers, they think, get a routine attitude about their books. "Here comes another John Doe novel," publishers are supposed to say and the old John Doe machinery is set to work. Someone has said, "the publisher's favorite author is the one who always writes the same book." An author once flew into a rage when his publisher's chief salesman said his book would be hard to sell because "it had no handle." Asking what that meant, he was told that it was always useful to compare a book with another book. "You can't say, for instance, that the author is an American Kipling. Or that this book is 'in the author's most popular vein.'" The trouble was, explained the worried salesman, scratching his head, that this book was brand-new —"nothing like it has ever been done before." "Why not say *that?*" said the author and went out to seek a publisher who might be more eagerly experimental.

There was complaint in other days of Scribner "conservatism" or "old fogyness," though Scott Fitzgerald wrote of "the curious advantage to a rather radical writer in being published by . . . an ultra-conservative house," and today the charge could hardly be brought by a reader, say, of *The History of Rome Hanks.*

C.S. and his editors surprised some departing authors by wishing them Godspeed.

> *"It is never agreeable," he wrote Anne Douglas Sedgwick in 1902, "to continue to publish books which the author would prefer elsewhere."*

> *"There are a few authors," he wrote in 1906 to F. Hopkinson Smith (who, however, never left him), "like Barrie, Cable, Page, Fox and others, who are thoroughly identified with this house; they give strength to us and in return we do our best for them. Of recent years I have counted you among the number.*

> *"But you will please understand that we make no claim upon you and I sincerely wish you to do what you believe to be for your best interests. . . . Whatever you do will be accepted by me in good spirit."*

And to Robert Grant who stood, in 1902, upon the threshold, he wrote, "I recognize your right to do with your work as you think best," and Grant turned round and came back.

Brownell, whose pen could be acutely sharp, once (with C.S.'s concurrence) invited a successful but complaining author in these terms:

*"I may say that we are quite unfamiliar with the criticism
contained in the remark of the gentleman you quote about
our books . . . but that if you yourself share his distrust we
should very much prefer you to give your book to some other
house. We could not, in such an event, count on the confidence which we are accustomed to enjoy in our authors,
and the circumstance would be too novel to justify us in
incurring it."*

And C.S. was not diverted by the most successful author
from his sense of justice. Once a writer who commanded, at
the moment, a very large public, brought in a complaint against
an editor. C.S.'s eyes blazed in their peculiar, alarming way
and the editor whom he immediately called in, trembled. But
then he turned to the author and one of the most Olympian
tirades C.S. ever released was directed, wholly, at him. It is
a fact, still cherished in the editorial department, that the
author was so terrified, he literally ran from the room. Nor
did C.S., in the tradition of military generals, then scold his
employee. The chapter simply closed and the next one began
with the author's return.

This, perhaps, is digression for such a scene might occur
wherever there are relations between fair-minded men, whether
it be a publishing house, a theatre or a filling station. But the
point at which the work of a publisher becomes most special
and delicate, and where the justness, intelligence, tact and
patience both of him and of his author are most severely tested
is in the opening phase when a written concept first takes on
the flesh of print.

Any piece of writing when it is fitted into uniform lines
and blocks of metal is, in a sense, reborn. The words seem to
take on new relations to one another; a new rhythm appears.

A novice writer sometimes hardly recognizes his own job: he sees defects which never appeared in his script or, perhaps, the work jumps into new life.

Henry James, in his early days, was so struck by the defects he believed he found when he read one of his stories in a magazine, that he virtually rewrote the story on the margins of the pages and submitted these to his book publisher as copy. It probably distressed the Scribners to get this tough compositor's puzzle instead of a fresh transcript, but the relic is interesting to students of James in 1946. It is useful, here, in showing the immediate impact of the print upon his mind.

Some letters of Sara Teasdale, however, show that her first sense of a poem's proper rhythm was confirmed by the printed page. Brooding over some verse which had been accepted by *Scribner's Magazine,* she sent in a revised manuscript changing the punctuation. But the printer's proof of the poem crossed this in the mail and she wrote the editor.

> *"Just after sending you the newly typed version of my poem, comes the proof, which follows the punctuation of the first copy. But since it looks very well in type as it is, I see no reason to reset it."*

James Boyd's view of his first novel was altered as he read its galleys.

> *"In general,"* he said in a letter to his editor, *"I got the impression from reading it in print that it is a better* tale *than I had hoped but not as well written — though I hardly dare make a statement so painful to the shade of my old master, Flaubert."*

When Edith Wharton's *The House of Mirth* was first set up, the reading of it in galleys made a precisely opposite impression on author and editor.

"I am so surprised and pleased, & altogether taken aback,"
Mrs. Wharton wrote Brownell in answer to his letter of
praise, "that I can't decently compose my countenance about
it. I was pleased with bits, myself; but as I go over the proofs
the whole thing strikes me as so loosely built, with so many
dangling threads, & culs-de-sac, & long dusty stretches, that
I had reached the point of wondering how I had ever dared to
try my hand at a long thing. So your seeing a certain amount
of architecture in it rejoices me above everything. . . ."

Here the transfer into print obscured the author's own view
of her work. Perhaps her own closeness to it and fatigue at
rereading had dulled her. Perhaps, too, seeing it in print for
the first time she centered her attention on detail and lost her
vision of the "architecture" as a whole. But it is more probable
that when her book was in type it began to challenge comparison with other printed books, and, as most of her reading had
moved in the highest reaches of literature, her own work seemed
far below the standard. A sentence of her letter to Brownell
suggests this answer:

"My theory of what the novel ought to be is so exorbitant,
that I am always reminded of Daudet's 'Je rêve d'un aigle,
j'accouche d'un colibri.' "

Yet her fear that she had been delivered of a humming-bird
instead of an eagle had not struck her as she prepared her
manuscript for the printer.

It is, of course, the business of an editor, as he reads each
manuscript, to visualize it as it will appear on the printed
page. This kind of imagination comes through long intimacy
with every phase of the transfer from writing to print. Moving
through each hour of the working day from writer to writer —
from subject to subject and style to style — his view is detached

and continues fresh, free from the intense inward focus which torments the author. He is aware, too, of other matters outside the substance and technique of writing: of costs, of rigid printer's rules, of the artistry of the printed page and of the total effect of all these things upon the job of merchandising. He knows what a printer can and cannot do within economic publishing limits. He knows, for instance, that corrections on a manuscript cost nothing compared with the expense of shifting set type metal. He knows that if a manuscript can be prepared to conform to printers' rules of uniform spelling, punctuation, and so on, it will save time and money. So, if he is a good editor, he will see, as he looks at the untidiest manuscript, a printed, bound, advertised and sold volume.

His first job, then, before a book is put "in hand," is to give the manuscript a careful reading. While he reads, he unconsciously adjusts the material to the requirements of the printed page. A letter which the blue pencil of an editor of *Scribner's Magazine* once brought from Sherwood Anderson reveals the difference which sometimes exists between an author's and an editor's vision of this.

> "I see," wrote Anderson, "you prefer not to break the sentences . . . up into paragraphs.
> "It really doesn't matter.
> "As a matter of fact I know that I am essentially a poet. It just happens I don't want to be proclaimed one. It's too much like being proclaimed a lover. I'd much rather sneak poetry across.
> "I break up paragraphs like this sometimes because it seems to me to make a kind of rhythm in the reading that I want. I want the mind of the reader to be singing as it reads without quite knowing what has happened.
> "However surely I do not stand for it as a vital matter."

And the editor catches errors of fact as he reads. E. L. Burlingame, who had a fantastic flair for this (and once even found an error in Bartlett's *Familiar Quotations*), caught one of Edith Wharton's heroines looking across Madison Square in New York at a clock where none existed. Knowing every stick and stone and legend of his home town, he wrote also to the confirmed Bostonian, Robert Grant, in 1894:

> ". . . In writing these papers it is especially important that they shall not have too much the point of view of Boston alone, or of any city where, as there, the conditions are at their easiest rather than at their hardest. The regular New York lot, and consequently the regular New York dwelling house of normal size, is only 25 feet wide: and houses (good homes too) exist . . . down to 18 and even 16 feet; but a house over 25 feet wide here in New York means a very rich man — one quite outside of the conditions of these papers. Don't you think this is an important point?"

But Burlingame, too, a lifelong city dweller, caught Harold Frederic, in 1887, planting buckwheat in the Mohawk Valley at the wrong season, and, though he never went to church (especially the Church of England), spotted an error by Mrs. Wharton in the interpretation of the Book of Common Prayer.

Maxwell Perkins, who can hardly be considered an expert in crime, wrote S. S. Van Dine that, "I think it highly doubtful that one could count upon killing another instantly with a 32-caliber. You often read of a suicide shooting himself in the head or heart with even a larger caliber, and not dying for hours or even days."

William C. Brownell, more aware in his reading of manuscript, of subtleties of style and literary technique, was occasionally so subtle in conveying his criticism, that authors must have scratched their heads over his letters.

". . . The book," he wrote Frank H. Spearman about Helen Eliot, "would be a shade more important, as a contribution to literature, if the plane of the treatment were here and there a little more elevated above the plane of the subject matter. As Emerson says, 'No man can do anything well, who does not come to it from a higher ground,' and Arnold points out as to translating Homer that it is a mistake to make the language too familiar, inasmuch as Homer — unlike a Dutch master, e.g. — 'does not sink with his subject.' . . . In dealing with Chicago boarding-house life, to be specific, it seems to us that there is every advantage to be gained by avoiding in one's own — the author's — diction a sympathetic color. Then what the characters have to say acquires more relief. The ends of realism are better served. The picture gains in vividness from the detachment of the author. The author and reader sympathise instead of the author and characters."

Brownell himself usually came to the manuscripts he read from a "higher ground." Yet his suggestion here serves "the ends of realism" today as well as it did in 1902 and the detachment he tried to make Frank Spearman adopt has become the basic method of such writers as Ernest Hemingway.

It was in the reports on manuscripts which he wrote to Charles Scribner, however, that Brownell really let himself go. Of *The Sacred Fount* by Henry James, he wrote:

"It is surely the n + 1st power of Jamesiness. . . . I have had the greatest difficulty in following it — indeed I couldn't follow some of it. . . . It gets decidedly on one's nerves. It it like trying to make out page after page of illegible writing. The sense of effort becomes acutely exasperating. Your spine curls up, your hair-roots prickle & you want to get up and walk around the block. There is no story — oh! but none at *all. That is the* point *no doubt. It is a* tour-de-force; *as if James had said 'You don't like my psychology & hair-splitting & analysis and no melodrama, eh! Well I will carry it all the farther for your opposition. I will carry it so far there shall be nothing but that, nothing but what you object to, just my little game, without any of my "criticism of life" (for which in general you put up with my subtleties); and I will do it so well & make it so salient, give it such relief, by such exclusive treatment that you shall at least exclaim "wonderful!" whether it pleases or exacerbates you.' And it is wonderful. There is no doubt about that. . . . But I am prepared to maintain it will take a nimble intelligence to follow the thread. . . . Innuendo is mighty hard to do satisfactorily it seems to me — i.e. have the meaning clear to the reader and obscure to the character in the book who is listening. But here we have not only the innuendo of the characters, forced by the subject into the dialect of innuendo but James's own inveterate innuendo besides. The result is Ossa on Pelion of suggestion instead of statement, of hint instead of expression — & hint & expression when there is no means of guessing except thro' them, no sidelights since the* subject *is something to guess, guess, guess all the time. . . ."*

When Brownell couldn't follow James, it was news. And C.S., who spent considerable effort in following Brownell, must have been bewildered at this report about a book already asked for from an author whose cohorts of admirers were growing year by year. The report, of course, was confidential in 1900, and C.S., who decided, in spite of it, to go on with *The Sacred Fount,* had to use discretion letting it get around the office and thus damp the enthusiasm which must accompany every product a publisher launches upon his market.

So C.S.'s armor had to protect him against his editors too.

[37]

It was a part of his job to see beyond their individual likes and dislikes and even their most cogent criticism to the public which demanded certain things. And it is the duty of a publisher to supply those things, even when they are contrary to his own personal tastes, his personal politics, his religious beliefs or his philosophy of life. Charles Scribner's political leanings, for instance, were far more Tory than those of John Reed, Max Eastman or Leon Trotsky, whose books he published.

C.S. had, like all good publishers, an intuition about public demand. He knew the seasons of its ripeness. "This is the psychological moment," he wrote to H. G. Wells, who had suggested delaying the publication of *Kipps*. Later he realized the public trend after the first World War and published the books of Scott Fitzgerald, Hemingway and others against all the discreet tradition of the firm — and somewhat to the horror of his contemporaries in the office, including certain editors and several salesmen.

The Scribners made mistakes which will appear in other chapters. They lost Conrad, for instance, as C.S. admitted in a letter to Conrad's English publishers. "Probably in your own experience," he wrote, "there has been some similar case — where a book slipped through your hands from failure to adequately examine it." Possibly there was a like slip on Bellamy's *Looking Backward,* though the record is not clear on this. C.S. certainly made some bad guesses in the other direction as when he paid a huge advance for the autobiography of Benito Mussolini which ran as a serial in the *Saturday Evening Post* and was a spectacular loss as a book. Such a gamble, however, is not an error on the conservative side, and may be explained by one of C.S.'s pet theories of publishing. He believed, and kept impressing on his associates, that in big competitive events of this sort a good publisher must occasionally throw his hat into the ring even if there is a chance of heavy loss; otherwise he may acquire a "Milquetoast" reputation among authors, trade and public, which will lose him more in the end.

In the history of a century of publishing it is easy to find the false steps, the wrong starts, the wasting conflicts, the blunders which, in hindsight, seem to have been so avoidable. Yet all these things stick the story together; they are a kind of human gelatin and it is perhaps this human thing, streaked with weakness, which, more than in other commercial enterprises keeps the publishing business from falling apart. Most of the pluses and minuses here must be written by men in moods: made nervous, changeable, headachy, zealous or exalted with joy by the shiny, slippery material they work in. That is the fascination. There are few others. The profit, compared with other commerce, is insignificant. The credit goes to the author. As John Fox once wrote to Charles Scribner, a publisher is "a man who is blamed if a book fails and ignored if it proves a success."

IV

FIRST MEETINGS

Thomas Wolfe, in the flush of excitement after his first meeting with his publishers, told a friend about it in a breathless letter. Wolfe's letter gives a universal picture; with all its telegraphic style, its impatient frankness, it is fresher than the tale of Pendennis and captures the thrill of every author who was ever young.

"... I was taken to his office where I found Mr. Charles Scribner (simply there, I think, to take a look at me, for he withdrew immediately saying he would leave us alone). Mr. Perkins is not at all 'Perkinsy'—name sounds mid-western, but he is Harvard man, probably New England family, early forties, but looks younger, very elegant and gentle in dress and manner. He saw I was nervous and excited, spoke to me quietly, told me to take coat off and sit down. He began by asking certain general questions about book and people (these weren't important—he was simply feeling his way around, sizing me up, I suppose) then he mentioned a certain short scene in the book, and in my eagerness and excitement I burst out, 'I know you can't print that! I'll take it out at once, Mr. Perkins.' Take it out? he said. It's one of the greatest short stories I have ever read. He said he had been reading it to Hemingway week before. Then he asked me if I could write a short introduction for it to explain people —he was sure Scribner's magazine would take it; if they didn't someone else would. I said I would—I was at once elated and depressed—I thought now that this little bit was all they wanted of it. Then he began cautiously on the book. Of course, he said, he didn't know about its present form — somewhat incoherent and very long. When I saw now that he was really interested I burst out wildly saying that I would throw out this, that and the other — at every point he stopped me quickly saying, 'No, no — you must let that stay word for word — that scene's simply magnificent.' It became apparent at once that these people were willing to go far farther than I had dared hope — that, in fact, they were afraid I would injure the book by doing too much to it. I saw now that Perkins had a great batch of notes in his hand and that on the desk was a great stack of handwritten paper — a complete summary of my whole enormous book. I was so moved and touched to think that someone at length had thought enough of my work to sweat over it in this way that I almost wept. When I spoke to him of this he smiled and said everyone in the place had read it. Then he went over the book scene by scene — I found he was more familiar with the scenes and the names of characters than I was — I had not looked at the thing in over 6 months. For the first time in my life I was getting criticism I could really use — the scenes he wanted cut or changed were invariably the least essential and the least interesting — all the scenes that I had thought too coarse, vulgar, profane or obscene for publication he forbade me to touch save for a word or two — there was one as rough as anything in Elizabethan drama — when I spoke of this he said it was a masterpiece, and that he had been reading it to Hemingway. He told me I must change a few words. He said the book was new and original, and because of its form could have no formal and orthodox unity, but that what unity it did have came from the strange wild people — the family — it wrote about as seen through the eyes of a strange wild boy. These people, with relatives, *friends, townspeople he said were 'magnificent'— as real as any people he had ever read of. He wanted me to keep these people and the boy at all times foremost — other business, such as courses at state university, etc., to be shortened and subordinated. Said finally if I was hard up he thought Scribner's would advance money. By this time I was wild with excitement — this really seemed something at last — in spite of his caution and restrained manner I saw now that Perkins really was excited about my book, and had said some tremendous things about it. He saw how wild I was; I told him I had to go out and think — he told me to take two or three days but before I left he went out and brought another member of the firm, John Hall Wheelock, who spoke gently and quietly — he is a poet—and said my book was one of the most interesting he had read for years. I then went out and tried to pull myself together. A few days later the second meeting — I brought notes along as to how I proposed to set to work, and so on. I agreed to deliver one hundred pages of corrected mss., if possible, every week. He listened, and then when I asked him if I could say something definite to a dear friend, smiled and said he thought so; that their minds were practically made up; that I should get to work immediately, and that I should have a letter from him in a few days. As I went prancing out I met Mr. Wheelock who took me by the hand and said, 'I hope you have a good place to work in — you have a big job ahead.' I knew then that it was all magnificently true. I rushed out drunk with glory. . . ."**

This first sense of response is unique in a writer's lifetime. None ever forgets it. Perhaps it is only a verse he has had accepted by a magazine, an essay he will blush, one day, to reread. He cherishes the editor's letter, is almost reluctant to

*From a letter to Mrs. J. M. Roberts, Wolfe's former schoolteacher.

cash the cheque. His emotional experience is big in proportion to the time of his loneliness; if he has lived in solitude with a novel as Wolfe had done, it is like daylight through an opened prison door.

First meetings have occurred in various parts of the world and in circumstances more casual than those of a Fifth Avenue office. The Scribners, for instance, traveled widely. Arthur Scribner met Henry M. Stanley, the African explorer, in Cairo, and Mussolini in Rome. The record is full of English week-ends which C.S. or his son spent with George Meredith, John Galsworthy, Rudyard Kipling, and an occasional author widely popular here who never left England.

In the days of the Magazine, many an author found it a vestibule to the House — a fact which made it profitable apart from its circulation and its advertising and gave reason to keep it going even in the years when the big, popular monthlies cut its business and it failed to break even on its own. In it an author had a chance to grow under the guidance of editors who cared about good performance even when the audience was limited. As Don Marquis once wrote about a story in *Scribner's:*

> *"Sometimes a writer who does really fine work —(and an editor who publishes it) — must get to wondering: 'Is there a public for this sort of thing, after all? Enough of a public? How much of a public is there for it? To which, as one of that partially submerged, but still existing, public, permit me to answer: Not so much as there is for rot; but enough, always enough, to make it worth doing."*

The editors of *Scribner's Magazine* would find and meet their authors at their homes in London and Paris; at dinners in Boston or Washington or, later, at cocktail parties where people of literary taste gathered genially together.

[43]

"I have had a good talk with Barrie," wrote Burlingame from London in 1891, "who is a queer, shy, silent little fellow, but with good stuff in him. . . . As to his future book-work, of which he told me a good deal in a general way, he agrees to communicate with us about anything whatever that he has in hand, before making any arrangements for America, and seems very friendly and quite touched by his work's having attracted us."

Burlingame, in the heyday of the Magazine, used to go to Europe almost every summer. He "stopped" at Garland's Hotel, an ancient little place in the Haymarket where Turvy ("not Topsy, sir, Turvy") the ageless valet brushed his clothes and his boots. Sometimes Mrs. Burlingame would go along and once he even took his two-year-old son who caught *la grippe* and almost died on the steamer and later was so dangerously exposed to literary infection that he never recovered from it. Burlingame had a cosmopolitan view, having lived in Peking, Heidelberg, Paris and St. Petersburg at various times. He had been educated too, in diplomacy, and spoke French and German with some fluency. He also loved conversation and a good dinner. So he would come back from his excursions packed with information about both literary and political trends in a day when the American intelligentsia watched Europe with intense and perhaps snobbish eyes.

As far back as 1879 — before the Magazine — he had spotted Henry James, and his letter to C.S. led to a first meeting. "Doesn't it seem to you," he wrote, ". . . that it is worth while to make him a decidedly good offer . . .? He is entirely *unattached* in the matter of publishing; and his future is certainly valuable enough to make an effort to connect him here."

Burlingame's later meetings with British authors, however, did not satisfy the impatience of a magazine editor.

"He is an incorrigible procrastinator," he wrote after a talk with James Bryce, "and it is evident we are to have a hard time with him. He alleged a new access of parliamentary duties and the sudden necessity of the changes in the American Commonwealth as an excuse for still further delay about our articles. I am trying my best with him but . . . he is inclined to be a little of a 'h'arbitrary gent' and kicks at any kind of spur. Altogether he is a good deal what his correspondence shows him; but a good fellow at bottom."

From this distance, such a picture of the writer of the classic on American government seems unhallowed but it reveals one publishing problem as it always was and always must be.

In that twilight of Victorian security, before world wars and quick transit had persuaded Englishmen how fast the people "out there" in America were moving toward civilization, England presented a cool façade to our literary travelers. British faith in the sacred Empire tradition which it took the Boer War in '99 to dent, kept us in the long British memory as rebellious colonials — at best spirited but naughty children. ("Why should they call us 'lion's whelps?'" wrote Charles Scribner in 1898. "We are almost big enough to stand alone.") But more specific than this was the soreness of British authors from their treatment by American pirate publishers who, before the International Copyright Law, printed every book they could grab, without paying a penny of royalty. Thus an American — inherently semi-barbarous — appeared, if he had anything to do with publishing, as a potential bandit to boot.

Naturally, then, an outlander like Burlingame was pleased by, and made the most of, any spot of warmth when he found it.

"Our day at Meredith's," he wrote in 1895, still glowing from the hospitality at Box Hill, ". . . was a great success. Meredith himself was in fine form. . . . The Barries were

staying there. M is delighted — I think sincerely & without reserve with all his relations with us. . . . He expressed himself as even pleased with the cutting of The [Amazing] Marriage, *which of course pleased me; & with its apparent reception in both countries . . ."*

So the cutting of British goods for the American taste was even then going on!

"The Barries," Burlingame continued, "being at Meredith's gave me a chance to know B better than ever. . . . I am convinced that he has a lot in him, & if his health (which is wretched) improves, has his best work still to do. But he is a phenomenally slow producer, &" — Burlingame's eternal bête noire —*"a procrastinator in the matter of letting his work leave his hands. I am quite sure, for instance, that my coming to wrest it from him is going to quicken by six months our receipt of 'Sentimental Tommy.'"*

That Barrie was not devastated by this snatching away of the work he forever wanted to keep for polishing is suggested by what he wrote to New York two months later: "It is a natural pleasure to an author to work with an editor who is in sympathy with him and certainly that is the man who draws his best from him."

Other evidence that Barrie liked his publishers is in the letters in which he tipped them off on new writers.

"I hear," he wrote, "that Quiller-Couch is getting on with a 70,000 words or so story. I only know the beginning but nothing cd be more romantic and attractive. An ideal start off to my mind. The hero is captured by the heroine in a boat, & she won't land him without a promise of marriage."

While such a springboard for a novel is unlikely to lure a

publisher in 1946, the author of *Ia* and other popular books became a Scribner find in the mauve decade. And Barrie brought E. W. Hornung, too, author of the famous "Raffles" stories whose hero was a gentleman burglar and hold-up man and which, oddly, raised no eyebrows in an age when moral sensibilities were supposed to be tender. He also tried to help them land Conan Doyle — without success. It would have been nice for the columnists (called "paragraphers" then) if Sherlock Holmes and Raffles could have been quartered in the same stable.

Stevenson, too, wrote Burlingame: "Why don't you get Charles Warren Stoddard on your Magazine: he has a small touch of genius"; and: "I send you herewith a set of verses by Mr. Henley which I think very remarkable."

After the First World War, about the time that it began to be discovered that a generation had been "lost," American writers commonly escaped to Europe. Some of them were stirred by post-war curiosity, some by decadence in the Paris "Dome"; others believed that they could write better about America from a distance and many went because the living there was cheaper. However curious such a migration may seem today, some of the best writers of a great era emerged from it.

"This is to tell you," wrote Scott Fitzgerald in 1924, "about a young man named Ernest Hemingway, who lives in Paris (an American), writes for the *Transatlantic Review* & has a brilliant future. I'd look him up right away. He's the real thing."

"Thanks for the tip," Maxwell Perkins wrote back and it did not take him long to discover the Hemingway potential, though it was scarcely known, at the time, outside Paris.

Fitzgerald himself came through the Irish writer of *The End of the Chapter,* Shane Leslie.

"In spite of its disguises," Leslie wrote of This Side of Paradise *in its unfinished form, "it has given me a vivid picture of the American generation that is hastening to war. I marvel at its crudity and its cleverness. . . . About a third of the book could be omitted without losing the impression that it is written by an American Rupert Brooke."*

Leslie continued on the watch and in 1921 wrote, "if ever I spot anything unusual I will pass the word to the great House of Scribner."

It not always happened, however, that authors' suggestions of other authors struck fire. In 1896, when Rudyard Kipling was being published in *Scribner's Magazine,* he was so enthusiastic about a novel he had discovered that he even offered to write a preface for it if Scribners would make a book of it. He described it as a "wild and wonderful tale — of which I think a heap. It's awful bad in places," he admitted, "and very fine in others. Now, what will the firm of Scribner's do for it?" When it arrived, however, the "awful bad" parts convinced them that not even a Kipling preface would carry it. "Where did he get his curse of formlessness?" Burlingame wrote Kipling after his disappointed reading of the manuscript: "Outside some bits of description like the very beginning, it is a sucession of starts for nowhere, each time with a lot of brilliant hopes that are promptly unloaded." Burlingame regretted "heartily and uncommonly" that the Scribners must say no. "But there seems nothing to be done, — not the least use tinkering with it."

Kipling was more successful with a later suggestion.

"I have rather a treat," he wrote in 1898, "— a story by W. S. Scully . . . who has been practically brought up among the South African races and has no small reputation of his own as the author of 'Between Sun and Land.' . . . Now that your land is going to have subject races of her

*own, she must take an interest in the thoughts and fancies
of such folk."*

America, at that moment, had achieved her much trumpeted victory over Spain; Cuba was under her protection; the Philippines offered prospects of both headaches and glory; the American people were divided between "isolationists" and "expansionists"; and Kipling, who thought of the white man's burden as a high moral duty, looked at the prospective American empire with sympathetic eyes. Scully's story was accepted.

Some authors who have achieved a lifetime of glory made slow entrances. Whether, in the 1870's, the firm of Scribner, Armstrong & Company was going through a somnolent period just before its rebirth in 1878 as Charles Scribner's Sons or whether the time-honored publisher's alibi of "bad times" had then an acute justification, it is certain that their evident boredom with such an up-and-comer as George Washington Cable showed a lapse of literary cunning that nearly lost them sixty-eight years of unbroken success.

It is true that Cable's best foot probably didn't come forward in 1871 when he sent in a round-up of clippings from his column in the New Orleans *Picayune* and offered to pay to have it published as a book. His letter stating that "it will be 120 pages . . . but with probably 40 pages of occasional verse" could not have given an editor much courage. The Scribners, furthermore, were proud of never having operated a job-printing establishment as part of their business and of not having emerged (as certain other publishers had) from a pressroom, smelling of ink. Writers did not simply pay them thus to print a book.

Besides this, Cable came from the dark and very dubious (in 1871) South and his paper was operated by "Rebels." Neither he nor it had any standing in the Northeast and New Yorkers had little means of discovering that in New Orleans, Cable was a veritable Alexander Woollcott of his era. At the same time, it is surprising that no editor, in the two months in which Cable's bundle kicked around the office, detected in it any germ or spark.

Four years later he tried again; this time with a group of orthodox stories which met with equal unsuccess. When he pressed the firm for reasons, J. Blair Scribner (the eldest son) wrote him:

> *"Although we can assure you that we fully appreciate your Stories both for their originality and merit we must . . . after due consideration decline their publication . . . the* times *are not particularly promising and collections of short stories almost always unsaleable. Your proposition to furnish a list of 500 subscribers is of course an inducement but not a sufficient one."*

Meanwhile, however, a magazine named *Scribner's Monthly* had sprung up and was attached to the House by a thread which its editors always claimed was a slender one. It was owned by a kind of joint-partnership called Scribner & Company in which Josiah G. Holland and Roswell Smith held most of the stock. Holland was editor; his assistant was Richard Watson Gilder.

Now *Scribner's Monthly* had become a highly successful venture. Aware that despite rebellion a decade before and despite the darkness of reconstruction days, the South was really part of the nation, its editors had sent a lively journalist, Edward King, to explore it. King, returning from what he called "The Great South Journey," brought with him, among other treasures, reports of his "discovery" of Cable. The *Monthly* then printed three of the stories out of the book Scribner, Armstrong & Company had rejected. King and Gilder became Cable promoters. They slipped paragraphs about him into New York newspapers and brought clippings of them to Blair and Charles Scribner.

"It is said that the name of Geo. W. Cable is a coming one in literature. . . . He is doing for the Creole life of the South something like Bret Harte's work for the characteristic California 'society.' "

Finally Professor H. H. Boyesen, who held the literary chair at Cornell University and was a Scribner, Armstrong author, joined the two zealots and, according to a letter published in Lucy Cable Bikle's *Life* of her father, "actually *bribed* S. A. & Co. to take the short stories"* as a volume. There is no record of the "bribery" in the Scribner files but in January 1878, seven years after the first knock on the door, J. Blair Scribner wrote Cable:

> "We have been intending to write to you . . . in regard to the short stories. . . . Your friend Prof. Boyesen has called our attention to them afresh and as the times have improved since you last heard from us on the subject we are now disposed to consider their publication more favorably. Your original letter to us has somehow got mislaid and we do not remember the nature of your proposition — but we will say briefly that we should be willing to bring them out in an attractive volume . . . early in April and bear all expenses attendant on publication. . . ."

Soon after this letter, the Scribner brothers, Blair and Charles, bought the Armstrong interest, and the reorganization of the firm as Charles Scribner's Sons delayed Cable's *Old Creole Days* another six months during which the search for its title

*Lucy Leffingwell Cable Bikle: *George W. Cable: His Life and Letters.* New York: 1928; pp. 50 ff. Italics hers.

(described in another place) was one of the most nerve-racking in all the strange history of title fever.

The "pay-off" (as modern vernacular would call it) on this story is in a letter to Cable from the firm in 1920, five years before his death, enclosing a semiannual royalty report: "560 copies of *Old Creole Days* is not bad." Forty-two years after publication, this was not bad at all — not, at least, for a volume of short stories "almost always unsalable!" One suspects that in the interval "the times" must have had ups as well as downs.

In 1946 — another twenty-six years after this letter, *Old Creole Days* is still selling. The total sales of Cable's books run into six figures. The charming, courtly author, for whom it took three strong men four years to push open the door, became a fast friend of the Scribners and their editors — he golfed, dined and spent countless week-ends with them and was one of that solid group which, in the romantic era, included Thomas Nelson Page, Francis Hopkinson Smith and Richard Harding Davis. He was, too, the forerunner of a whole library of fiction about the South; by Joel Chandler Harris, Page, John Fox, Jr., Stark Young, James Boyd, Marjorie Kinnan Rawlings and many others.

These reminiscences of authors meeting publishers through the scouting of editors and pressure of friends would, if they stood alone, imply that there is something in the old legend, built up by generations of amateur writers, that the unsolicited are ignored. Manuscripts, according to this myth, which are simply sent in with return postage, are not read and the old authors' device of sticking pages together is used to prove it.

Professional authors know that, while there is no obligation, moral or otherwise, upon a publisher to read anything that is sent him, he would be extremely foolish to send back any manuscript without examination. He would be equally foolish, of course, to read every word of every submission. He must find a course by which the substance and technical performance in any piece of work is quickly recognized. Practiced readers make it possible to handle the immense volume of manuscripts which come in daily with few mistakes. And, as Burlingame used to say, a certain portion of any job could damn it even "if Shakespeare had written the rest."

This does not prove, however, that the worst kind of writing in parts of a manuscript need condemn the author. Beginners are notoriously uneven in their work and an experienced reader will detect sparks of real talent in a wholly unpublishable book or story. Then the author must be encouraged and we have seen examples of this kind of encouragement in the letters of William C. Brownell.

Edith Wharton's connection began with a poem entitled "The Last Guistiniani" which she sent out of the blue to *Scribner's Magazine* and for which a cheque was sent her for $20 in July, 1889. Her next effort — a month later — was promptly declined: "We are sorry that we cannot like this poem quite as well for our purpose . . . so that we must hope that you will give us another choice." In September she sent in a batch of poems from which the editor chose "Happiness," rejecting the others. In May, 1890, she landed her first prose piece, "although we cannot often use a sketch as slight. . . ." During the next two years, her manuscripts were alternately accepted and declined but evidently personal meetings had taken place for she had progressed from "Dear Madam" to "Dear Mrs. Wharton," an immense stride for 1892. During these years, also, there was mounting interest in her work and evident co-operation, for in the fall of 1893, she wrote, "I shall never forget your encouraging kindness to me ever since my first literary endeavor had the good fortune to fall into your hands."

In the 1880's the phenomenon of the literary agent began

to make itself felt in England and some publishers were afraid that this was a serious threat to personal meetings with authors and, indeed, to the whole friendly relationship. Charles Scribner shared this fear and with reason when bidding began. He wrote of this to his English representative, Lemuel W. Bangs, in 1893.

> *"Just now there is a 'boom' on with English authors owing to the Author's society and the effect of Agents who put everything up at competition but it cannot last forever. A telegram to-day about the new Meredith serial shows that it has struck him also but there is a limit to what things are worth and publishers and authors will both find it out."*

Again in the same year he remarked on the practice and its ruinous effects, but he was optimistic.

> *"There certainly is a great strike among authors and the open bidding which is sometimes insisted upon forces prices too high in many cases but perhaps it is a temporary phase of business which will disappear — as many others have. . . . I think author's agents will go the same way."*

The bidding phase disappeared sure enough, but the agents continued — learning, as time went on, to adjust themselves to the subtleties of publishing. Yet in 1906, when they had spread to America, C.S. was still worried. Of one case involving an important author, he wrote to Bangs:

> *"It is an unfortunate situation in what I thought was a promising connection and I am particularly sorry on personal grounds . . . but my experience is that when an author deals with us through a literary agent, the days of our relationship are numbered. The agent is sure to 'crowd' us to such an extent that there is no profit or pleasure."*

But agents became increasingly popular with authors and, eventually, when events brought movie, radio and television rights into what had been a simple book and serial picture they were necessities. Today the business of a successful author is so complex that his affairs must be handled by an intermediary executive if he is to survive.

So it has become common for first meetings to be arranged by an agent. Agents have learned much since the profession began and today many charming and intelligent men and women are working at it. Publishers recognize their value and often enjoy their friendship. But the best agents do not intervene in the relations between an author and a publisher when this is established and such friendships seem, on the record, to be warmer and less formal in late years than ever before.

The record does not show all of this warmth. The letters from the beginning refer to off-stage conversations. And there are gaps in the correspondence which must have been filled by pleasant afternoons and evenings and which no living memory can bridge. The older episodes were perhaps less sensational than that hinted at in the correspondence between Perkins and Scott Fitzgerald in which, while driving each other home from Ring Lardner's one warm Long Island evening, both ended in a lake. But they included golf, horseback, walks in the snow, oysters and old madeira.

"I hope you will be coming down this winter," wrote *James Boyd to Perkins from Southern Pines, North Carolina. "We can spend many a profitable evening drinking rum & thinking of a title, I supplying one & you the other. Anyhow let me know as soon as you have an idea of sufficient merit to justify an invitation on my part."*

"The papers here," wrote *Charles Scribner, Jr., to Winston Churchill in the grim prohibition year of 1923, "a*

week or two ago were full of a rumor that you might be the next British Ambassador but I doubted if such a post would attract you. It would have been fine, as I should have had to call on you in Washington and have a drink of ambassadorial whisky — not that there is any lack of quantity or consumption here, but you never know how poisonous it may prove."

It always worries publishers to talk at length with an author before any of a book is on paper. There was an extreme case of this once at Scribners' and editor Charles Dunn, who has a sardonic flair, said of a certain much-discussed novel project that "the book has become a classic before a word of it is written." But once a manuscript has been accepted and put in hand, editors like to have an author available to talk things over rather than to have to write him. The correspondence with Stevenson in Samoa, with Wolfe in Germany and Switzerland, with Fitzgerald and Hemingway in Paris, with Edwin Arnold and Fox and Davis in Japan, with Admiral Dewey in Manila, with Stanley in Africa, with Marine Captain John Thomason in the Caribbean, all shows business which appears complex in letters but which might be cleared by a few minutes' conversation.

"I do not want," wrote Stevenson to Burlingame from a distant point, "to go into matters (which I seem to have mismanaged once) under the spur of hurry: your letter reaching me to-day about 2 P. M. and the mail leaving tonight. Will it suffice if I make you my apology for any offence I may have unwittingly offered? and if I add what is the fact, that I regard you with affection and would be very glad to shake hands with you and have a walk and share a luncheon this moment? I think we are both peppery, and perhaps not always clear either of us; so we must agree to take our cor-

*respondence not too heavily. And at any rate we seem to
have reached an agreement though by somewhat bewildering
paths. I do trust this will now be all well; I should count it
dear money that made a breach in our delightful relations."*

Perhaps the most inaccessible author on the record is Maxim
Gorky, who was in prison in Russia in 1901 when he got a letter
from the Scribners with terms for the authorized American
publication of *Fomá Gordyéeff*. Isabel Hapgood, the translator, explains this in her Preface, adding: "from prison he
despatched the cablegram of acceptance, — an incident which
is worth mentioning for the suggestion as to methods of the
Russian Government toward prisoners, which differ from the
popularly-received notions in that regard."

The first "first meeting" on the record occurred in 1846 with
a minister of the Gospel whose literary production reached
such a volume in this and the following year that, according to
the *Dictionary of American Biography,* "an attack on the brain
induced him to spend the summer of 1847 in the Adirondacks,
then a wild and little-known region." On just which day after
its founding, Rev. Joel T. Headley entered the small office of
Baker and Scribner — the original Scribner firm — on Nassau
Street, New York, and met Charles the First, father of "C.S.,"
is a matter lost to history, but it is on the books that within a
year four of his volumes, *Napoleon and His Marshals* and
Washington and His Generals (each two volumes), had been
written, printed, bound and put on the counters and that the
ultimate sales of these books passed the quarter million mark.

The title *Washington and His Generals,* the first success of
the first publishing Charles Scribner, brings to mind that of
Douglas Freeman's *Lee's Lieutenants* published nearly a century later by his grandson. A comparison between the books
hardly sustains the halo which once glowed round the head

of the Reverend Headley. But a glance at the titles standing at either end of the hundred-year span, suggests many things about the history of authorship, of publishing and, indeed, of the nation itself. Headley's book, written, hand-set and printed within a few months while scavenging pigs were said to have galloped through the New York streets, trumpeted about the birth of the nation, stirring flamboyant patriotism to justify the grab of the Mexican War; Douglas Freeman's volumes which took years to write, at a time when millions of machines roll off countless assembly lines every few seconds, calmly reviews the lives of men who fought to divide that nation and appeared while eleven million united Americans struggled on two fronts half a world apart to save civilization.

Publishers who still adhere to the old ethics are careful not to approach an author until they are sure he is free. They know that to invade a competitor's reserve with offers to an attached author is destructive of the whole personal and friendly basis on which this peculiarly delicate business is based. When an agent sent in a novel in 1906 with a note that "the author's name is John Galsworthy," it was promptly returned. Galsworthy at that time had friendly relations with another American publisher. Not for four years was Charles Scribner sufficiently assured that the author himself was determined to change. In 1910, Galsworthy's agent wrote:

> "*I can assure you that there is no question of your inter-fering with Mr. Galsworthy's relations. . . . His instructions to me are that while he wishes, naturally, to have fair and reasonable terms, it is more important to secure a publisher sufficiently enthusiastic about his work to push it energet-ically, and therefore he does not want you to take it up unless you do feel keen. . . . My experience makes me slow to*

blame publishers when books do not sell but in Mr. Galsworthy's case I get so many indications of a large and growing interest in America in his work, I cannot help feeling sure that handled as you can handle books, when you choose, his work will find its public. Although Mr. Galsworthy is not indifferent to the financial side, it is less that consideration than the desire, natural to a serious writer, that his message should be spread. I should not write to you at such length but for my anxiety to find exactly the right publisher, and to avoid another change."

To which C.S. answered:

"I acknowledge with thanks your letter . . . concerning Mr. Galsworthy's books. . . . We should be glad to publish them and you would be sure of our best efforts, for we think this author's books harmonize well with our other publications. But we are opposed to a large advance, both from experience and because we do not wish to outbid . . ."

These letters contain much that is inherent in the gentler publishing tradition. It is true that courtesy is exchanged in all kinds of business relations between rivals, but the grounds of competition in publishing are subtler and are more deeply channeled by human currents than most affairs of manufacture and merchandising. Enthusiasm, "keenness," harmony with other authors and other books are all variables, and writers, salesmen and public follow their mystic signs as planters watch the shadows of the moon. All good publishers understood these things in the old days and bitterness about an author's change was felt only when there was dirty work at the crossroads.

In late years, certain other businesses have become less personal; modern machinery, chains, monopolies and whatnot have changed them, in the public view at least, into great corporate forces which seem to move apart from and sometimes even athwart human impulses. If this ever happens to publishing the jumpy authors will take an angry stand and whip it back into line.

V

"NOT WITHOUT MERIT"

When a book by a new writer becomes a best-seller, a body of legend grows about it. It appears that it was declined by a dozen stupid publishers until some genius saw its worth and brought the author from his garret into the daylight. It is not explained that the genius who discovered Author A, the week before let Author B's manuscript slide through his fingers to another genius who may, indeed, be the very oaf who originally saw no prospects in Author A, but now is acclaimed as the discoverer of B's masterpiece. Nor is it told how long and patiently both these publishers have labored with the beautiful lost words of Authors X and Y, upon whom, year after year, the public has inscrutably turned its back.

To those who know the facts beneath the legend, therefore, it is not surprising that good publishers waste so few tears over mistaken judgments of manuscripts. Over a long career any publisher can find in his record dozens of declinations of books which later brought fame and profit to someone else. If, in that career, he has built up a solid body of good authors who enjoy working with him and bring him a steady income, year after year, and if, besides, he has laid a backlog of departments producing steady-selling religious, educational, juvenile, subscription or technical books, he has spent his energies more wisely than in the restless search for big sellers. The proof of this is in his survival. Those publishers who have approached their job in this way have lived the longest, and the wisest young publishers in the field today are those who are steadily building, regardless of brilliant, quick and sporadic successes.

The public, too, amused by the best-seller legends, is seldom aware of the peculiar reasons behind some declinations or of how beneficial to an author the rejection of a manuscript may be. A publisher whose list is full, say, for two seasons ahead will reluctantly let go a book which seems sure-fire to himself and all his editors. He is already committed to the limit of his capacity. If, now, he takes on another large job, he knows either that he cannot do it justice or that, if he does, the books for which he has already agreed to do his best will suffer. Both his conscience and his practical judgment tell him that half a dozen old, loyal authors and another half-dozen new ones who came to him in good faith and on whose work he counts for the future, cannot be slighted for the prospect of one brilliant success. And as authors will not wait until a publisher's list clears itself, rejection is the only course, however it may hurt. There have been cases in which a publisher has hired extra staff and made other expansions for one tremendous book, but, normally, the subtleties of the business do not allow this kind of stretch and the tales of its failures where it has been tried are not told. So, though it would be surprising to find an author pleased at a rejection — even when these things are explained to him — yet it is common enough, afterward, for him to look back over his manuscript's stormy voyage and thank his lucky stars that it came to haven at last in the place where the fullest measure of attention could be accorded it.

But it is true that a hardy, realistic decision of this sort is often difficult. It would be a boon to authors if publishers would make them oftener. Many a young author has been hurt by a timid acceptance: the taking of a book which has the cards of circumstance stacked against it but which the publisher hopes "somehow" to push through. And young authors are so likely to be excited by the mere fact of having a book published that they fail to see the half-heartedness of some acceptances. But any author, young or old, has a right to expect full honesty from anyone who reads his manuscript. He has far more right, for instance, to ask a publisher why he accepts a book than why he declines it. Indeed, in the latter case, he has no rights at all. The rejection of a book is wholly the publisher's business. But an acceptance immediately becomes the author's concern. If a publisher tells him frankly, as all publishers do, at one time or another, that he has taken the book not for its own perfection but because he sees a flair in the author which will produce valuable future work, well and good. But if he shakes his head, complains of a crowded list, divided enthusiasm, sales resistance to this sort of book, yet decides to "take a chance and print it anyway," the author had best say "thank you" and go elsewhere.

Enthusiasm among a publisher's staff is something an author is justified in expecting. Brownell used often to write in his gracious way, "that we are reluctantly declining your manuscript because it is difficult to foresee, in our office, the unanimous enthusiasm which is so necessary to advantageous publication." Enthusiasm, of course, is not always easy for an inexperienced writer to discern. Editors acquire, through the years, a surface coolness which may not accord with an author's exalted view of his own effort. This was deceptive in Brownell, for instance, whose expression sometimes made one think that any literary or other effort put only a drop of amelioration in the world's ocean of sadness; yet Brownell was able to write to Edith Wharton, "You can assuredly plume yourself on having joined the 'note' of universality to that of distinction," and "you have the happy hand. How it can model so much and touch so lightly is a mystery." And Perkins, who has been accused of difficulty in articulating enthusiasm when he talks, could have left no doubt of it in James Boyd's mind when he wrote of *Drums*, "Of course we want to publish it. . . . It is a very large canvas and beautifully painted, and we have naturally found it a great pleasure to read."

With older, more famous authors, the question of price is sometimes a factor. In old times it was thought worth while to give as high as twenty-five per cent royalty on a book by a highly successful author. Today most authors are content with a sliding scale between ten and fifteen, and it is generally conceded that it is a mistake to ask for a high advance on royalties. The publisher wants a margin at the start, so that he can be reasonably free with the money he spends on promotion. With a crushing load hanging over his first activities, the enthusiastic intention to "go to town on a book" as the modern vernacular graphically expresses it, may grow damp throughout the office.

> *"It is said," wrote Charles Scribner, Jr., to a world-famous author in 1930, "that an advance acts as a spur to the publisher but it might as truly be said that if the first sales do not promise to meet the advance, the publisher is apt to cut advertising and limit the possibility of loss to what the author has already taken."*

And his father, forty-five years ago, made a revealing statement of his policy to the English mystery-writer, E. W. Hornung:

> *"The report will show you that your books have a better market here than formerly . . . we think we may attribute a small share of their success to our confidence. Under these circumstances it is a little hard to see your next book issued by another publisher here. . . . We are always prepared to pay whatever the book is fairly worth. In competition, for the sake of getting a new author, a rival publisher might outbid us for some particular book by paying more than it*

was commercially worth and this is all that interferes with a general statement that we would be willing to pay whatever any other publisher might offer. I always assume that an author does not wish to get the best of his publisher any more than I wish to get the best of an author."

This letter was written in the days when publishing "ethics" leaned backward. But it is still believed by wise men on both sides of the author-publisher fence that an auction-block practice in books would be ruinous to everyone concerned, not to mention the personal relationship which seems to have been so beneficial to literary production. So an author whose book is declined because he or his agent insists on an exorbitant advance may well be wary of the next offer.

The declination of books on the grounds of readability or literary excellence is another matter. It is hard to understand, for instance, how a novel which has become a classic, is included in literary courses in schools and colleges and still sells, forty years later, many copies a year, should have met with an inhospitable reception in manuscript. Yet here is the report of a Scribner editor, Edwin W. Morse, on Arnold Bennett's *Old Wives' Tale.*

"Mr Bennett's novel belongs by subject and largely by treatment in the class of 'Kipps.' It is realism dealing with the tradespeople of a small mid-England town and their petty affairs spun out to the proportions of an epic. The leading figures are the two Baines girls, daughters of the principal draper in Bursley, one of the Five Towns in the Manchester district. Their careers are followed in the most minute particulars from the time when, during our Civil War, they were fifteen and sixteen respectively, until their deaths in this country. The changes in the town, social and

[65]

commercial, which took place between the crinoline and the motor-car periods are dwelt on with care and particularity. The main story however concerns itself with the dull, empty and wasted lives of the two Baines girls, Sophia and Constance. . . . A remark of one of the sisters, Constance, as she looks back over the career of her dead sister and of herself, seems to present the author's justification for such a study —'Well, life is like that!' Mr. Howells might say 'Amen!' to such a sentiment, and no doubt life is just like that to thousands, perhaps tens of thousands, of English of the class here described. But, granted the truth and the vividness of the portraiture, the people themselves are so deadly and monotonously dull, so devoid of aspirations or even thoughts above the yardstick standard, so depressing and even saddening in all their social relations, that they make a most fatuous assembly to find between the covers of a book. The book, in a word, leaves one with the impression of a fine talent spending itself lavishly, but wasting itself, upon an unworthy theme."

This is certainly a persuasive statement to one who has not read the book. If we project ourselves back into the period — which was one of flux between the romantic and realist eras — it seems more so. It is safe to assume that the book had other readings and that the editors agreed. But surely no publisher can look back from 1946 upon such a rejection without putting a black mark against his record.

A more arguable case was that of *Zuleika Dobson*. This was declined in 1911, by Scribner's English representative, Lemuel W. Bangs. They had published one of the author's previous books under the forbidding (to Americans) title *Max Beerbohm: Works,* and it had come a cropper. "*Zuleika,*" Bangs wrote, "I did not think would interest us. The author is more highly estimated by himself than by anyone else, and has never reached any high standard in his literary work."

Several of Gertrude Atherton's books were declined on moral grounds. George Moore's *Esther Waters* went back because the combined morals and snobbery of the period were not expected to tolerate the illicit love affair of a chambermaid. But the discussion of times and morals forms a chapter by itself.

The Scribners have been given great acclaim for the discovery of Scott Fitzgerald. Yet *This Side of Paradise,* when it first came in, went back. Perkins liked it, saw in the manuscript the possibility of great improvement and suggested transposing it to the third person from the first in which it was written. Brownell could not stomach it at all and Burlingame described it as "hard sledding." The first World War was in mid-career at the time and it was hard to convince older editors of the significance of flappers and the Jazz Age. Fitzgerald himself was in training camp and about to go overseas, an event which the abrupt Armistice finally forestalled.

At Scott's request, Perkins peddled the revised manuscript to other publishers, terrified that they would accept it, for all the time he saw how vitally it might still be improved. The other publishers, however, sent it back without comment and Scott, the war over, decided to spend six months on its rewriting. When the new version came, the pressure of Perkins's enthusiasm plus the wholehearted support of Charles, Jr., exerted on C.S., put it over.

Here was one of the exceptions, which must occur to prove the rule, to undivided enthusiasm. As with James's *The Sacred Fount,* editorial opinion certainly differed on *This Side of Paradise.* And the galley proof was hidden as long as possible from the sales department.

An important member of the sales department in those days was a person who had certain peculiarities of expression. One of his favorites was "I speak advisedly," when he was uninformed and meant "guardedly." Often mistrusting his own literary judgment he spoke "advisedly" about many books, and used to take them home to an erudite sister to read. His sister was supposed to be infallible and it was true that many of the novels she had "cried over" sold prodigiously. So when it was known that he had taken *This Side of Paradise* home for the week-end, his colleagues were agog on Monday morning. "And what did your sister say?" they asked in chorus. "She picked it up with the tongs," he replied, "because she wouldn't touch it with her hands after reading it, and put it into the fire."

Brownell, however, was won over, in time, by the new author. "May I read you something beautiful?" he said, coming out of his office one day into the open space where several editors were gathered, and he read aloud, in his fine diction, two pages of *The Great Gatsby*.

Brownell used to read his manuscripts lying on a couch. He was the only Scribner employee who was ever granted such a luxury. Perkins, who never even sat down and had a lectern built so that he could do all his work standing up, and Burlingame, who sat, if at all, on the edge of his chair, used to regard Brownell's practice with amazement. Charles Dunn and other irreverent editors maintained, in spite of their adoration of Brownell, that they could hear undeniable sounds of dozing from his office.

Yet Brownell wrote letters about manuscripts which showed he had not missed a comma or a semicolon. His declinations were so meticulous and so gracious that authors were almost tricked into believing them acceptances.

"We have been extremely interested," he wrote a Miss Pusey in 1898, "by your novel 'Society' and in finally coming

to the conclusion that we shall be unable to undertake its publication we beg you to believe that we do so very regretfully & for reasons which by no means impeach the many excellences of the book. Your own statement that it is not a first effort was not needed to convince us that it is the work of a practiced hand and we cannot too warmly congratulate you on many of its felicities of literary expression and really dramatic situation. If we may venture to make the suggestion, however, we think you will agree with us that the public taste of the day, rightly or wrongly, has concluded it to be the wiser course to demand observation rather than imagination of all authors of whom the strenuous personality is not already eminent or overmastering. There is a great deal of heart in your book, and certainly none too much, but is it not here and there treated after the dictates of your own sympathies (with its shade as well as with its light) rather than scientifically, impersonally, artistically, universally? And doesn't the etiquette side of it encroach a little now & then on the human interest? We should not obtrude any reflections of this sort if we were not desirous of attesting our interest in the book & our hope that you may permit us to examine whatever else you may do as carefully as we have done 'Society.' "

New York in the 'nineties moved in gentle tempo. Past the Scribners' windows on Fifth Avenue and Twenty-second Street, "stages" were pulled over the cobbles by big, straining horses, and the horses were followed by flocks of sparrows and white-clad men with brushes. Hansom cabs, their high-perched drivers braced and rubbered against the weather, ambled along the curb or sped, hell-bent, at eleven miles an hour, down the center. The rich and great moved about in polished landaus or victorias behind "spanking" high-checked, dock-tailed cobs over which whirled the long lash of the liveried coachman, and beside the coachman, in speckless boots, his arms folded like an artilleryman's in caisson parade, sat the footman, poised to spring at his master's signal to the coach's door.

All the world seemed secure. Such things as the panic of '93 and the threat of "free silver" were short-lived. New Yorkers lived serenely behind impenetrable bastions of defense, stuffed themselves with food, took naps, smoked immense cigars and worried, mainly, about catching *la grippe* or having their daughters slighted at a ball. That, at any rate, was the ambience in which literature and the arts blossomed: there was time for culture, haste was vulgar, there were few telephones and people were kind to one another in a remote and courtly way. Even the "war," which brought an orgy of bunting, bands, parades, triumphal arches and hero-worshipping ballyhoo to New York three months after Brownell wrote Miss Pusey, touched no one deeply.

Even nine years later (in 1907), when typewriters clicked in the offices and the smell of gasoline was mingled with the sweet horse redolence of the streets, Brownell wrote, in the beautiful longhand he had learned in school from the celebrated Spencer in person, a masterpiece of careful regret.

"I liked it," he told an authoress of her manuscript, ". . . for its altogether extraordinary cleverness. And this I didn't believe the public would like as much as I did. At least I didn't think they would be as willing as I — an old hand or jaded palate or whatever you like — to dispense with other things which it lacked. Substance, for instance — sentiment, character, story. You can 'broider that text as well as I. You are very good at embroidery! In a word I didn't think there was enough warp & woof for the embroidery, to make a story appeal to our public. And this sense

[70]

was helped by the spirit in which the embroidery is stitched — an elusive & elliptical & tricksy genius. The public likes a bite better than a whiff. I won't say that, in some moods, I don't agree with it — but certainly not enough to fail to appreciate the savor of méringue of modernity which you have so happily confectioned without putting a very thick pie under it."

A purist in metaphors might quarrel with some of Brownell's imagery here and a later stylist might wish it sharper and more succinct, but the letter (which goes on for three more pages of minute script) is undeniable proof of leisure in an editorial world now forever dead.

Brownell was always distrustful of half a manuscript and thought it unfair to an author to read unfinished work.

"It would," he wrote Upton Sinclair in 1902, ". . . be of no use to submit to us a portion of a work, the judgement of which would depend largely upon the ensemble *— as in the case of a novel."*

Perkins, in a later day, was more pressed by circumstances and sometimes had to read a book in bunches. But, as he wrote Sidney Howard in 1927, "if you feel reluctance about showing an incomplete manuscript as I could easily think you might, because it is not well to talk about work of that kind before it is finished, it won't much matter." And "I ought to learn," he wrote James Boyd, "to resist the temptation to read a book in sections. . . . Doing this makes it impossible to get the complete impression."

Probably in every publishing house, an occasional personal literary prejudice, inexplicable in hindsight, interferes with the acceptance of valuable material. This happened rarely at Scribners', but it happened. Brownell's feeling against Edgar Allan Poe came too late, of course, to affect the Scribner publication of Poe's *Tales,* but Burlingame's curious indifference to Emily Dickinson was probably responsible for the Scribners' not becoming her publisher. The strangest antagonism Burlingame expressed was to Stephen Crane, whom he described as "standing on his head and waving his legs with a crimson roar." These things stand, nakedly and alone, upon the record and it may be unfair to print them thus without their lost context of thought and reason. Burlingame was, at the time, the editor of a magazine and magazine work was, as we shall see, peculiarly hedged and conditioned. Perhaps in the vast realm of his thought outside his job his attitude had another color.

There are skeletons then in many of the dusty closets where the tell-tale letter copies of dead men are stored. Probably once in a while it does no harm to give them an airing; to show the weakness of the wisest minds in this intuitive and fallible profession.

VI

TIMES AND MORALS

The history of the minutest phase of a nation's life which lasts a hundred years is bound to be complex. If it centers round dates, names and places, its chronicle is profoundly dull. Only the human impulses in their variety; only the quirks of individuals, leading or punctuating trends of custom, have the slightest attraction for a reader who is not directly involved. No such reader cares, for instance, that the "original" Charles Scribner was the son of a Uriah Scribner, who in turn descended from a Connecticut Scrivener (except, perhaps, for the remote hint of a play on words). He is not moved by the fact that this "original" deserted an 1845 law office from ill health and entered the supposedly more restful commerce of books. He cares far more what this zealous and charming gentleman said when a Nassau Street mouse ran up his trouser-leg and, if he said it in the presence, say, of the Rev. Headley, for the comment of this theologian as the hundred thousandth copy of his latest work tumbled from the press.

He cares also about what Maxwell Perkins couldn't say, in the office of this original's son eighty years later, as he sat with a manuscript by Ernest Hemingway on his lap. (The normal reader must care about this or so many versions of the dialog would not have been printed and told.)

Perkins, according to Malcolm Cowley's profile in the *New Yorker*, explained that there were three probably unprintable words in the script of *The Sun Also Rises*.

" 'What are they?' Mr. Scribner asked.

"Perkins, who never uses a stronger phrase than 'My God,'

[73]

and that only in moments of great emotion, found that he simply couldn't say them.

" 'Write them then,' said Mr. Scribner.

"In his chicken-track hand, Perkins scrawled two of them on a memo pad and handed it to him.

" 'What's the third word,' Mr. Scribner asked.

"Perkins hesitated.

" 'What's the third word?' said Mr. Scribner again, giving the pad back to him. Finally Perkins wrote it. Mr. Scribner glanced at the pad.

" 'Max,' he said, shaking his white head, 'what would Hemingway think of you if he heard that you couldn't even write that word?' "*

Unfortunately there was no Malcolm Cowley and no *New Yorker* in the Manhattan of 1846, and if there had been the first Charles Scribner would have shuddered at the possibility of any but the most dignified of his gestures or utterances being bandied about the little town. The only periodical which reported the doings of publishers in any detail was *The Literary World*, which obscured its dehydrated material with long and pompous words. There was not, indeed, much dignity to report. The quality of American literature, in spite of Emerson, Hawthorne, Melville and a few others, was at a low level; the best of it was printed in Boston, the cultural center, and the bulk of good books was imported from England, where the great Victorian era was already in blossom.

Yet there was a great rash of print over the country. Fiction, poetry and juveniles dropped daily from the presses, not to mention the droppings of "moral philosophy." To glance over these books (without other information) one would suppose Americans to have divided their time between prayer and covetousness, license and repentance. Every year a thousand

*Reprinted with permission from the *New Yorker*, April 1, 1944.

books proclaimed the wages of Sin in terms of hell-torture; a thousand others made Sin delicious for forty-nine chapters and paid it off only in the hurried fiftieth. In the reading East, "females" had already largely taken possession of the printed word, men being too busy, and most books were designed for their swoons and tears. Magazines and especially newspapers thundered about moral decadence alongside advertising columns of sheer pornography.

It seems an unpropitious time for a gentleman educated by Princeton College and European travel, a person of deep and dignified religious convictions, to establish a serious publishing enterprise in a nest of cutthroat materialists like the city of New York. Only the brick chapel in which, in 1846, Baker & Scribner opened shop on the corner of Park Row and Nassau Street protected them.

The name of Isaac D. Baker would perhaps be lost had he not been the first partner of the founder of a house which has endured through three generations of the Scribner family and a century of American culture. Hardly a glimpse or tale of Baker survives beyond the fact that he seems to have worked at dry goods before books tempted him and he himself lived in the Scribner partnership only four years.

A faint flicker of the geniality which may have glowed in the chapel office is reflected in the first author's letter in the files.

"I should like hugely," wrote the Reverend H. N. Hudson from Keene, N. H., in October, 1849, "to walk into your store again, as I did in days of yore when I was a young man;"— and this is doubtless facetious as the store was then but three years old —"and if you were not so far off, I rather think I should do so: but alas, a lass! age, old age and the distance prevent me. Which being the case, my heart and other bowels yearn to hear from you: in the first place I

want to hear from yourself; in the second, that your precious
wife and sisters are well; in the third, whether the book is
selling . . ." He continues through financial items to "the
sixth, whether New-York is right side up. . . ."

Hudson concludes his letter with the suggestion that neither
Scribner nor Baker were the ceremonious characters age has
made of them: "Please shake Mr. Baker's hand and crack a
good joke upon him, for me, and slap your two clerks on the
back. . . ."

Scribner started with a policy. No reprints. No throwing
together of a popular English book in a new cheap form and
printing and selling it without benefit to the author. (When
he at length decided to import, he started a special company for the purpose.) New current writers—no regilding of
classics. Religious books, yes, lots of them, but by professors
of theology and dignified (preferably Presbyterian) divines,
not fly-by-night circuit-riders and camp-fire evangelists. Novels
—presently—in spite of the New York *Herald's* editorial in
1848, condemning all fiction (including Bulwer and Dickens)
as "trash." History of the Headley variety whose astonishing
inaccuracies later made the hairs of the orthodox historians
stand on end, but which combined the jingoism and religious
fervor of the 1840's in popular proportions; poetry—of N. P.
Willis, God rest his soul; and, once the business got going, the
sleepy reveries of Ik Marvel. But current stuff, mind you, all
of it, not the dead men's relics which the snobs thought the only
fit literature for respectable Americans to read.

But it was all highly moral. Morality exuded from the Brick
Church Chapel. It moved with Scribner commerce to Broadway, to Grand Street, back to Broadway, up to Fifth Avenue,
through all the firm's permutations. It still dominated the
House in 1887 when Gertrude Atherton sent in a manuscript.

"I have no hesitation," wrote the Scribner reader, J. R. G. Hassard, "in advising you to decline Mrs. Atherton's novel, 'The Randolphs,' principally for the reason that it is an apology for adultery. . . ." After describing the book, Hassard added, "Besides this radical immorality, the novel contains many passages of pseudo-philosophy which would give offense to religious persons."

Of another Atherton book the discerning but delicate Hassard wrote of the loving hero and heroine that "the author, with a superfluity of prurience which fixes her quality, gives us to understand that they have anticipated the marriage ceremony."

Hassard's reticence is hardly equaled by Edwin W. Morse, who, some twenty years later, encountered the earlier gems of Elinor Glyn. Speaking of the heroine of *The Visits of Elizabeth,* Morse wrote:

"All the men, married and single, make love to her in various ways, and she comments naïvely on their behavior in squeezing her arms, holding her hands, kissing her, etc. One tries to make an assignation with her. . . . At the end one has the uncomfortable feeling of having been a spectator of the operation of rubbing the bloom off a girl by a lot of worldly and more or less vulgar people. . . . The theme is one that requires the most delicate handling — such as Henry James or Bourget would give it. Mrs. Glyn presents it with brutal bluntness and directness."

No wonder, with such a background, that even in the 1930's Perkins's pencil broke over a certain Hemingway word! It was not, perhaps, merely — as Cowley implies — a question of Perkins's personal delicateness. Perkins was flexible enough before truth in writing — Tom Wolfe was witness of that. It was that, looking into the stern eyes of the Founder's son, with the Founder himself staring down from the wall, in all the dusty ambience of the old theology and old morals, he did not realize that C.S. had grown flexible too!

The firm's permutations began in 1850. In those days, when you wanted to do something different, you started a new, additional company for the purpose. It was the opposite impulse from the great merging trend which followed it. So, seven years after Baker & Scribner in 1850 had dissolved into Charles Scribner & Co., there came a side-show called Scribner and Welford for importing, and the brilliant English Charles Welford became a fixture, going later to England to represent Charles Scribner's Sons. In 1879 came another collateral, Scribner & Company, dedicated to two magazines, *Scribner's Monthly* and the beloved juvenile, *St. Nicholas,* operated by J. G. Holland, Roswell Smith and Richard Watson Gilder. Smith eventually removed it by an orthodox business transaction from all Scribner connection and turned it into The Century Company, as which it became an immense influence on American letters. There is no rattle of skeletons in this transfer and the friendliness of all concerned was widely proclaimed in 1881.

Meanwhile, in 1871, Charles Scribner died, untimely, at fifty; there was a brief interval of Scribner, Armstrong & Co., until, in 1878, the sons, Blair and Charles, joined after a time by Arthur, took full hold, giving the firm its permanent title.

That, in the fewest words, is the chronicle; it is not spectacular. But through it runs a highway of strong and singular consistency. This, perhaps, is what has drawn all the authors and held so many: the sense that on that road they knew where they were going because it ran so straight, clearly and simply sign-posted. On it they could never be betrayed into outlands of bog and quicksand.

Through the years, conventional shades of morality altered. When the Queen died and insurgent waves, so adroitly and so long held back, began to dash upon the British islands, their echo came across to us whose last frontier had closed. Machines, incandescent light, fast movement, upsurge of the underclassed, the manœuvre of violent guns and ships, sharpened and defined the lines of social patterns. The Victorian petticoats came off and were discarded as the costume of hypocrisy. Men did in the open what they had done in dim, gaslit corners and women came out of bondage. Children were told truth; writers wrote it and publishers, perforce, printed it. Creative writing graduated from the wishful into the actual, and even the reading public finally woke from its dreams.

All this would scarcely need saying in 1946, except that it has taken us until 1946 to understand how much struggle this change has involved. Even now, the history is written with such oversimplification that our schoolboys (unless a war drags them away before they have the chance) conceive of the thing happening all at once between, say, a Thursday twilight and a Friday dawn.

Authors and publishers who have lived through it know that it came at molasses pace. For years, authors fought with publishers and publishers with the public. Truth, realism, clarity, economy, all the things we praise in our brave world, got into print almost word by word. The very linotypes seemed to jam when some of them appeared. The public screamed and called out the police; ministers (forgetting the ugly words in Scripture) rocked their pulpits; moralists shouted about sex depravity, snobs about vulgarity, managers about the labor octopus, patriots about Treason.

If all this had not occurred, however, and if the changes had gone through overnight, the world might now be in even greater chaos than it is. Not until long after a revolution do we know the usefulness of the restraints with all their seeming dumbness, ignorance and reaction.

In this aspect, the conservative publishers played a balancing role. It was no more valuable, in the long sweep, than the role played by the radical publishers. Each watched his special public. Between them came the change and it was not violent enough to swing the whole literary trend too suddenly or too far.

The Scribners were conservative publishers. Some of the advance guard of authors called C.S. (without strict justice) an old dodo. It is true that there were head-shakings throughout the office over books it finally printed as far back as Maxim Gorky in 1901. In a letter in that year written by W. C. Brownell to Isabel Hapgood, Gorky's translator, the conflict between fidelity to artistic integrity and fear of the public's recoil is clear enough.

> *"The episode,"* *Brownell wrote of a scene in* Fomá Gordyéeff, *"makes us fear effective criticism whatever its justice. The psychologic purpose and real force and feeling may easily be missed by a public unused to the* genre. *It is difficult to debate such things, but the fact that they suggest debate is of itself enough to menace misconception and we feel inclined to omit this episode. If we did so, however, would the same general question come up again in anything like the same baldness? Not having read the* ms. *further than this I am unable to answer this important question and must appeal to you."*

And now, note, another fear of criticism from "broader-minded" readers:

> *"Of course we don't want to publish a patently expurgated edition. Therefore it would be salutary to know now, if this*

episode stands by itself to a very considerable extent . . . or if there are other things in the matter yet to come which, having omitted this, consistency would involve the omitting of also, thus really maltreating the book."

Brownell concluded by saying that, as there would be other English translations, "we should not like ours to be . . . the only one prudishly devitalized to the misrepresentation of the author."

Miss Hapgood's prompt reply is a milestone on the road of change.

". . . There is another episode . . . but much less crudely expressed. In fact, robust Paul Bourget-ism, if one may describe it so, and considerably less offensive. . . . I think you will be more severely criticized, in one direction, for omitting this passage, than in the other for leaving it in its place . . . but . . . it has seemed best to me to let the Scribners sit in judgment, from the outside-public's and the inside-publisher's point of view."

After naming some current books to illustrate, Miss Hapgood adds:

"In short — the public has become used to rather strong meat, in recent years, or I should not have dreamed of suggesting this book! It dazes me."

And Brownell closes the incident on a note of triumph for art and truth at the beginning of the new century:

"We decided to keep in the scene I wrote you about. It is nobly treated and too characteristic to be omitted fairly. . . ."

In the century's first decade criticism came from the clergy.

Henry van Dyke, a beloved Scribner author with an enormous
following among all sorts and conditions of religious-minded
folk was distressed by Maurice Hewlett's *Rest Harrow*. "I think
it is pretty rotten,"—he wrote in 1910—"and gravely, blas-
phemously, sentimental."

Dr. van Dyke, while not wholly innocent of (non-blasphe-
mous) sentimental bursts on his own account, was nevertheless
far from a prude. But his note on Hewlett's novel is an index
of restraint as the literary picture broadened. He later protested, "I like the 'Younger Writers' vastly more than you
suppose. They refresh and cheer me up." Incidentally van Dyke
came in for a "moral" censure himself when, in 1920, Scribners
circularized a picture of him with a pipe in his hand.

> *"I have taught my boys," wrote a member of the Cali-
> fornia State Legislature enclosing the shocking portrait, "the
> sin and evil of tobacco, and had rather they were left on
> the battlefield of France than come home addicted to to-
> bacco. . . . It seems to me that the enclosed cut of yourself
> will do more harm . . . than your books can possibly do
> good."*

When a Galsworthy novel arrived for magazine serialization
in 1915, Robert Bridges trembled over a galley proof which
he returned to the author.

> *"The Magazine," he wrote, "goes into a great many
> families as appropriate reading for young and old. It also
> is used as collateral reading in some schools of both sexes.
> We fear that some of them would find this paragraph too
> frank for reading in public."*

This was the passage:

> *"Was not all man's unhappiness caused by nervous an-*

ticipations of the future? Was not that the disease, and the misfortune, of the age; perhaps of all the countless ages man had lived through, since that first genius among his Simian forebears made the great discovery that the supreme act of love should be committed face to face and eye to eye? Whence, slowly, consciousness and soul had crept into male and female bodies and man had come about . . ."

"I consent," replied Galsworthy, "to the deletion of the paragraph from after 'countless ages man had lived through.' I regret however that what is probably a piece of scientific discovery, administered in delicate lines should have to be withheld from your reading Public. And I reserve all rights in my contribution to man's knowledge of his origin."

Bridges, however, made a point to be considered in comparing a magazine with a book. The buyer of a magazine buys a variety of literature. He may buy it for one thing, yet have another, for which he also pays, thrust upon him. The buyer of a book on the other hand knows — or should know — what he is getting in for.

It is interesting, as a conclusion to the above incident, that Galsworthy, despite his reservation of "rights" to his triumphant scientific discovery, seems to have forgotten it when book publication came along. At any rate, the dubious passage appears in no edition of *The Freelands* and is here, for the first time, given the light of day.

But it was long before this that C.S. himself began to have doubts about his own conservatism. He felt them in the 1890's. In 1887, he was still alarmed by radical writing especially if it offended religious sensibilities. When churchly Americans were shocked in that year by the translation from the French of Renan's *Life of Christ*, he used the device of Scribner & Welford to escape responsibility for its publication. Scribner

& Welford, which existed wholly for importing books, put its imprint on foreign books it brought into the country. The imprint branded the book as foreign — printed elsewhere and originally arranged for by a foreign publisher. Scribner & Welford simply did Americans the service of buying the books in sheets, binding them in the United States and putting them on sale.

"We cabled," reads C.S.'s letter to Bangs in 1887, "to put S & W imprint on the Renan . . . as C.S. Sons don't want the responsibility of publishing for such a radical."

But in 1894 we find him wishing his public more flexible. In that year George Moore, for whom the Scribners had already published *Vain Fortune,* was encouraged to send over the manuscript of his new novel, *Esther Waters.*

"It is the life struggle," Moore had written of this book while he was in the midst of it in 1892, "of a servant girl, the drama of motherhood, a servant girl who devotes her whole life to her illegitimate child. The girl I am trying to depict represents the simple sturdy steadfastness of the Saxon race. All characters in the book are servants, betting men and jockeys. For it is a racing book in low life or rather betting in low life. Both masters and servants are ruined by betting. The book is one of the most honest ever written. . . ."

Moore followed this, as he got deeper into the excitement of his creation, with another.

"I have just written the scene between Esther Waters and the rich woman whose child she is nursing. I think I have succeeded in bringing out the callousness of the rich woman and the heroism of the working woman who at last finds words, simple words, and tells what she thinks. Then there

is the scene with the baby farmer. 'Give me five pounds and
I will take your child off your hands for you. Of course if
it lives I shall be out of pocket. I must take my chance at
that.' A drama of motherhood in the middle of a complex
civilization and yet beset with dangers worse than those of
a primeval forest."

It is hard to imagine a description of a book more prejudicial
to a respectable New York publisher of the 1890's. Added to
the American public's then moral attitude to such subjects,
there was the snobbish attitude. The now forgotten institution
of "servants" was then in full swing at least in the eastern
portion of our Democracy. Servants, when not functioning in
starched uniforms and expressionless faces, were hidden away;
they slept far upstairs in small dark rooms, ate in the kitchen
and were paid approximately four dollars for a seventy-hour
week. The notion that a servant could suffer passion and have
a sex life, if held at all, was not publicly expressed. Furthermore, Moore's whole thesis was a slap at the novel-buying
public, most of whom either were well-off or wanted to be.

In spite of this, Charles Scribner eagerly sent for the book
when it was done. It came with instructions to pass it on to
other publishers if declined. Only after long consideration,
Brownell wrote Moore:

"*. . . We wish very much to publish it if we could and*
so to give it and ourselves every chance we waited till the
second batch of sheets came. You will easily understand the
obstacle in one way to be the plain-spokenness which our
public finds objectionable & unnecessary, and will certainly
not believe us blind to the elevation, force & touching quali-
ties of the work. We regret sincerely not to become its pub-
lishers & regret also to be obliged to enclose (as we do) the
notes of declination we have received from Messrs Harper

[85]

& Messrs Appleton, to whom, in this order, we sent the sheets."

And to Bangs in England, C.S. wrote:

"Mr. Brownell and I have been talking over the story by George Moore. . . . We like the story ourselves but there are scenes in it such as a child birth in a hospital with full accounts of labour pains etc. which would hardly go down here and it would certainly excite surprise if published by us. . . ."

By 1911, the doubts were still there about the public but slow change was foreshadowed in another letter to Bangs:

"Indeed," wrote C.S., "that is one of the great difficulties now; so many of the well-known English authors — like Wells, Arnold Bennett, George Moore, and others — are too free and coarse in their handling of delicate questions to suit us. I enjoy their books personally but our imprint would sometimes be injured by association with such books. It is very hard to tell where the dividing line comes and we sometimes make mistakes, for the public is becoming more and more callous."

The imprint had already, however, gone on Wells's realistic *Kipps*. It went, after a while, on Galsworthy's *The Dark Flower*. After the war it went, dubiously, on the "radical" Fitzgerald. Perhaps it would be too simple to say that when the Scribner imprint went on a book it put the seal on the *genre* — that, after that, any one who objected branded himself as far behind the moral trend.

By the time Hemingway arrived, America had profoundly changed in its appreciation of fiction. The war had turned American writers toward what the French in Zola's heyday had called "naturalism." Dos Passos's *Three Soldiers,* E. E. Cummings's *The Enormous Room* and other books had led a new way to frank expression. "Sex" had become a new word — formerly merely a noun modified by the adjective male or female, it now meant a thing by itself, an abstraction. Children learned about it honestly at a tender age from parents and teachers, rather than in the back yard. And the war had brought all kinds of physical realities, once hidden, into public view. Yet, with all this change of feeling there was a curious hangover about words.

For instance, the word "prostitute" was freely used but the old Anglo-Saxon word "whore" (used even in a book title by Daniel Defoe) was taboo. Even "bitch," though proper in its technical place, was shocking in human application — not to mention its male offspring. "God damn" came to be accepted in dialog when it was written "goddam." These prejudices and especially that against obscene slang (words marked "vulg." in such dictionaries as printed them at all) broke down slowly and some words are still the sole excuse for the banning of books in certain communities.

While prejudices existed there was a plausible literary argument brought by editors against using the words. A word which, because of prejudice or very exceptional usage, *arrests* the reader or concentrates his attention on a passage which should not be unduly emphasized, may damage a story.

This was expressed in a letter from Maxwell Perkins to Ernest Hemingway in 1926 when *The Sun Also Rises* was in hand in the Scribner office.

"The book is of course a healthy book with marked satirical implications upon novels which are not, — sentimentalised, subjective novels, marked by sloppy, hazy thought. That is one of the first things it is. But as I have said, people

[87]

are afraid of words. We don't want to divert attention from its intrinsic qualities to details of purely extrinsic importance. It would be a pretty thing if the very significance of so original a book should be disregarded because of the howls of a lot of cheap, prurient, moronic yappers. You probably don't appreciate this disgusting possibility because you've been too long abroad, and out of that atmosphere. Those who breathe its stagnant vapors now attack a book, not only on grounds of eroticism which would not hold here, but upon that of 'decency,' which means words."

So custom altered and the publishers with it, and, before looking back over the history, more gradually than it would seem. Today such a great proportion of readers has come over to realism in fiction, that its sales match those of the best-seller romances of other years. Yet there is still a large public group which wants romance and dream and "uplift" and there would be no more sense in quarreling with such a group than to quarrel with men and women who prefer golf to gardening. On any street corner an author may be greeted by a reader who says: "I meet unpleasant people and things in business, and sad things in all of life — why should I come home and read about them?" This distresses the realist but such an approach to fiction is legitimate enough. Fiction is fully capable of providing escape and there is no reason against such a use of it. But when the craving for escape from life possesses an entire people (as was almost true in the '80's and '90's) and when no means is given any of them, through the arts, to face it, there is occasion for social alarm; and it may be, as some assert, that we are reaping today a whirlwind sown in the romantic years.

VII

IN HAND

Somewhere near the office of C.S. on the editorial floor, there was always, in the firm's middle years, another office slightly smaller, perhaps, but with a similar group of waiting men outside it. In it sat "A.H.," a kind and much beloved man. Arthur Hawley Scribner was younger than Charles; he had been still happily at Princeton College in 1879 when Blair Scribner died and Charles took all the reins in his hands. By the time Arthur arrived to take his place as partner, the reorganized business was sternly on its way and Charles was its undoubted dictator.

A.H. had neither the iron will nor the finality of decision of his elder brother, and his experience in the business was more specialized. At any rate, he acted as a cushion or shock-absorber between Charles and the staff. You did not take a question to C.S. if you thought there was a chance that A.H. might answer it. On the other hand, if it was a question of major importance, you could be sure of a more conclusive, if balder, reply from C.S., because the procedure on large questions was that, if you put it up to A.H., he would evade you with a smile and, after you had left him, walk softly across the hall with it, to his brother's desk. One thing you could be sure of was the smile. That and his cordial welcome, whatever the press of mood or business and the quickness of his humor were the things for which he was loved. A.H. never scolded and rarely frowned. He tried, sometimes, and broke down, was laughing before he finished and though occasionally men left his office uncertain as to immediate action, none ever left it hurt.

If you wanted a raise, or time off, or had trouble at home you told A.H. He did not give you the raise, perhaps, but you knew, if you had reason, that he would be your advocate; that you would get it later. His courtesy was infallible and very old-world; to the end of their lives, for instance, he addressed his elders as "Mr. Brownell" or "Mr. Burlingame" and even referred to them so in his private letters to his brother. He was sometimes accused of pinching pennies because he was so meticulous and tireless about figures and it was true that he would not use a new pencil till the last half inch of usefulness had been got out of the old one. But he did not pinch dollars and the record shows at least one transaction where enthusiasm carried him far beyond prudence. He liked enthusiasm and, when he found it in his workers, gave it rein.

Once a new publicity man brought him an unheard-of proposition. A novel had been published and died. The young man was certain it could be revived with the right advertising. He wanted to spend $5000 on it more than a year after publication. He brought his campaign beautifully laid out on cardboard. A.H. shook his head. That wasn't the way the publishing business was run. A book sold or it didn't sell; it caught on if it was going to catch on in a few months — after that it was a terrific job to get the retail stores to carry it. Yes, there was the classic story about a George Meredith book brought back to life after the plates had been melted, but such phenomena were too rare to prove anything. . . . Then, suddenly, in the midst of this dialog A.H. caught the gleam in the boy's eye; it was irresistible and he laughed.

"I can't destroy your faith," he said. "Go ahead and I'll back you."

He did not even ask C.S. The young man went ahead and learned his first lesson in the art of publishing. It cost Charles Scribner's Sons approximately $4500.

A.H.'s mastery was in the art of manufacture. He knew all about paper, binding, type-faces, gilt, stamps, cut and uncut leaves. He knew the cost of these things to the last mill; he knew their durability, their fitness and their tradition. He was expert, too, in word estimates and could tell just the number of pages a manuscript, when printed, would fill; he had a fine grasp of the balance of plant and royalty and even the imponderable of "overhead." He had an affection for all the physical properties of books; he would handle a finished job with tender, tactile appreciation.

Arthur Scribner comes into the story here because, once a book was accepted, its terms arranged and its manuscript edited, it was put "in hand," and from that point until it reached the ultimate consumer it was largely his concern. In modern lingo his job, therefore, was "operational"; policy, and the subtler contacts with authors or critics were managed elsewhere.

"What is 'in hand'?" wrote Scott Fitzgerald to Perkins in 1924. "I have a vague picture of everyone in the office holding the book in the right hand and reading it."

It means — though it never quite finally meant that to Fitzgerald — that all the preliminaries are over: the bickerings on clarity, taste, meaning and morals, as well as business terms. It means that someone has taken the manuscript and tried to make the punctuation, spelling, use of capitals and italics uniform. It means that the words have been counted — not every word, which would be highly inaccurate — but counted for estimate of the white space which would become black when printed, and allowing for short lines, paragraphing, dialog. It means that the manuscript has been sent to the printer along with memoranda about sizes of type-page and type. And it means that a first printing or "run" has been estimated and paper ordered.

During the period that a book is in hand and, especially

when galley proofs come in, jittery authors are likely to make frequent calls or write anxious letters. If they are new authors, the print surprises them. Galleys are long, unmanageable sheets, each containing without breaks about four book-size pages. An author, accustomed to think in pages, is upset by these long columns of print. Galleys, also, are almost impossible to read in bed or, indeed, in any comfortable position. They fall at angles on the floor and become entangled with the feet. They require vast desk space to sort and arrange.

Down the margins of the galleys, printers' proof-readers put exasperating and often incomprehensible hieroglyphs. Printers work with rigid, humorless minds. They underline a capital S on "gal. 23" and remark, in telegraphic comment, that the same word was spelled on "gal. 21" with a small initial letter. "But that's the way I want it!" exclaims the author. It makes no difference, my young friend, that that is the way you want it. The editor probably knew you wanted it so, when he sent the manuscript out (hoping the compositor would miss it), but to the compositor you have done a shocking and inexcusable thing. If you insist on using two "cases" of S for the same word in the same book, it will probably take the whole editorial department in a body to sell the printer on your inconsistency. If eventually they beat him he will put an A with a circle round it in the margin as testimony that the inscrutable and possibly demented Author, not he, is responsible for the lapse.

Men in composing rooms are disturbed by the slightest departure from the rules of punctuation they learned by thumb as apprentices. Authors like to break these rules for rhythm or emphasis. If they do, a question mark and the laconic scrawl "punc" are sure to jump at them from the margin. The word "construc?" is especially infuriating to a writer who estimates his style highly. What does a proof-reader know about construction?

"Herewith the proof," wrote Stevenson in the eighties, "which I trust will put your printers on their mettle. Possibly a word from you might help: depict me as a man of a congested countenance and the most atrabilious disposition: you will only anticipate the truth, for if they go on making hay of my punctuation, I shall surely have a stroke. I am up to my neck in attempted papers; three of them, no less; and not one will come off well — better Luck! — but this morning has gone to your printers and to the composition of insults to the reader. I hope he is a man of sensitive vanity. Then I shall have touched him on the raw."

It is astonishing, however, thinking back, to remember how much proof-readers in the old days did actually know. When the Scribners began to do their own printing they had a proof-reader whose erudition and memory were a perennial surprise to the editors. He knew Latin and Greek thoroughly; could and did read all the classics in the original. He could spot a misquotation anywhere in the realm of poetry. But he also had the sciences at his finger tips. He caught errors in the transfer of Fahrenheit into Centigrade, in statements of Boyle's Law or the acceleration of a falling body. Many printers forty or fifty years ago had such geniuses on their premises; men who from inertia, bad habits or contentment had remained proof-readers to the ends of their lives.

The editors were supposed to read the galleys before the authors got them. If they could, they would answer the printer's queries and spare the author. Then they would add suggestions of their own; seeing new things — for no editor is infallible.

"You work subtly," wrote Perkins as he sent the galleys of Marching On *to James Boyd, "and in reading the proof, I find there are things I had missed."*

He then made some marginal suggestions and was careful in his letter covering them.

"You speak," wrote Boyd back, "of fearing that criticism may confuse and trouble me. If you have such a fear it troubles me more than any criticism could. I have spent a lot of time trying to get intelligent criticism of my stuff. Of the many who have commented you seem to me to have a good deal the most sense. So I beg you not to go back on me. On the other hand don't fear that my high opinion will over balance my independent judgment. It's my stuff & every decision must be mine. . . ."

Reflecting on the demands of "the lonely art," Boyd added:

"In a word whenever I can feel the force of your criticism I'll seize upon it avidly & use it without acknowledgement, & in any case when I can't, I will wrangle bitterly, denounce you passionately but all on purely professional grounds . . .

"So sing out loud and clear. Then we'll have something to work on."

The attitude shown in this letter might well be taken as a model by young authors who mean to make writing their profession. In it is a sense of dependence upon an editor up to the moment of publication balanced by a firm stand on his own rights. But it is most notable for its divorce of the professional from the personal regard. The mixing of these things is dangerously easy in the writing trade and many a writer has remained an amateur because his emotion or, as he once called it, his "temperament" prevented his keeping them hardily apart.

In contrast to the above, the record shows an acute case of "temperament" when an author caused to be written into her contract this passage:

It is further understood and agreed that said publishers shall restrain themselves and their staff severally and individually, from any harassment of said Author in the course of her work, and that they shall wait patiently to allow her to do it in her own way and in her own time, as she pleases; and that if it seems to said Author that she has been unnecessarily pressed, obstructed, or irritated by the importunities or by the apparent indifference of said Publishers, she shall be free to cancel this agreement.

The conflict here between "importunities" and "apparent indifference" indicated a delicate procedure on the part of the staff. They knew the author well enough to be sure of her resentment if they failed in constant inquiry about the progress of her book, but at what point did such concern become "harassment" or "importunities"? It is significant, perhaps, that this contract is now seven years old and that in spite of the most adroit fulfillment of its demands by the "said publishers," the manuscript it called for has not yet arrived.

Timing is the most stringent control while a book is "in hand." The presses must be fed. The printer has set a date for making galleys into pages and type into plates for the press. This date fits into a schedule which includes all of the season's books. Yet, as the printer sends out his galley proof he faces imponderables. He has no idea in what shape the proof will come back. A brainstorm may induce the author to cut, enlarge or rewrite. Perhaps even an editor may induce this. So, in a sense, both editors and authors are the printer's natural enemies. There are degrees of enmity here, of course, for the author may be assumed to have virtually no concern for the printer's troubles. The editor, too, is more directly accessible.

"Hold up galley forty for big change," cabled Scott Fitzgerald from somewhere in Europe while *The Great Gatsby* was in hand. "The correction," he wrote in his following letter, "—and God! it's important—. . . is enclosed herewith." But as a postscript to this same letter he added with characteristic inco-ordination of the constants of time, space and type-metal, "I hope you're setting publication date at earliest possible moment."

Sudden changes of this kind are not peculiar to the later writers.

> "P.S. and a P.S. with a vengeance," appended Stevenson to a letter headed "Raw Haste Half Sister to Delay." "Pray send me the tale of the proof if already printed — if not, then the tale of the M.S. — and — throw the type down. I will of course bear the expense. I am going to recast the whole thing [The Master of Ballantrae] in the third person; this version is one large error."

It took an even temper like Arthur Scribner's to stand between a printer and the author-editor coalition. A.H. knew, to be sure, that printers, for all their pretended rigidness, could be as elastic as rubber bands if they had to. It was in their tradition to stop presses in the midst of runs because someone had died or a war had begun or ended or a last-minute lawyer had spotted a libel or a misprint had made a word obscene. The decision was whether or not they had to, but this was policy and the ukase must probably come from C.S.

But A.H. had his hand on other things besides printers' schedules. One was the timing of the salesmen. This takes place while a book is in hand. The traveling men — the "boys," they are always called, though several may be well into middle age — leave to sell retailers over the country the books then in hand for a spring or fall season. They go, of course, well in advance of publication. Retail booksellers being traditional skeptics, the

boys take with them "dummies" of the forthcoming book. A
dummy looks as much like a book as possible and even contains
a title-page, contents table if any, and a few pages of text. The
rest of it is blank. With this tangible evidence of good faith in
hand, the most Missourian bookseller can hardly doubt there
is really going to be a book.

A.H. used to gather the boys together before they left, along
with a discreet editor to talk about the season's offerings. These
meetings were genial and A.H. kept their tone gay and hopeful.
The salesmen were supposed to have read galleys of the books
before, and at the meetings the editor would tell why they were
good and what sort of people would like to read them.

All this of course took time and effort. The dummy involved
full manufacturing plans. A wrap or dust-jacket with a blurb
on it drew the publicity department into advance action. If,
after all this, an author delayed his proofs so that the book had
to be "put over" to another season the results were disastrous
indeed. These were once summarized in a letter written to H.
G. Wells by C.S.:

> "*We are much disturbed at the idea of postponing the
> publication of 'Kipps'. . . . You probably do not realize
> what a disappointment and injury the postponement would
> cause here '. . . 'dummies' are in the hands of travelers in
> various parts of the country, and already many orders have
> been received. The book has been included not only in our
> announcements but in a number of advertisements, and the
> way for its publication has been prepared by advance notices
> . . . 'all our expenditure of time and money would be thrown
> away by the postponement and we should lose the best season
> of the year. This is the psychological moment and delay
> would cause an anti-climax.*"

Wells's threat of delay in this case was due to an English

serial jam, not to the author's procrastination, but the results would have been the same whatever the cause. It was straightened out as it happened and the salesmen never knew of the threat.

A cause of delay and of general distress familiar to all publishers is the disease of title fever which, oddly, often becomes acute while a book is "in hand." Outsiders think an author writes his title before he starts his book. Actually this rarely happens or, if it does, his title is usually bad and shocks the publisher when he sees it. Publishers and authors have different ideas about titles. To an author, the title is usually involved with his feeling about his book; it brings out some aspect which is dear to him. To a publisher, it is a means of selling it.

Publishers know that, unless an author is famous, his name means little to the average book buyer. He may have been wined and dined and lionized in literary circles and his picture spread over the literary pages of newspapers and magazines; yet unless he has been exceptionally honored by Hollywood, Pulitzer or wide comment on his personal behavior, the large reading public — who simply want a good book to read — neither know nor care who the author is. So it is the title which, over his head so to speak, sells his book.

A woman who (as one did in the Scribner Bookstore) wanders among the counters, saying: "I want a book for a man thirty-four or thirty-five;" will make her choice from those the salesman spreads before her by title. She will glance at the picture on the wrap, read the blurb, look, perhaps, for the publisher's name as one might look for "Schenley" or "Hiram Walker" on the label of an unfamiliar bottle and buys the book because the title has provoked her.

Dear to the heart of Harold Frederic was the title *Douw Mauverensen* for his second novel. When the Scribners saw it on his fine manuscript they shuddered in unison. The very stenographers and office boys shuddered. Possibly in sections of up-state New York, which were the setting of Frederic's story, the name would be pronounceable. But in the deep South, the Middle West, Philadelphia or even Boston tongues would twist over it until they gave up. "Give me that book beginning with a D by that man who writes for *Scribner's Magazine.*"

It was not easy, however, to divert the author.

"The more I think of this," he wrote *(in 1887), "the more it appeals to me as a name which will wear.*

"And isn't it true that to give a personal narrative the name of its chief figure, is to help individualize it in the public mind? It would be an impertinence to quote the great books —'Robinson Crusoe,' 'Tom Jones,' 'Henry Esmond,' 'David Copperfield.' . . . I have always believed that 'Christie Johnstone' and 'Peg Woffington' were read so much while other and to my mind greater books of Reade's were neglected, because their titles conveyed the direct tangible idea of a personality, while 'It is Never too Late to Mend,' and 'Put Yourself in His Place' didn't."

Still missing the point, he wrote again, "it occurs to me that perhaps the best way out of our dilemma would be to call it —'The Story of Douw.' " But when, fully confused, he suggested *Where the Mohawk Gently Glides,* the publishers decided they must do it themselves.

So Burlingame, the greatest title-hound in the establishment at the time, set to work. And, one night at midnight, pacing his dining room after his noisy family had retired, he trapped *In the Valley* which stood forever on the cover of Frederic's long-celebrated novel.

The record shows that a long struggle ended when Edith Wharton wrote Brownell in October, 1904:

"I am fatuously pleased with 'The House of Mirth' at this moment after going through a phase of black despair!"

And an audible gasp of relief goes up from Burlingame's letter to her:

" 'The House of Mirth' captures us all. I think it is the inspirational title we have been hoping for. I was satisfied with and even liked 'The Year of the Rose,' as you know; but this is very much better, crisper, more vigorous, without a suggestion of preciosity, and telling its own story to perfection. We all adopt it without a dissenting vote. . . .

"I have since learned that 'The Cost' has just been used as the title of a novel by David Graham Phillips so it would be out of the question anyhow."

But there was the same siege over her next novel.

"How do you like 'The Cup of Mercy'? It enunciates itself easily, & is a beautiful phrase," Mrs. Wharton wrote in March, 1906. In June she suggested "The Boundary." In July:

"I launch this . . . to ask you, before the die is cast & the type is set, whether you like 'The Chariot of the Gods' better than 'The Boundary'? It is certainly showier. . . ."

A week later:

"On second thoughts I don't like 'The Chariot' . . . I don't like 'The Boundary' either; but if I may have till the end of August, a miracle may happen before that. . . ."

In reply to this, a comforting Burlingame letter said:

"We have still a little time to think, for it will be late August they tell me before anything goes out in print; and

I remember 'The House of Mirth' was found in the very last few days, so perhaps an inspiration will yet come."

It came, and just in time.

"A new thought!—'The Fruit of the Tree'. . . . Do let me know if you approve."

The approval was quick, yet no sooner had the announcement been made than a book was found in England with the same name. This was such a frequent happening, however, in the book world that publishers had long given up trying to fight it and the copyright law has rarely been enforced against a title.

There was a like attack of the fever when James Boyd, after the great title-success of *Drums*, was in a frenzy as his next book moved through its galley stage.

"You can find," he wrote in November, 1926, returning a set of proofs, *"in this first chap., the significance of 'The Bright Horizon.' I have also tried* Free, Free White, Free Man, Prisoner, Deliverance."

"I am still perplexed about the title," Boyd's editor answered. *"I think you have sent a number that are quite good, —'Deliverance' and 'Barrier's End' among them. The trouble with* Deliverance *is that somehow it does not have much* lift *in it. The trouble with 'Barrier's End' is that it has rather the sound of titles that were used in the great days of Arnold Bennett, say . . . There is another trouble with 'Barrier's End,'—it may seem a rather artificial view but I do think a one word title, following the one word 'Drums' would be better. . . . I do not care for 'Marching' . . . 'Wrath' would be a possibility.—But a word like that does not fit with the early part of the novel. . . ."*

Boyd wrote back:

*"Your letter . . . just came. [Laurence] Stallings was to
be in N. Y. Sat — yesterday. His suggestion for a title . . .
was 'Grapes of Wrath' from the Battle Hymn of the Republic. Another which I like better from the same poem is
'Marching On.' "*

That clinched it. But after the book came out, the Scribners
were obliged to write Donald Brace of Harcourt, Brace:

*"We are truly sorry that we used Ray Strachey's title,
'Marching On' for James Boyd's new novel. Please believe
it was altogether unintentional. . . ."*

After a series of brainstorms in 1924, Scott Fitzgerald sent
from Rome the titles *Trimalchio in West Egg, Trimalchio,
On the Road to West Egg, Gold-Hatted Gatsby* and *The High-
bouncing Lover* for his third novel then in hand. They were
discarded and he finally consented with reluctance to *The
Great Gatsby.* This was attached accordingly, the book printed
and bound and the publication date set — April 10, 1925. On
the nineteenth of March, however, he had a final inspiration,
induced, perhaps, by the dream world air of the island of Capri
from which he cabled, frantically:

*"CRAZY ABOUT TITLE UNDER THE RED WHITE
AND BLUE STOP WHAT WOULD DELAY BE."*

It would, Maxwell Perkins wired back, be fatal.
Perhaps the most critical case of title fever occurred when
Scribner, Armstrong & Co., before its reorganization into
Charles Scribner's Sons, had the first of George Washington
Cable's books in hand.

*"The name of the book," wrote Cable in January, 1878,
"if it pleases you shall be* Jadis. *If you would like me to try*

again, however, I will do so; I appreciate the importance of a name that will, so to speak, go where it's sent."

Blair Scribner (Brownell, the French scholar, not having yet arrived) replied that he didn't know what Jadis meant, and added, in effect, that he didn't think it would, so to speak, go anywhere.

"I have beat my brain," answered Cable, "for a title almost the only result being that the brain is well beaten. Jadis . . . signifies, as near as I can give it in English, once, in the faery-tale sense 'once upon a time.' . . ."

Cable proceeded then to suggest the following:

Prose Idyls for Hammock and Fan; Half Hours for Hammock and Fan; The Old Regime: Créoles et Créoles; A Peculiar People; Creoles; Créoles du Vieuxtemps; Hammock and Fan.

Dizzy, perhaps from the swing of the hammock, the Scribners lapsed into silence. Cable, evidently fearing that the profits on his book would be used up in postage, sent three penny post-cards a week.

"I want to satisfy you . . . 'Odors from the South' or 'Odors of Cypress & Orange.'
"I can think of nothing else but 'Under the Cypress & Orange.' "
"I am trying the changes on another phrase. 'Creole Burr & Blossom,' 'Clusters from a Creole Vine.' "
"If you think you can stand one more —'Creole Antiques.' "
"As a sort of final effort I send you this 'A Gallery of Creole Antiques'— and shall rest on my oars until I hear something."

While he was resting (no longer, happily, in his hammock) Burlingame arrived in the Scribner house, and in April, 1879, the whole affair — cypresses, burrs, oranges, vines, fans and antiques — was evidently thrown in his lap. At any rate, on April 14, he wrote to Cable:

"Won't 'Old Creole Days' satisfy you as a title for your volume?"

Without waiting for his reply, the reorganized firm of Charles Scribner's Sons evidently rushed the book into its binding, for the next letter in the files (on May 20) expresses Cable's thanks at receiving "5 copies of 'Old Creole Days.'" So that was that and nearly seventy years later, in 1946, the book still sells under that title.

The benign influence of Arthur Scribner was inside rather than out; his work was intimate with many of the staff and only occasionally came in direct meeting with authors. His concern was great with contentment and unity among the men and women whose co-ordination in the work of publishing must always be complex. He got up baseball teams (ably assisted by Joseph McElroy Mann of the cashier's office, who in his youth had invented the pitcher's curve and was famous for having pitched the first curved ball at Princeton) and he organized luncheons, dinners and outings for the staff. And here he conceived the radical idea of "author meets salesman." Why these two vital factors of publishing should have been so long and sternly separated is not clear unless we suppose that any interest in sales was beneath an author's dignity — a supposition not borne out by the correspondence.

"We have recently given each year," wrote A.H. to Henry van Dyke in 1926, "a very informal dinner to our salesmen before they start out on their fall trips, and this year the dinner is to be next Friday, May 7. . . . This is the climax

of a week's intensive work with them on our new books and serves to start them off in good spirits particularly when we can have an author or two present, as they then feel that they have been let in behind the scenes, which gives them an added importance with their customers. Last year Struthers Burt, Will James and [Captain John] Thomason were present, and we have just asked Kermit Roosevelt if he can come this year, and I wonder if it is possible for you to join us. . . . They would particularly appreciate meeting you and would receive directly from you a much clearer idea of the purpose of your book than can be conveyed to them in any written paragraphs — indeed you could quite inspire them. They are a fine set of young men, about twelve in number, of whom we are proud, and it is an encouragement to our authors to know the class of men who represent them."

That this idea had thoroughly caught on by 1929 is shown by a letter in that year from Charles Scribner, Jr., to Winston Churchill.

"I am looking forward very much to seeing you and I hope that you may find time to come to our office and meet some of my associates as I am sure that it would have the effect of redoubling their efforts in behalf of your books."

One of the associates to whom Charlie Scribner here referred was Whitney Darrow, head of "Wholesale." Charlie Scribner's term "associate," used to an author about a sales executive, indicated a change which had come over the face of the House. That such a change impended had been evident when C.S. first took Darrow from his own Princeton University Press and gave him charge of the commercial end of the business. It meant that the important work of selling books was at last assuming the dignity it deserved.

[105]

It was never strictly true, as sharp-tongued authors were once wont to remark, that "a book salesman can't read." He did frequently present, however, a striking resemblance to salesmen of soap or brushes, products which do not directly demand understanding of the printed word. For this reason and to protect sensitive authors and editors from exposure to commercial "taint," sales-folk were hidden. So when, in 1916, authors first encountered a person of Whitney Darrow's charm, education and familiarity with letters representing liaison with the marts of trade, they were surprised and secretly delighted. Later, when they were not only permitted but encouraged to discuss with him the matter uppermost in their minds, repression-neuroses in the writing world went into a sharp decline.

Today, a new literary visitor, wandering through a building in which nothing else has ever altered, is a little startled by the unique magnificence of Darrow's office. His feet touch carpet and suspicion creeps into him. Has he stepped from the dusty purlieus of art for art's sake into a Babylon dominated by a golden temple of trade? His doubts are soon allayed as his eyes move to the walls closing him in. For here, every square inch up to the tops of the partitions is covered by photographs, drawings, sketches, caricatures, affectionately inscribed — of authors! This final evidence of breakdown of traditional barriers so affected Tom Wolfe when he first saw it, that he confessed to an editor that he would never believe he had "arrived" until he should find himself on a Darrow wall.

To present a picture of the "In Hand" period in which the headaches appear largely as those of the publisher would be misleading indeed. It is almost an axiom that the necessary grief which accompanies any phase in the great and beautiful process of transferring thought to print must be predominantly the author's. His concentration on the immense job in his hands must be pure, single and in a high altitude. The confusing tricks of selling and advertising with all their necessary vulgarization cloud his vision of his creation. If he is cajoled into altering his text to tickle a popular whim, his sense of honor is hurt. If a blurb distorts his intent, the injury is deep. If a half-baked, smart-boy critic perverts, for his own *réclame*, the whole of an author's motive, it seems to destroy the years of his effort.

For the years of his effort with all its pain and stern devotion, the average author of a book gets little money value. To make $5000 in royalties on one book is very fair success. Yet if it is a good book, it has probably taken him a full two years to write. The cases are innumerable in which five years' work has netted him no more. Many a non-fiction writer whose book involves research has spent more in cash than the book brought him, so that he has actually lost money.

So, for most authors, satisfaction must come indirectly or in imponderable terms. It is true, for instance, that the immeasurable profit of "prestige" comes only from a book. A "great name" in literature comes wholly from a writer's books. No amount of magazine publication, lecturing, radio broadcasting or movie production has a comparable effect. Yet all these highly profitable things are often made possible to an author because of the reputation he gains from one book which may be unlucrative or even costly in itself.

For it is a curious fact that a book need not sell in great numbers to build a wide reputation. Libraries, reviews, quotation, prizes and honors are all concerned in this result. And many writers are able to continue comfortably in their profession because, through the prestige earned by a single book, come orders and demands for lectures, articles, short stories or broadcasts. These are the indirect terms. The great imponderable is the satisfaction of a published book — greater, for a sincere writer, than all the temporary, high-paid achievements in the whole of this articulate world.

But is it a wonder that the author watches like a cat every move his publisher makes? Is it surprising that every proof-correction, every detail of wrap, cover, paper, type which clothes his precious product, keeps him edged and wakeful? Is it surprising that he suspects every editor, manufacturing man, salesman or publicist of perverting, hiding or ignoring the fruit of his anxious years?

And the publisher, on the other hand, works in a world which from long contact he understands. He has far more rules to guide him. He has a great organization of many minds; his job is delicate surely, but not lonely. And he has a "backlog" to save him from loss.

Yet these solid things — the publisher's sanity, experience, security — give the author courage. And the smooth, even functioning of the machinery which gives shape to his work steadies him against his own shifting moods. If the balance of its motion is upset, his poise is lost.

To keep the rhythm, there is a governor or balance-wheel in every sound publishing machine. Often it is beneath the surface, far inside, without show or glitter. It works evenly, in silence, and has some effect upon every motion. The author feels its presence even when he never sees it.

In the House of Scribner one of the steadiest of those controls, for forty years, was the hand of Arthur Scribner.

VIII

O U T !

Whoever has watched an author take his new book fresh from the press into his hands has been in the presence of a unique emotion. Nothing is quite like it. The thing is his, yet it is not wholly his; it is his creation which someone else has admired enough to beautify, to multiply, to make solid and permanent. The thing in his hand is himself detached, microcosmic, but one of thousands which will soon go out to other minds, to become part of other lives, other households — small bundles of himself traveling far into the world.

If it is his first book, it is unfamiliar, he does not recognize it. The warm, used quality of his manuscript, its pages curled by his handling, is gone; here is something clean, to be carefully touched, a little cold and respectable, with a dignity given it not by himself but by sharp-edged people and processes, machines and pressure. He must live with it awhile before its presence on the table is no longer odd; before he will like its clothes. Sometimes he is afraid to open it lest he find some forgotten horror beneath the decent dress. Presently, though, he must open the cover to the blank flyleaf waiting for his signature and a few carefully written words — something smart, worthy, succinct, to make the book a treasure for a friend "without whom . . ." So he goes out smiling, he will walk through the street with the book casually in his hand as if it were any book, its front turned modestly inward.

The next day he is back. His wife cannot bear the jacket. A friend has pointed out three misprints in the first chapter. How had he missed that change he had intended in the love scene?

Those verses he had quoted in chapter twelve were Pope, not
Goldsmith — he was certain he had fixed it on the page proof.
The blurb says he graduated from Wisconsin in 1930; what
would his classmates of the famous year of 1931 say to that?
His wife's cousin has been to Brentano's; there isn't a copy of
the book in the store and publication day is only two weeks off.

A publisher learns to take these things without aspirin. He
knows that a book with no misprints would be a new phenomenon. They occur even in law books, dictionaries and telephone
directories, where a comb is used that is far finer-toothed than
any trade publisher employs. An occasional misquotation is not
taken seriously even by the critics. They enjoy finding it and
they smile at it but the book is not hurt with the public. Publishers know that mistakes in first editions are so usual that the
rare-book business is largely built upon them; misprints in the
first printing of a valuable book enhance its permanent value.
And the fact that a writer or his family does not like a wrap
is generally in its favor from the publisher's view.

As a rule, however, the author is not there in the flesh, to
take his new book into his hands. Then the letters pour in. A
distant author's jitters begin the moment the last page proofs
leave his hands, when the die is cast.

*"I sent you today," wrote Thomas Nelson Page in 1898,
"a telegram asking you to correct without fail a slip in a
legal phrase . . . as it appears now* in vinculis matrimoniæ,
and should be in vinculo matrimonii. *I knew the error was
there and intended to correct it; but forgot, and it struck
me all of a heap this morning. I don't want bad Latin and
bad law together. There is one other error that I meant
to correct. . . . Dr. Cary says, 'Syria is confederate with
Ephraim.' It should be, 'Ephraim is confederate with Syria.'
No it should not — I have written it wrong now. It should*

be 'Syria is confed'te with E.,' which is what I meant to make Dr. Cary say; but I wrote it wrong and forgot to correct it. I do not know just where that speech is. . . ."

The next day he wrote again:

"Cannot a slip be printed and bound in the vols. as errata? I am worried about the thing because it was so stupid of me. . . ."

These letters were written not to an editor but to Charles Scribner himself, who was expected to drop all his other work and thumb through the book until he found an error which even the author was not sure of. Whatever may have happened in the office when C.S. got these confused notes, he kept his temper when he answered them.

"I received your letter . . . concerning the errors in Red Rock. . . . It was impossible for us to . . . print an errata slip and insert it in 10,000 copies of a novel without delaying the book. The Latin phrase has been corrected and will appear all right in the new edition. . . . We can also correct the other mistake if you will send me word where it occurs. . . . Otherwise it will be necessary for us to read the whole book through. . . . I regret that either mistake should appear in the first edition but doubt whether a single critic will notice them."

Critics, however (among them the meticulous "F. P. A."), discovered about 100 misspellings in the first edition of This Side of Paradise. This was too many and the fault was plainly the publisher's. Fitzgerald's spelling was notorious. It was persistent, often picturesque and bore little relation to sound. To the end of his life he wrote "etc.," "ect.," and "yacht" "yatch." "Week" and "weak" were interchangeable. "Descision" and "tyrrany" were favorites; so was "dissapation," and always he wrote the name of his friend Hemingway with two m's. The difficulty with *This Side of Paradise* was that Maxwell Perkins would never, at any stage of its making, let it go out of his hands, and Perkins, but for the stern supervision of his secretary, Miss Wyckoff, would probably be something of an orthographic phenomenon himself.

It was the fault of the Scribners, too, that Theodore Roosevelt's *Outdoor Pastimes of an American Hunter* was advertised in the New York *Times* as the pastimes of an American Homer, bringing a facetious burst from Brander Matthews.

> *"Dear Mr. President," he wrote to the White House, "... You may be the American Xenophon — altho the Rough Riders were not Ten Thousand and did not retreat; and you may be the American Herodotus or even the American Thucydides. But the American Homer! Really the sycophancy of some toadies is appalling. As I like always to think well of my friends — especially when they are practical politicians I shall try to believe that this advertisement is wholly unauthorized."*

And, from the White House, the President wrote his editor:

> *"Oh, Bridges, Bridges — why didn't you make it Lucretius instead of Homer? Of course I appreciate the flattery, but I am so afraid that an unkind public will take the view ... expressed by Brander Matthews in his offensive letter which I enclose."*

There was another case of a blurb which, in its wording, was discovered to take a backhanded slap at William Lyon Phelps. "Among all those," it read, "who have the least interest in literature, he is an ever more valued friend and adviser. He writes about nothing but he illuminates it."

But authors who should know better, make astonishing mistakes which publishers can hardly be expected to catch but which are seized upon by the leering critics. Edith Wharton, who had done much research on cotton mills in preparation for *The Fruit of the Tree,* had eight technical mistakes in her descriptions of cotton machinery and practice called to her attention — discovered, fortunately, in the serial version. An author who shall be nameless, who has a most uncomfortable conscience for accuracy, put a footnote in a historical work saying that tomatoes once grew wild in the New England colonies. It was an inexcusable statement, for this man grows his own every year from seed and he should know what frost does to them. The thing got by the critics, who know tomatoes only when sliced and who rarely read footnotes anyway, until it reached Lewis Gannett of the New York *Herald Tribune.* Gannett, who is one of the world's great experts in tomato history (having traced it far back of the love-apple stage), was justly incensed.

And this same author, who is proud of knowing every comma and semicolon in the works of Lewis Carroll, named his country place "The Borogroves" from *Jabberwocky.* When he was told there was no r in the last syllable of Carroll's "borogoves" he refused to believe it and got seventeen editions of *Through the Looking Glass* out of the Public Library before he was convinced. Even then he claimed that Carroll must have written it wrong, but as Carroll had invented the word and had died long ago his claim could not be proved and seemed implausible to say the least. But this sort of thing happens to the surest authors and, curiously, their mistakes seem to occur oftenest in the material most familiar to them.

The wrap or jacket (once called "dust cover") worries authors less now than in the days when it was predominantly pictorial rather than decorative. In his mind the publisher always saw a new book in its wrap on a counter or in a store window while the author visualized it on his drawing-room table. So the publisher tried to make the wrap attention-catching — to make his book stand out among other books. He used to give the book to an artist to read; the artist would pick from it — if it was fiction — a sensational scene and paint it in lurid colors. To the author this seemed cheapening; his dignity was offended. He criticized the drawing as if it had been a work of art.

When James Boyd saw the wrap for *Marching On*, the picture horrified him.

"*. . . The troops," he wrote, "are not marching on. They are strolling.*

"*There is neither the mass nor the movement which make* momentum. *And momentum is the thing you feel when you see a division on the march. . . .*

"*Incidentally the horses are out of drawing & don't move the way horses do on the march. . . .*

"*If the present artist can't do the trick, I implore you to get one who can.*"

Perkins's reply did not satisfy him.

"*Your letter . . ." Boyd wrote again, "says, 'whether the difference on a wrap, which aims to give merely an impression, is very important or not . . .' Of course your experience is great & may justify that belief. But I can't help feeling that in the production of a book everything is important; from the writing down to the typography & stock & though economic considerations must govern this last & many other items, within those limits I'd like to see everything as perfect as it can be made.*"

This hit the book designers in a sensitive spot and Perkins's

next letter is such a final analysis of the whole wrap situation
that it is worth quoting at length.

*"I am terribly sorry to have given you the impression . . .
that I do not appreciate the great importance of attention
to every detail in the production of a book . . . it is the
very essence of publishing. . . . There was opposition to the
change, [based on Boyd's criticism] but only because the
wrap as it stood, had been vastly admired by the selling force,
and by the booksellers. Nobody could argue against the force
of what you said, and we decided to make the change; — but
with some little anxiety.*

*"A good wrap is not easy to get. We go through an enor-
mous amount of casting about, planning, discussing, trying
out; and when we get a good result, we are often afraid to
try to improve it . . . for fear that we shall lose the single,
bold effect a wrap should give. . . .*

*"We take infinite pains with our wraps, and we have no
hack artists do them, nor anyone on our staff. We constantly
set aside drawings altogether, that have been made and have
not been successful. The house realizes that bad wraps can
actually kill books, and that there is nothing so important
in connection with exploitation as the wrap. I want you to
realize this. We shall have a new drawing for your wrap
today."*

In the end, in Boyd's case, everyone was satisfied but it was
a delicate business. In his final letter on the subject Boyd
summed the author's point of view.

*"The wrap, to my eye, is vastly improved. Perhaps some
recondite principle may now be violated but to me it now
has a thrill lacking before and if it also has for the reader
the purpose is served."*

[115]

Note the emphasis: "for the reader." It is of the reader that the writer thinks. Not, as the publisher thinks —"for the buyer," for the potential reader, the customer who sees the wrap first and reads the book after; for the extremely important salesmen, retail and wholesale, whose enthusiasm must be won. The author does not consider these factors — perhaps he should not; once his mind is encumbered with details of selling, exploitation, advertising, his writing may suffer.

Yet the authors who are willing to leave all these things to their publishers are few indeed.

The advertising or publicity department which begins work on a book while it is "in hand," starts with the initial handicap that most of what it does will be wrong to the author. Hawkeyed, on the day of publication, he will search the newspapers. If his book is not advertised on that day — though later display is often far more effective — the publisher will hear of it. Thereafter, whether the book responds or not, it must be continuously and heavily exploited. Any failure in sale is likely to be attributed entirely to deficiency in advertising space.

> *"I don't like to complain," wrote Harold Frederic, "but I* do *feel keenly that men who do work much inferior to mine get advantages in advertising . . . which my books, poor devils, may not hope for. I see your advertisements in a number of different forms, notably* The Nation, *the magazines &* the N. Y. *papers. It may be all illusion on my part, but I seem to get less show in these than any other writer whose name is on your books. Even when* The Boston Herald *started a boom for 'In the Valley,' I heard of it from eight or ten strangers who wrote to me from different parts of New England, but I could not learn that my publishers had lifted a finger to utilize the thing.*
>
> *"Doubtless you hear this plaint, or some variation of it,*

from many people. That will help you to receive this one with the better good-nature. But it is a grinding and aggravating thing that books of their character — which you and I don't differ much about — should be left to make their own slow way along, always doing a little I grant you, but doing that little strictly off their own bat, while the whole impetus of organization is put at the disposal of books which, if they *were left to themselves, would go into the ditch within a twelvemonth."*

Even in 1894, this wail was so familiar that you can almost hear the sigh with which Charles Scribner took up his pen to answer.

". . . We never," he wrote, "worked harder over any books than we did over 'In the Valley' and 'The Lawton Girl' and yet their sale was not proportionate to our efforts. You, of course, will recognize that the taste of the public in these matters is altogether capricious and the success of the inferior books . . . is really due, not to any effort of the publishers, but because they happen to please public fancy."

"I do not think," wrote Edith Wharton to Brownell in 1899, "I have been fairly treated as regards the advertising of 'The Greater Inclination.' The book has now been out about six weeks, & I do not think I exaggerate in saying that it has met with an unusually favourable reception for a first volume by a writer virtually unknown. The press-notices have been, almost uniformly, not only approving but very flattering. . . .

"So much for my *part in the transaction; now as to Mr. Scribner's. I have naturally watched with interest the advertising of the book, & have compared it with the notices given by other prominent publishers of books appearing under the*

*same conditions. I find that Messrs. Macmillan, Dodd &
Mead, McClure, Harper, &c advertise almost continuously
in the daily papers every new book they publish, for the first
few weeks after publication, giving large space to favourable
press-notices; in addition to which, they of course advertise largely in the monthlies. So far, I have seen once, in a
Sunday paper, I think, an advertisement of the 'Greater
Inclination.' . . .*

*"If a book is unnoticed, or unfavourably received, it is
natural that the publisher should not take much trouble
about advertising it; but to pursue the same course towards
a volume that has been generally commended, seems to me
essentially unjust. Certainly in these days of energetic &
emphatic advertising, Mr. Scribner's methods do not tempt
one to offer him one's wares a second time."*

Perhaps Arthur Scribner's reply — for to him usually fell the
thankless job of answering such complaints — persuaded Edith
Wharton; at any rate, she did not carry out her threat and
The Greater Inclination proved to be only the starter for a
long line of highly successful books published by the Scribners.

It was Charles Scribner, however, who took on the mollify-
ing job in the case of Robert Grant, who, in 1901, launched
a protest over the advertising of *Unleavened Bread.*

*"Comparisons are dangerous," wrote C.S., "but I do not
know another book which has been so largely advertised in
proportion to its sale. . . ."*

*In a P.S., he added: "R. H. Davis has just been in and
speaking of his next novel for which he has many offers. He
wants it 'pushed' but says he will be perfectly satisfied if it
is advertised as much as* Unleavened Bread.*"*

Here a special view of authors as it appears to publishers is striking. Again and again it is in the record that an author thinks some other author gets more advertising space than he. A says, "if I got as much as B, I should be satisfied," but B says, "why do I get less than A?" Often, too, authors would apparently be happy if their friends would leave them alone. But their well-wishing friends hound them, urging them to badger their publishers.

"The statements of an author's friends . . ." wrote C.S. to Mrs. Humphry Ward in 1917, "must always be taken with great allowance, as you must have found in your own experience."

The whole question of a book's advertising, however, is seen by a publisher, as C.S. explained to Robert Grant, "in proportion to its sale." The sale of a book must justify what is spent upon it or the publisher loses money. So publishers usually budget a percentage of a book's retail price to be spent on paid publicity, per copy. Supposing this portion to be thirty cents on a three-dollar book, then, if the book sells 10,000 copies and $4000 is spent on advertising, the book may be unprofitable to the publisher. So the publisher must do some adroit guessing before he makes up his advertising campaign.

On the other hand the author, especially if he has friends in the advertising business, says that, as the advertising must take place before the sale, the publisher should take a chance, launch a big campaign at the start and proceed on the assumption that the more a book is advertised, the more it must sell.

Professional advertising agents, thinking in terms of food or soap for which there is a universal demand, say that this is true, providing they out-advertise their competitors in quantity and quality. But publishers know that it is not true of books.

The demand for books is limited. Among the four million readers of a national magazine, the big majority probably read that magazine *because they don't want to read books.* For a publisher, therefore, to advertise books in that magazine and pay for four million circulation (every reader of which at some time buys soap) would be a foolish waste. He must pick his mediums with the greatest care, using book sections or pages in newspapers or the columns of literary magazines where every reader is a potential book buyer. He must work out the quality so that every word, every square inch of margin, every typographical appeal will be to that peculiar class of folk, who buy bound volumes. And he must place his advertising at precisely the right moment in a publishing "season."

"The Republican Convention," wrote C.S. to Mrs. Humphry Ward in 1916, "comes on June 7th and it will be hard to get a hearing for any new book a week or two before and after."

"I enclose herewith," Perkins wrote James Huneker in September, 1920, "an advertisement of 'Steeplejack' which appeared in the Saturday [Boston] Transcript. We are preparing another . . . which contains a considerable quotation [from Steeplejack] which will give the flavor of the book and make people want more of it. It will fix an impression of it in their minds better than any descriptive paragraphs by an advertising man could do. We have so far published in New York and Philadelphia only smaller advertisements. . . . We do not wish to spend all our money in one brief explosion of advertising, but to carry it through a number of weeks and then revive it with greater emphasis just before the holidays. . . . The second week we are to advertise in . . . Chicago . . . and Los Angeles. . . . The books will then be certainly on sale in distant points. . . ."

This letter answers most of the questions a publisher must ask himself about advertising. Will the ads appeal to a special audience? Can we keep the interest alive but still have money left for the holidays? Will the books surely be in the bookstores in the places where the advertising appears? And in it is implied the so-called guesswork as to probable sales which a publisher must always do if he expects a reasonable profit.

This is not all guesswork. A large proportion of the preliminary promotion — the "spadework" done by a publisher — the author seldom knows anything about. Months before a book is published, salesmen are at work, feeling out the retail market. News items are sent to trade journals, advance trade advertising placed in them. News, literary "gossip," are sent to literary editors. Advance circulars called "spring list," "fall list" are widely distributed. So by publication day, the trade is well aware of the book and the publisher already has some sense of how it is likely to hit the public caprice.

Sometimes there is an advance sale which shows how the wind is blowing. This has been known to hit a hundred thousand or more in the case of a popular author. Even a book by a new author may appeal to the retail trade and sell several thousand. If this happens a publisher knows he can do his first advertising profitably. Advertising which exploits an advance sale, which can tell that the book is already popular, that a lot of people are eagerly waiting to read it — is effective.

So there is usually more to go on than mere guesswork. If, however, there is not, then the shot in the dark must be taken. The book may catch on even if the retailer has been wary in advance, even when no omens are good. An exceptionally popular critic or columnist may start it. So may that mysterious factor "word of mouth."

A wise publisher then starts an advertising campaign and watches results carefully. If there are orders and reorders, he plans extension of advertising. If not, after a certain point (and a dozen things determine the point) he knows that no amount of plugging will do any good. Something inherent in the book has made it fail to meet the caprice. Or some other book, too much like it, has killed it. The disappointment then is bitter to the publisher as well as to the author. The publisher (contrary to authors' occasional opinions) wants to sell the book. Why not? He has gambled real money on its manufacture and promotion. And he has given it mental effort, astuteness and the benefit of experience which cannot be balanced up in dollars on the ledger.

The author counts, as a rule, from the day of publication — the great "day," a milestone of his life. He has worried before, like Fitzgerald: "My God! Suppose I fell flat. . . . May the saints intercede for me to the Christian God who comforteth the afflicted." But he begins to watch his publisher and to praise or blame him on "the day." He knows little of what has gone before. He has not investigated the deep factors which determine whether a publisher is good or bad: experience, wide trade confidence, keenness and patience in promotion spadework, sensitive fingers incessantly on the public pulse. Instead he bases his estimate on display advertising. It is an entirely natural practice because publishers have been reluctant to take authors into their confidence on the other matters. From all the complaints and unhappiness which have circulated so long in the literary world, it would seem that a publisher who gave his author a brief glance at the landscape and horizons of the publishing business beforehand would save himself a lot of headaches.

Praise given by an author to his publisher for excessive promotion has more than once been misplaced. The publisher may "shoot the works" on one book to the point where he is no longer in business when the next comes along. Or he may lose the confidence of the bookseller by overselling.

A few years ago, a publisher made a strike with a long

picaresque novel by an unknown author. The book sold in the hundreds of thousands. He immediately encouraged the author to do another of the same sort. Months before the second was published, he drummed it among the trade as better than the first. He sold it by the carload and, when the book appeared, spent a small fortune on advertising it. The author praised him.

Meanwhile, however, the public caprice had changed. It had tired of picaresque romance. It had shifted away from long novels. Furthermore, the author, writing under pressure, thinking of the public and of his royalties had produced a lesser job. When the ultimate buyer came to the bookstore he had "heard" the book wasn't so good. Or, he thought he would try a shorter novel. So the booksellers were left with piled shelves. The big advertising was useless. And the author suffered as well as the publisher when the third book came along.

One of the author's hurdles of the "out" period is posed by those persons whom Fitzgerald described as the "ex-policemen who are now critics." It is a common authors' belief that the real critics in the United States can be counted on the fingers of two hands and that the rest are either ambitious folk who use a book review as a show window for their own cleverness or girls recently graduated from high school whose work is grossly overpaid at $5 a column. Many editors share this view and one of them expressed part of it succinctly in a letter to Ernest Hemingway when *Men Without Women* was criticized.

"It was a most enraging review," he wrote, "first because it appeared a week too soon — and because of women without men," there being, he explained, "only editresses," on the paper in question, and finally because the female reviewer "spent a large part of her time in talking about the function of criticism instead of functioning as a critic."

Shane Leslie, who, though not an American, had the warmest feeling for the United States and its people, was scornful of our critics.

> *"Is there no reviewer," he asked in 1919, "who can recognize an interesting book or point it out in this country? . . . Not a review of value saluted Henry Adams' unique Education which will be studied in universities a century hence. I think American reviewers ought to be spued [sic] out because they are neither hot nor cold but tepid. . . . Wild reviewers seem more necessary than authors but I suppose publishers have tamed them."*

Leslie's last remark will not find much agreement among publishers. For whatever may be said about ignorance or incompetence it would be hard to deny that book critics in America have, and assert, more independence than any in the world. The cases in the whole history of American publishing in which influence has been successful with a reviewer are rare indeed. And publishers have discovered that attempts to exert it through eulogistic letters sent out with review copies have tended to build prejudice against the book.

Often a publisher will find an angry or controversial review more helpful than a song of praise.

> *"Enclosed," wrote Charles Scribner, Jr., to Winston Churchill after the publication of* The World Crisis *in 1923, "are some reviews which have appeared since those forwarded. . . . As you will see, they are all complimentary and unusual; perhaps the best thing that could happen would be for someone to start a little controversy by 'knocking' what you say."*

Authors with long experience take the review hurdle in their stride.

"About the Reviewers," wrote Henry van Dyke (distinguishing them, nevertheless, by a capital), "I am in the dark. Some seem to hate me because I keep my finger-nails and my English clean. Others despise me for the lack of explosive or salacious quality. . . . They are all right — from their various points of view. But I have never written for reviewers."

Dr. van Dyke knew, of course, that the critics who made fun of his books had not the faintest effect on their sale. So did James Huneker, a very different author, who was much praised.

"Philip Hale," he wrote Perkins in 1920, "in Boston *Herald* wrote a gorgeous review of S. [Steeplejack] a pageful! Did you see it? (It may sell 3 copies in that frosty town. . . .)" Of another "gorgeous, flaunting page" in a theatrical paper, he wrote: "At least 3 cocottes and 2 shoe-string gamblers will buy the book."

Carolyn Wells, who took nonsense seriously and got a long-continued sale for the collections of it which she compiled, wrote in 1902:

"I have received a great many notices of my Nonsense Anthology, *and some of these are by way of adverse criticism. But after careful consideration . . . I have reached the conclusion that the most censorious judges are those who know the least about the subjects they discuss. . . . I have in mind most prominently the* Sun . . . *whose reviewer seemed to score my book with a sort of misguided malice which made me wonder if he had any grudge against me personally. However, my friend the editor of the* Bookman *said only space counts in the* Sun, *not matter — and since they gave me, in all, nearly two columns, I should feel flattered rather than chagrined."*

Incidentally, with one of its rare smiles, the Boston *Transcript* noted:

"Miss Carolyn Wells, appreciating the facilities for research offered by the Boston Public Library, has come to this city in order to complete the collection of verse for her Nonsense Anthology. . . *!"*

Generally, both publishers and authors are aware that reviews have surprisingly little effect on sales.

If blame and criticism were all a publisher got from authors in the tense "out!" period, he might well feel that he was nurturing an ungrateful lot of vipers. But the record shows otherwise.

"I feel," wrote Henry James, on receiving his author's copies of The Wings of the Dove, *in 1902, "that I have never been so well presented, materially, & that my prose itself very essentially gains thereby. . . . As I compare the London edition dejectedly with yours, I feel yours to be beyond comparison, the book. I promise you, however, not to abuse, in future, the privilege of finding such happy antidotes of form to my long-windedness."*

"I heartily congratulate you," wrote Sidney Lanier of his King Arthur *in 1880, "on achieving what seems to me a real marvel of book-making art. The binding seems even richer than that of the* Froissart; *and the type and printing leave a new impression of graciousness upon the eye with each reading."*

"You see I have felt," wrote John Thomason, the Marine captain who made the First World War live for many readers in Fix Bayonets, *"— and do feel — that my relations with you*

gentlemen are based on something different from the routine money arrangement. And that in itself is worth a lot to me — I would not willingly part with that feeling. Also I am not blind to the fact that the money value of my work with the other [magazine] outfits proceeds very largely from the circumstances under which I was, as it were, brought out — and you all brought me out. That leaves a very heavy obligation on me — the kind of obligation you like to incur, even though you can't ever discharge it."

In the "out" period also comes the occasional worst of all tribulations for both author and publisher, the lawsuit. In the 1930's plagiarism suits multiplied until they took on the look of a racket, though the theatre suffered more than book publishers. Young tyro authors have a hard time learning that in literature as in other departments of life there is "no new thing under the sun" and that similarities of their own first brilliant ideas expressed in a trial play or story to passages in successful books or Broadway productions are nearly always coincidence. In the 1930's a small army of lawyers of the ambulance-chasing variety was ready to take up the cause of any amateur writer who had a hint of a case. Two of Sidney Howard's successful plays were attacked in that way and, though both suits were lost, the defense was costly and troublesome.

And no matter how careful an author and his publisher may be, a suit for character damage or libel sometimes turns up. After the charming Knopf novel, *A Bell for Adano*, by John Hersey, had been out more than a year, the alleged original of its hero brought suit for defamation, though most readers thought Major Joppolo one of the most admirable and endearing characters in a generation of fiction. In nonfiction, an accidental misquotation, a factual error or a statement which the law brands as technically libelous may bring a suit.

But it is generally conceded that the suit brought against Arthur Train, Maxwell Perkins and Charles Scribner's Sons some six months after the appearance of *Yankee Lawyer: The Autobiography of Ephraim Tutt* was the oddest in modern publishing history. The charge was of fraud. The plaintiff had bought the book supposing it to be a bona fide life-history of a living person and had discovered it to be fiction and therefore "tosh and piffle."

The book was the thirteenth in a series of fictional volumes whose world-famous stories had centered round the created character, Ephraim Tutt, a criminal defense lawyer, enemy of unfair legal prosecution. It was Perkins's idea that Train should write the full, definitive biography of his celebrated hero whose adventures had delighted millions of readers over a quarter-century — readers both of the *Saturday Evening Post* and of the Tutt books — and publish it under Tutt's name. This gay literary *coup* was hailed with almost universal pleasure by the press and fiction public across the country.

Novelists and publishers, however, are likely to acquire the mistaken habit of thinking that every one who can read at all reads and understands fiction. Lately the spreading response to radio skits and comic strips has revealed that there are millions of our fellow Americans who are basically incapable of understanding an imaginary story. Professional readers of fan mail tell of the daily thousands of letters addressed in good faith to Superman and Popeye and Victor Gook. But that this sort of thing could happen in the case of a printed book was a surprise to Perkins and Train when, as Train describes it:

"Every mail brought letters to the publishers from people anxious to have Mr. Tutt's address, in order that they might retain him to defend them on criminal charges. . . . Then Mr. Tutt made the 'sucker list,' and we had many laughs

*over the seed catalogues and printed circulars soliciting his patronage of mail-order houses, concerts, charity entertainments and War Bonds. . . . One young woman who was accidentally switched onto Max Perkins's private wire refused for a long time to accept his assurance that there was, in fact, no Ephraim Tutt. 'But there must be a Mr. Tutt!' she almost sobbed, and, when finally convinced, burst into tears."**

None of these people, evidently, were fiction readers or even readers *about* fiction; otherwise they would certainly have heard of Tutt. They simply had the fictional blind spot. But when a practising lawyer of Philadelphia (home of the *Post*) added his demonstration of ignorance of the most popular legal character in current American fiction by bringing his complaint, it was truly astounding.

Had this Mr. Linet merely sued for personal damages in that he had paid what he called a biography price ($3.50) for a novel (said by him to be normally $2.50 or $3.00) it would have been one thing. But his charge went on into his mortification at the hoax and the waste of his time in reading *Yankee Lawyer*. It concluded by demanding an injunction against further publication of the book. Thus he brought into the picture the threat of a precedent (if his suit were successful) which would affect the whole future of creative writing and its publication.

The story, when it broke in the press, was so incredible to the normal reading public that Train and Perkins and the Scribners were at once accused of having cooked the whole thing up as a publicity trick. The public has since learned that there were no grounds whatever for this suspicion and that such things may spring, not out of the lunatic fringe, but from staid,

Mr. Tutt Finds A Way, by Arthur Train, Scribner, 1945, pp. 6–9.

respectable and presumably informed elements of the population. Possibly the whole wartime confusion of the public mind;
perhaps the haphazard intermingling of fact and fancy by the
radio and by movies, have helped implement such curious dis-
tortions of innocent literary intents. They are reminiscent of
the panic once created by Orson Welles by his rendering of a
radio fantasy. They are important, profound and worthy of
study.

Arthur Train engaged John W. Davis for his defense. The
application for injunction was dismissed "on the ground that
no man could of his own volition constitute himself the cham-
pion of the public and demand relief on their account." Un-
happily Train did not live to enjoy the conclusion of the suit.
It was in mid-career when he wrote of it in the closing chapter
—"Mr. Tutt Pleads Not Guilty"—in his last book of stories,
Mr. Tutt Finds A Way.

During his last illness, the complaint was withdrawn. But
for Arthur Train, who began as a lawyer and devoted much of
his life to translating with unfailing accuracy the eccentricities
of the law into the currency of exciting and beloved fiction, this
suit provided a dramatic curtain.

IX

BEST-SELLERS

The use of the term "serious books" as distinguished from fiction was until a few years ago universal in the strictly business provinces of publishing. Even today many salesmen cling to it and it is hardly possible to get much below the august editorial offices of any house without hearing it.

According to this classification books on how to shoot craps or win at poker; how to mix drinks or teach acrobatics to fleas; the essays of Stephen Leacock or Robert Benchley are serious books and Flaubert's *Madame Bovary* and the acute tragedies of Zola or Theodore Dreiser are not. Thus a novelist who has devoted a life's study to bitter human conflicts and desperate social problems, may be said to have turned "serious" if, in his dotage, he takes to comic verse or the design of crossword puzzles.

Publishers who have seen novelists explode on encountering this barbarous relic now caution their people to say "nonfiction"—at least when authors are around. And sensitive trade journals like the *Publishers' Weekly* edit "serious books" from their columns. This is sensible because otherwise those novelists who consider their work literature will one day organize, throw their typewriters out the window and stay on strike until every last offender has been properly and publicly chastised.

Once this is settled, the historic causes of the custom may be explored. It may, of course, be a legacy from the Calvinistic era in which all novels were regarded as trash if not actually sinful. Perhaps, however, we need only go back to what some call the "gay," others the "mauve" Nineties.

In that decade, there seemed to be a definite retrogression in seriousness of fiction from those immediately preceding it. The promise of realism suggested by the regional novels of Hamlin Garland and Harold Frederic, the public of the Nineties was willing to leave unfulfilled. *Looking Backward,* Edward Bellamy's probing into the evils of capitalism, stood high in the market in 1888; his *Equality* in 1897 (the most serious of the 90's) got nowhere near best-sellerdom. Instead there was a flood of romance, humor and what we, today, consider the most saccharine of "sob" sentimentality.

There were the stories of Ian Maclaren, Hall Caine, Anthony Hope, S. Weir Mitchell, Paul Leicester Ford, F. Hopkinson Smith, Frank Stockton, Charles Major — some of them "bully" stories, sure enough, and some fine romances, but certainly not serious compared with the nonfiction of William James and George Santayana which accompanied them and sold, comparatively, not at all. The best fiction came from abroad — Kipling, Barrie and the celebrated *Quo Vadis* of Sienkiewicz (though that too was romance).

It is customary to speak of this *fin de siècle* decade as the all time low, but actually the best-seller lists show a drop in seriousness after the century turned.* Kipling and Barrie were no longer among the ten at the top; Gilbert Parker, William J. Locke and Mrs. Humphry Ward took their places. Triumphant among Americans were Winston Churchill, Alice Hegan Rice, Kate Douglas Wiggin, Meredith Nicholson, Robert Hichens, Harold MacGrath, George Barr McCutcheon, Robert W. Chambers. And however fondly we may remember the stories of John Fox, Jr., or Thomas Nelson Page or Mrs. Burnett or Owen Wister, we cannot call them serious literature by today's standards. And the only best-selling realism in the

*Information on this subject is from Alice Payne Hackett's valuable *50 Years of Best Sellers.* New York: R. R. Bowker Co., 1945.

American scene came in Edith Wharton's *The House of Mirth,* in the terrific Upton Sinclair exposé, *The Jungle,* and in Frank Norris's *The Pit.*

As we look back over the twenty years, the one classic which time has proved seems to be Stephen Crane's *The Red Badge of Courage.** Yet at its birth, the excellence of this book was not unanimously admitted even by otherwise discerning critics. In 1897, for instance, the year after it was published, Edward L. Burlingame wrote to Charles Scribner about the possibility of getting something of Stephen Crane's for the Magazine.

> *". . . I confess," he wrote, "I can't get up much enthusiasm over this, even irrespective of a Kipling in the field — and without bringing in the literary discussion (in which I believe you and I think alike about the "Red Badge," &c). Although I think Crane did an impressive & on the whole genuinely fine thing in the "Open Boat" (coming in our June number), I don't think he is going to outrun the limits of a sensation. (This dangerous piece of literary prophecy will probably recur to you when he is seated on the pinnacle of fame; but he never will consent to sit there; he will insist on standing on his head & waving his legs with a crimson roar.)"*

So here are C.S. and Burlingame agreeing about what modern critics consider the brightest spot of literature in the American "mauve decade" and not, apparently, favorably, either toward the book or the author.

Men like Burlingame and Brownell were, however, suspicious about best-sellers. About one of Edith Wharton's books, Brownell wrote her that it had done well. "If it had done very

*Published by D. Appleton & Co., 1896. Eighth on the best-seller list for that year.

much better one might have wondered if it were really as good as it seemed. . . ." When *The House of Mirth* became a best-seller, however, Burlingame was forced to a concession.

> *"I am especially glad to find," Mrs. Wharton wrote him in 1905, "that you think its large circulation is a sign of awakening taste in our fellow-countrymen — at least in 100,-000 of them."*

On the other hand, one of the most noted critics of the time, Bliss Perry, for many years editor of the *Atlantic Monthly* and later professor of Literature at Harvard, sided with the general public about a Henry James novel.

> *"Did you," he wrote C.S. in 1901, "send me 'The Sacred Fount' because you thought me one of the 'remnant' who still remain faithful to Henry James, or were you trying to do missionary work?*
>
> *"It came when I was in bed with the grippe, ten days ago, & I read the book through religiously. (The day was Sunday, for that matter!) Well, I wanted to swear, very frequently, & probably I did, for Henry James's later developments as a juggler with the English language are irritating to one who admires his early stories and almost all of his essays. And this book, as your advertising paragrapher says, is the 'distilled essence' of everything one hates and admires in his later methods. (By the way, what an admirably phrased announcement that was! Surely you have doubled the writer's salary before this!)*
>
> *"I suppose it is good for one's wits to read a book of this sort, but I am not yet enough of a Bostonian to thrive upon it as a regular diet. 'The Sacred Fount' makes me feel insufferably stupid, like talking with some confoundedly clever woman who is two or three 'moves' ahead of you in the con-*

versational game, & doesn't allow you to catch up. Only a woman would *let you catch up, & James doesn't. He is so exasperating in his mannerism nowadays, & yet every three or four pages there is a clause, & sometimes, by great luck a whole sentence that is as exquisitely perfect as a bird's egg that has dropped from the nest & lies all unbroken upon the sidewalk. A miracle of a sentence!*

"But I am not reviewing the book—Heaven forbid;— only thanking you for remembering one of the most unprofitable authors that ever cumbered your list. Now that I have seen a little of the book publishing business, I wonder increasingly at your hospitality toward my unlucky shots at the great public."

The public, in those days, were not buying James's serious novels in any great quantity. Nor did that same public spend much more on the novels of H. G. Wells or Theodore Dreiser than they spent on nonfiction.

With the war came *Pollyanna* and *Just David* and the tremendous sellers of Harold Bell Wright, but with it, too, came Ernest Poole's *The Harbor** and *His Family,** Wells's *Mr. Britling Sees It Through** and, in 1919, Blasco Ibañez's *The Four Horsemen of the Apocalypse†* and Conrad's *Arrow of Gold.‡* And most important of all, with the war, the public began on a large scale to buy nonfiction. In 1916 and 1917, for example, the Scribners reaped an unprecedented current sale for poetry with Alan Seeger; in 1918, Harper scored heavily with the Mark Twain letters and Macmillan with the *Recollections* of Viscount Morley. Now a nonfiction best-seller list began to be published. It was topped in 1919 by the Houghton Mifflin *Education of Henry Adams.* One of the first nonfiction books which, in sales, actually exceeded some of the

*Macmillan. †Dutton. ‡Doubleday, Page.

fiction best-sellers of its year was *Theodore Roosevelt's Letters to His Children* published by Scribner in 1920. And, in 1921, came H. G. Wells's *Outline of History* (Macmillan), destined to remain a landmark in nonfiction, selling eventually over a million copies.

Thus, for nearly a quarter century, the publishers' salesmen in America had a pretty good alibi for their classification. It is natural for a salesman to gauge his thinking about any commodity by its best-sellers. The curious fact here, however, was his admission, in the language he used, that the product which sold best was the one entitled to the least respect! A parallel for this in commerce would be hard to find.

So when, in the 1920's, the whole scheme seemed to go into reverse, there was great bewilderment in the bookselling world. Heads were shaken in every part of America over Sinclair Lewis. Here was true realism coupled with satire of sacred institutions, yet, in the year following its publication, it was number one on the best-seller list. *Main Street** had crowded out a Zane Grey, a James Oliver Curwood and a Gene Stratton Porter. It sold just under 300,000 in its first year. Critics wrote long articles trying to explain it by the public's new maturity, by post-war "disillusionment" and a great fiction era was predicted.

The promise came true. The whole trend was away from romance. While only a few of the more realistic novels made the best-seller lists and while the old "sweetness and light" still predominated there, the lists did record at least one novel every year which even the sterner critics acclaimed as literature. This upset the old guessing-game in the editorial offices. No one could be sure any longer that a serious novel — even a somber, a tragic novel — might not become a best-seller.

Just off the best-seller lists but with printings so high that

*Harcourt, Brace, 1920.

they had the salesmen turning unexpected handsprings to keep up with them, were books of immense importance as reflections of the temper of the period. Mark Sullivan in his *Our Times: The Twenties* calls F. Scott Fitzgerald's *This Side of Paradise* "a book which had the distinction, if not of creating a generation, certainly of calling the world's attention to a generation." It was the first literary time-bomb, so to speak, the war had set. It waked all the comfortable parents of the war's fighting generation out of the hangover of their security into the consciousness that something definite, terrible and, possibly, final had happened to their children. And it gave the children their first proud sense of being "lost."

It was not, of course, in any sense a war book. War novels were, in 1920, under a public boycott. Yet it was a war product, curiously mixed up with some of the war's latent causes and an exposure of everything the war had released in the adolescents and newly-adults of America. Its influence was immense. It led the less articulate boys and girls in a pattern of behavior which expressed all their half-conscious revolt. It gave a name and set a beginning to an era which might otherwise have had no conscious integrity—"the Jazz Age"—but which now historians will record as long as American history is written. And the fact that it gave no more than a hint of the author's promise detracts nothing from its value as a landmark.

It produced a flood of realistic interpretations of themselves by youthful writers. Its British echo, *Dusty Answer,* was a near best-seller in America. *The Plastic Age,* by Percy Marks, a more subjective view, was second on the list in 1924.

The success, in 1926, of Ernest Hemingway's novel of postwar cross-currents, *The Sun Also Rises,* is an index of the altered public taste. Its scene was Paris without traditional glamour — a sordid Paris in which the international people of the story moved through thought rather than action. Critics held its motives to be obscure and quarreled over them. Yet the public read it avidly and its sale convinced editors like Maxwell Perkins that another generation, "lost" though it might be, had found an understanding of the writing craft of which most of their elders had little enough.

In the novels of John Galsworthy, whose success in this country was as great as in England, we see the effect upon an older writer of the changes wrought by the war. *The Forsyte Saga,* read as a whole, shows the full continuity from *The Man of Property* in 1906 to *To Let* in 1921 and the full impact upon his philosophical mind of youth's revolt. Galsworthy had, to be sure, long been a rebel against hypocrisy in pre-war England, as is evident in *The Island Pharisees.* But his sympathy with the war's generation, especially in matters of sex frankness and freedom, won him an immense following among the kind of young people who had begun to see their conflict with the past in books like *This Side of Paradise.* His *The Silver Spoon* (1926), *Swan Song* (1928), *Maid in Waiting* (1931) and *One More River* (1933) were all on best-seller lists and Galsworthy, today, is part of the Scribner "backlog."

Galsworthy's decision to combine all his novels about the Forsyte family into one continuous story in a single volume is on record in a letter to Charles Scribner in 1921. It is evident from this that he realized that he had produced a real saga — a monument to his life.

"I have always been exceedingly set," he wrote, "on having this long chronicle bound up in one volume, because it is emphatically my special book — the book by which I shall specially go down to posterity. I always hold that a writer goes down the ages identified with one book. . . . At my age I shall never do anything as big as this again, and I want to see it gathered up and bound in one tome as soon as possible.

It is a much more coherent piece of work than the usual trilogy; and this binding of it up in one volume will take it out of that category."

It was in the 1930's, however, that the Scribners saw much of their patient growth in the past bear fruit on the best-seller lists. Here besides the three Galsworthys were Stark Young's *So Red the Rose,* Thomas Wolfe's *Of Time and the River,* Robert Briffault's *Europa,* George Santayana's *The Last Puritan* and Marjorie Kinnan Rawlings's *The Yearling;* and on the nonfiction lists, Will James's *Lone Cowboy,* Clarence Darrow's *The Story of My Life,* James Truslow Adams's *The March of Democracy,* Peter Fleming's *Brazilian Adventure* and Douglas Freeman's *R. E. Lee: A Biography.*

On the "serious" side of the ledger, there was equal bewilderment in the 1920's when the tide turned.

"I think," wrote Robert Bridges to W. W. Ellsworth in 1922, "the most notable development of recent years is the increased sale of nonfiction, serious books* *at prices from three to ten dollars a volume. We have sold seven or eight editions of [Henry Fairfield] Osborn's 'Men of the Old Stone Age' . . . Lothrop Stoddard's books, 'The Rising Tide of Color,' 'The New World of Islam,' and 'The Revolt Against Civilization,' have had and are having a very unusual sale. The same is true of Whiting Williams's 'Full Up and Fed Up' and 'What's on the Worker's Mind.' "*

What was the matter? Were "serious books" becoming less serious? Had history shed its dignity — or at least its frock coat and tall hat? Was sensational debunking (which was, perhaps, merely making statuesque characters more human) responsible

*Bridges, who should have known better, wrote this without either italics or quotes.

for the terrific popularity of biographies like Lytton Strachey's *Queen Victoria?* Shades of Henry Adams, who feared that "history would soon become as popular as magazine writing, and the luxury of its social distinction would vanish"! (Though Henry must have had qualms himself when his great *Education* was a best-seller in 1913.) And it is true that some old-school historians raised their eyebrows at James Truslow Adams and suspicious critics stayed up all night combing his books for errors (just as they had with Carlyle).

Perhaps there was a new avidity for "culture" to be got in quick doses. This would account for the "Outlines" of which Wells started an epidemic. Perhaps it was sex — some of the biographies had racy passages, sure enough. But this wouldn't explain the hold books like James Harvey Robinson's *The Mind in the Making* (Harper) took on the public or the Walter Page *Life and Letters* (Doubleday), both on the 1923 list. No, writers of "serious books" must be learning to write in a new way — with more of the novelist's technique, making real people as alive as if they were imagined characters or bringing the thought of their essays home with common, lively examples. And, on top of this, there were at least a hundred thousand people with new wide interests — people who wanted to think. This figure, of course, based on sales, was only a fraction of the full nonfiction public, for the libraries in the 1920's increased as they never had before.

Historians are already finding this impulse toward better writing and reading curious against the madness of the 'twenties in other directions. It is at variance with the frenzy of the boom, with the follies of prohibition, with flagpole sitting, marathon dancing and the spread of general delinquency. It was coincident, too, with immense business activity.

Some of these are reflected in the vogue of the Coué book on autosuggestion and other "self-help" books, the religious books which were sought, perhaps, as a balance to the growth of the lunatic fringe. Reflecting the lunatic fringe itself was Chic Sale's "serious book," *The Specialist,* a treatise on privies which had to have a new publishing company organized to print it.* Success stories like *The Americanization of Edward Bok* and Bok's *Twice Thirty,* Michael Pupin's *From Immigrant to Inventor* were popular. In 1925 a book came along which combined success and religion.

The manuscript of this book came to Maxwell Perkins for the Scribners' consideration. Perkins read it with some horror and took it up with C.S.

"It treats Christ as a super-salesman," he said, "a go-getter, a man with a talent for business. Of course it might sell."

C.S., with his long background of grave religious publishing, was properly shocked and agreed that it should be declined. When it appeared, however, C.S. sent for Perkins.

"How about this book?" he said. "Why haven't we got it?"

"Why, we discussed that, Mr. Scribner. I talked it all over with you a year ago and we decided to decline it."

"*You* discussed it with *me?* You mean the manuscript came to us?"

Even Perkins was startled by this incredible evidence of C.S.'s power of forgetting.

"Why, certainly, Mr. Scribner. Don't you remember that I told you it portrayed Christ as a salesman? And I added that it might sell."

C.S. looked at him a long time without change of expression. Then, with only the faintest twinkle in his right eye, he leaned forward and pointed his finger at Perkins.

"But you didn't tell me, Mr. Perkins, that it would sell four hundred thousand copies!"

*The Specialist Publishing Company (1929).

In 1926, a new phenomenon appeared in the publishing world. This was the book club, a device for furnishing its members with a book selected each month by a board of judges. This convenience for readers who were too busy or inexperienced to pick the best books from the welter of reviews and gossip and then go to a shop and buy them, resulted in a large increase of sales. The "Book of the Month Club," which began its selling in 1927, gave members an option as to whether they would take the club's selection or some other book. Most of them relied on the wisdom of a jury composed of eminent critics and authors.

And, in general, the Board was believed wise by reviewers as well as readers — though occasionally there was acrid dissent. Publishers and authors had mixed feelings about this "club" and the many others which followed it. They could hardly help rejoicing when their books were chosen, for it meant a certain sale of nearly 100,000 copies (later four or five times this), though the author took a sharp cut in royalty. On the other hand, many thought it worked a hardship on the books not chosen, for it focused public attention so strongly on the selection. And, in the beginning, some publishers felt that certain books had as good a chance without the selection and would be more profitable both to them and to the author without it. But there was no question that the clubs had come to stay and they did offer a hope of great reward to new authors. And there can be little doubt either that they were an important influence in increasing the circulation of good books and "educating" a new, large public.

What makes a best-seller is a question which publishers agree is even harder to answer than "What makes a good book?" But, though the answer cannot be put into words, most publishers are less blind about it than the public believes.

It is impossible to devote twenty years or more to constant selection without acquiring an intuition which is right more often than it is wrong. It is not necessary to put such judgment into a formula. With a formula, a publisher would soon lose his elasticity. You cannot explain public delight in color, form or melody; if you could, the world would soon be regimented into dreariness.

Certain themes are sure-fire for a lot of people. A sizeable following is guaranteed for a novel with a religious background. Books on success, self-improvement, the technique of a popular game can be counted on. Mysteries have a special public. Certain authors have their own bodies of disciples. Someone said that "an author is likely to be successful if he writes the same book over and over again." But what makes a book spread over all the groups and classes is a known but inexpressible secret.

We can say that public taste has widened immeasurably in the last fifty years. Many of the old bars are down. The public will accept realism, tragedy, every aspect of life. Snobbery and squeamishness are gone. But it will accept sound romance too. It is probably safe to say that a good book has, today, a better chance of being a best-seller than ever in American history.

X

BACKLOG

Behind all the hits and misses — the sensational sellers that flash across the land making lions and sometimes millionaires of their authors; or the stillbirths which sadden every season — lies a province of quiet, steady work of which the public knows little. This is a building place where workers ignore caprice and the changes of the moon; brick on brick they make a solid structure to house the publisher when the rains come.

Many publishers have background buildings so strong and well equipped that they could live in them for years without ever publishing a new "trade" book. With this sort of shelter they can afford to take chances on a novel, to experiment with a new author and give the years of profitless patience that are sometimes needed for his success. With it, business is not interrupted by a public which suddenly decides, for instance, that, after wanting little else for five years, it wants no more war books; or that it is abruptly sick of "costume" novels, psychology, sex, adventure or stories about the South.

The term "backlog" is often loosely used to include everything which has a steady sale. More strictly it means business which moves through special channels. Backlog in this sense is possible because there are certain books people always want, regardless of tide or events. Some of these books are tools, year-round necessities: school geographies and arithmetics, books for college courses and collateral reading, technical manuals, dictionaries, encyclopedias, reference books, books on theology or medicine, agriculture or business. There are, too, the classics — Homer, Shakespeare and Dickens — which reach beyond the

[144]

so-called reading public and are wanted in a nice dress to fill a corner in a new living room where they will impress a visitor, at least, even if they are never opened.

To manage the making and selling of these different volumes, a publisher must divide his house into departments with an expert at the head of each and specially trained workers under him. Usually departments evolve over the years. One publisher, for example, began with religious books and for many years produced nothing else, then he branched out into the profane field and presently had best-sellers, tables of logarithms and How to Play Tennis all in their different markets. Another began his career with cross-word puzzles — a magnificent back-log — and is now able to experiment with the most advanced fiction. Others began with job printing shops or retail book-stores and tried no publishing at all until these things were steady, going businesses. Probably none ever began with all his departments at once, and the road of publishing history is lit-tered with the debris of those who started on the shoe-string of current books and tried to build a business by catching pop-ular fancy on the wing.

The broad divisions over which a publisher of long stand-ing may find himself presiding, in addition to "trade," are subscription, educational, religious and importation, with some-times a retail store, a magazine and his own printing establish-ment besides. Sometimes a special department is organized for juveniles, a steady kind of business, though children's books are generally handled through normal trade channels.

Subscription, according to F. E. Compton, who lectured about it at the New York Public Library, is the oldest technique of bookselling since the invention of printing.

"When William Caxton set about translating and printing

The Golden Legend in 1483, he used the subscription method of publication. . . .

"Then, as now, it made possible the publication of valuable books that could not otherwise be published — books too expensive for the risks of over-the-counter sales. And today it performs another function: it takes books to people who have never bought books before — those millions who are without library or bookstore service or who do not use those services."

What other means the great Caxton had of distributing his books in that dawn of the English renaissance Mr. Compton does not explain, but it is unlikely that, outside of London, the retail book trade was extensive. We do know that the means of payment was the reverse of what it is today: in advance — not eased over the months or even years until the volumes are dog-eared before they are fully owned.

But Mr. Compton quickly brings us up to date and, in a few words, gets to the crux of our modern American pattern.

"Of the people who live within driving distance of a bookstore, how many do you suppose ever enter it or buy a book from it? Your guess is as good as mine, but I think we should be vastly overestimating if we said that ten per cent of them ever saw the inside of a bookstore. And how many of these would ever dream of buying a work that cost fifty dollars, or a hundred, or a hundred and fifty?"

Yet in thousands of small, even primitive, homes we find books on shelves: Shakespeare, the Britannica, Dickens, Mark Twain, Longfellow, Kipling, Poe, histories of the United States by Andrews, and the Adamses from Henry to James Truslow. Many owners of these have never seen a bookstore and would be frightened of one. Someone has dropped in, collected a dollar or two or five "down" and left the books. These genial, irresistible visitors used to drive buggies over muddy mountain roads. Like the traditional peddlers in jingling carts before them, they were welcome, bringing gossip from the next county and fine tall tales of the big world outside; beds were made for them and food set on stormy nights. Today, children of a third generation thumb these ancient buggy-borne books in the lonely backwaters. So, through the history of subscription books in America, runs a thread of romance which is part of the weft of the national culture.

A good book agent was a kind of genius. He made more money sometimes than anyone in the company he represented. Yet he started from scratch with nothing but his carfare and his sample book. He had no drawing account, no salary. He sold books or he starved. His heyday was a time when frontiers were still open, the "land of opportunity" still infinite in its breadth and every American's credit good. He worked entirely on futures. His customer became the possessor of a beautiful thing on the payment—"down"—of the loose change in his pocket. But Americans were proud folk with consciences. They paid.

From the lofty moral pinnacle of modern business it seems as if the old book agent's zeal outran his scruples. He was, of course, doing a nobler job than the salesman of sewing machines. He was educating the people. This gave him a certain latitude of method. If he hypnotized the money out of a man's pocket he did it in a good cause. His toe in a closing door was the advance wedge of culture. And when he moved in lonely places he met the tremendous hunger for print that we know now was the by-product of this land's rocketing physical growth.

The old sleight-of-hand is a thing of the past. It has been beaten by the new communications, by standardization, by all the efficiency of modern business machinery. Carroll Merritt, head of the Scribner subscription book department, tells a story of its pay-off in the early days of the transcontinental telephone.

The Scribners had one special genius of the old school still on the road. One day Merritt got a message to report at once in C.S.'s office. C.S.'s eyes were glacial. His jaw was set and jutting.

"Mr. Merritt," he said. "Who is president of Charles Scribner's Sons?"

"Why, of course, Mr. Scribner, you are."

"Are you sure? Are you quite sure?"

"But yes. . . . Why?"

C.S. pointed to the telephone.

"My friend, George Spifkins," he said, "President of the United Pacific Coast Light and Power Company has just called me from San Francisco. He tells me the president of Charles Scribner's Sons is sitting in his office selling him a set of Henry van Dyke."

By wire, Carroll Merritt fired the old-line salesman. But a month later, while he was wandering about the fifth floor, Merritt glanced into C.S.'s office and was astonished to see his ex-book agent sitting, not on a chair, but on C.S.'s desk. Furthermore, C.S. was at the desk, his face obviously working against an explosion of unprecedented laughter.

"But don't you see, Mr. Scribner," the agent was saying, "you can't get to see a man these days unless you are on his level. Now George Spifkins was president of ——"

C.S. put out his hand and stopped him.

"Listen to me," he said. "You can be Vice-President if you want. That's Arthur's job. You can even be Secretary. But you've got to let me be President — at least to my old friends."

This same salesman whose art died with him once telegraphed Merritt from New Haven that he was in a hospital with a fractured leg in suspension. Knowing that the fracture had occurred in a good cause, Merritt went to see him. There he was, totally immobilized, his leg hung from a crane over the bed. They talked for a while and when Merritt left, the salesman said:

"I almost forgot. Here's something for you."

He picked up a pile of papers from the bed table. They were orders for a subscription set of Galsworthy at a hundred dollars each.

"But how the devil?" said Merritt. "When you've been flat on your back."

"Well," said the salesman, "you see all the docs in the hospital have been in to visit at one time or another. I kid them and I guess they like it. I think I've got the whole list there — and one nurse."

Somewhat more complex than the skill of the subscription agent was the technique of the boys who operated for the educational department. Books for the public schools were "adopted" by a state board or commission whose procedure varied in the different states. An adoption might mean the sale of a million or more copies. Representatives of the educational publishers arrived long enough before the meeting to give the members of the board a chance to consider carefully their samples. While this went on a small version of a political convention took place in the state capital and men in smoke-filled rooms promoted their candidates. Some of the legends in the history of educational sales suggest that schoolbooks have not always been adopted strictly on their inherent merits; that the fragrance of Corona cigars, the mesmerism of expensive food and even more subtle persuasions have played their part in plans for the teaching of the young idea.

In the early days of American textbooks, publishers used to become so inflamed with zeal for certain of their works that competitions in the state capitals took on the look of holy wars and salesmen who lost felt the burden of defeat upon their consciences.

The first Charles Scribner, whose business often seemed to him an instrument of his moral and religious aspirations, became possessed of a new set of geographies designed by a Professor Guyot. Guyot's system of teaching, while it has an odd look set beside our modern global design, was radical in its day. How the gentle Mr. Scribner came to own this series is lost in the limbo, but the record shows a mystic Mrs. Smith whose commercial motive, if any, is not apparent, but who seems to have preceded the salesman and softened up the boards. And the record shows, too, a live salesman, Gilman H. Tucker, on Mrs. Smith's heels in Boston.

"I am not surprised," wrote Charles Scribner to Tucker in May, 1867, "and yet not less rejoiced to hear of Mrs. Smith's success and that you have such a high opinion of her. It has always seemed to me that she was raised up specially by Providence for the work in which she is engaged. Aside from its commercial aspects, it is truly a great work, one in which we all can enter upon with pride and though attended with very great difficulties from its very nature, because it is a revolutionary educational movement, still one feels stimulated and nerved up to it by its very greatness & importance. Whether we realise ourselves the pecuniary advantages or not we may be conscious and thankful that we are the means of starting a great reform which must tell on the educational interests of the country for years. If our lives are spared a few years, we shall both see the day when the present text books on geog will be discarded, and our opponents will come over on our ground or be left out in the cold. I have been expecting what you tell me, a combination

of all the old style of geographical interests, against Guyot. They stand or fall together *and we are their mortal enemy, from the* very nature *of our books, not of course from any other considerations.* It is the old story. Pilate & Herod *have become friends to defeat us. Well I hope you are* not *intimidated. You* dont *write as though you were. But you have truly a* tremendous *fight before you. Can you see that you are making headway? . . . Their cause must indeed be desperate. . . . Whenever you think* I *can be of any service to you let me know, but I must tell you frankly that I have no talents for lobbying &c. If you think some of the members of your Board have more* brains in their stomachs *than elsewhere and that a* little feeding *would do them good though it is* not in our line *we wish you to feel free to entertain them. With some you know the* last dinner *is most effective, and one from us I suppose would digest as well as from Cowperthwaite &c. . . ."*

The intimidation suggested in this letter as tool of the evil rivals was apparently still going on in the twentieth century. R. V. Coleman, who later managed the immense enterprise of the *Dictionary of American Biography,* tells a story of his earlier days as a textbook salesman when parts of the West were still in the grip of Calvinism. One of the members of the adoption board had evidently been persuaded by one of Coleman's competitors into voting for a series of primary books which we may call the *Springfield Readers* but later had qualms. On the day of the adoption, this man went to the publisher's agent who had done the persuading and, with a haggard face, said:

"I have spent the night on my knees," he said, "praying for guidance and after my long vigil I know that God will not let me vote for the *Springfield Readers.*"

The agent turned to him with clenched fists.

"You vote for those readers anyway," he shouted, "and then spend tonight on your knees asking God to forgive you."

In the first years after the reorganization into Charles Scribner's Sons in 1879, the Educational Department lapsed under the strain of strenuous affairs and, in the 1880's, C.S. sold his list to other publishers except for a dozen or so college texts which needed no special promotion. Yet educational books haunted his mind. Perhaps his father's zeal about Guyot had planted the persistent idea in his childhood and acquaintance with Princeton professors in his college days kept it alive. C.S. had a habit of stubborn, silent pursuit of a thought; it used to appear in his face once in a while and alarmed his colleagues, so powerful was it. So in 1893, when other things were well in their stride, he wrote to ask a young Dartmouth man, who was working in the D. C. Heath Company in Boston, if he would care to have a talk with him.

Thus, with a boy in his early twenties, he began one of the most successful and long-lived educational departments in the general publishing business. Edward Thomas Lord had all the qualifications. He had graduated from Dartmouth at nineteen with a Phi Beta Kappa key. He was a shrewd, serious Yankee from the state of Maine; three generations of New Englanders stood behind him. The sternness of his face used to scare people at Scribner's, but it impressed professors. It impressed C.S. too, especially when, in their first disagreement, Lord's arguments were swift and final — for C.S. loved a fighter and Lord was it. He was an independent and a direct young man, but if a job compelled him he would put his soul into it.

Lord could and did relax away from the office. He was liked on the road. He played a good game of poker, knew his way about the state capitals, was a persuasive salesman — not in

spite of his honesty but because of it. When textbook sales-
manship was at its peak of swashbuckling, Lord could spike a
crooked game and was likely to win with a square one. When
his work became editorial as well as commercial he was able
to interest all sorts of writers in the House.

It was Lord, for instance, who first led George Santayana
of Harvard toward the Scribners. The intermediary was Barrett Wendell. Wendell was C.S.'s main standby in Cambridge,
which seemed remote from the warmth of Princeton. The Scribners had published Wendell's first books and were to publish,
one day, his greatest.

"Tell me," a boy once asked startlingly of Edward L. Burlingame, "how I can get an education all out of one book."

"That's simple," Burlingame replied, not at all startled. "The
book is Wendell's *Traditions of European Literature.*"

Wendell told Lord where Santayana lived; Lord sought him
out in his retreat in the Harvard Yard and reported back to
Wendell that Santayana had written a book called *The Sense
of Beauty* and was disheartened about getting it printed. He
had asked Santayana to let the Scribners see it — would Professor Wendell remind Santayana of this in case he forgot?

"The manuscript of this book," writes Santayana in his
The Middle Span, *published in 1945, "went from local publisher to publisher, and was rejected. I had given up all
expectation of getting it published when Barrett Wendell,
always friendly to me and the humanities, sent me word that
he thought Scribner's would accept it. I sent it to Scribner's;
it was printed and . . . it established pleasant relations
between me and Scribner's which have lasted for fifty years."*

Through Wendell, Lord also got to know the men of Harvard's great days: Nathaniel Shaler, George Herbert Palmer,
Ralph Barton Perry and Wendell's protégés in other univer-

sities: William Vaughan Moody, Robert Morss Lovett, James Weber Linn, Charles Foster Kent — and a line of college books grew up beside the school texts.

Once a Lord enthusiasm came up against C.S.'s sometimes quixotic practice of publishers' ethics. This was the great William James. Lord had dropped in at James's study on one of his visits to Harvard, not even knowing that James had a book ready for publication. Lord went because he liked and admired James, and was surprised when the great psychology teacher told him he wanted to change publishers and go to the Scribners with his new book. And of course C.S. was pleased when Lord told him.

Presently, however, there came a howl from James's former publisher and C.S. withdrew. That this gesture was too generous to be fully understood by the other publisher is evident from the letter C.S. later wrote him.

"As to James's book I must set you straight. We did not decline the book or refuse to go into auction for it until you made the definite claim that you should regard our publication of the book as discourteous to you and an unfriendly interference with the relations between yourself and Mr. James. We had almost agreed to publish the book when this question was raised by you. Nor is it true that an agent of ours 'went after Professor James.'

"Of course I know that the old relations between authors and publishers are pretty well broken but I thought you were trying to maintain them and that between our houses and one or two others there was still a semblance of the old customs."

The unhappy pay-off on this story is that James grew impatient with these publishing courtesies, said, "A plague on both your houses," and took his book to a third.

Texts for elementary and high schools came, however, to occupy the bulk of the Educational Department's attention under Edward Lord, and soon after the century turned there were always Scribner salesmen at "adoption" time in the various states.

Happily for the progress in American learning, adoption practices are more liberal, more democratic and hence far more complex today than they were forty years ago. Today, in many states, choice of schoolbooks is optional with counties, towns, or even individual schools in the same cities. Then, blanket state adoption was the rule. A set of books was picked by the adoption board and every school in the state must use those books in its grades, regardless of local conditions in the different communities. This kind of educational dictatorship naturally induced a lot of political legerdemain by the less scrupulous publishers' agents in the powerful centers and the pupils got the result. Politics was in some cases even applied to the contents of the texts, and certain facts of American history, for instance, were thumbed down by potentates who happened to be anti-British. Others were thrown out when they offended a dictator's religious or racial convictions.

For a long time before the board's vote, publishers' representatives could be observed being exceedingly nice to board members. It was not even unthinkable that a powerful politician who knew nothing about education was found smoking exceptional cigars during this period or attending an unusual number of pleasant parties in hotel rooms. A day came, finally, when "sealed bids" were turned in to the board and when the board met it is probable that thirty or more salesmen spent a restless night — for a state adoption could mean the sale of a million copies.

When the educational pattern changed in state after state, the salesman's acquaintance widened and his travel multiplied.

He was obliged then to visit many towns and to know school superintendents and principals everywhere. With the coming of "progressive" schools and novel modern methods of teaching, special demands came in the kind of books and the list was diversified and enlarged.

The educational part of backlog became one of C.S.'s pets. His growing intimacy with Princeton during his years as trustee increased his acquaintance with its professors and through them he came to be known by educators over the country. In later years he sealed the relationship of his own work as publisher to university education by founding and endowing the Princeton University Press. This Press made at least one highly important contribution to the House of Scribner. It gave Whitney Darrow, its first head, his early training in publishing. When the Press was firmly, successfully established, C.S. took Darrow, who became his own wholesale manager and later a director. Darrow has played a vital part in the House's success over more than a quarter century.

Schoolbooks sometimes and college texts often are by-products of trade editions. There is, for instance, a high-school edition of *The Yearling* by Marjorie Kinnan Rawlings. Special editions, convenient for college reading, have been made of the works of Stevenson, Meredith, Lanier; Brownell's classics *Victorian* and *American Prose Masters* are on the educational list. It is a happy day for an author when his volume is converted into a textbook. This removes it from the public caprice and brings its author continued security. Hundreds of writers have been able to live for years on the steady royalties of their educational editions. A young writer once asked a publisher how he could make the most from his writing. "Do textbooks or juveniles," he was told. "Do a few of both and you will never have to worry again." These two kinds of book have, of course, one property in common. Neither is chosen by its readers.

Teachers or parents are the arbiters and the ultimate consumers must do the consuming at their discretion.

Some books lie somewhere between the trade or subscription and educational departments and are used by all three publics. Histories and biographies are in this borderland. A house, as it grows, learns to take advantage of all these outlets and, today, many books are published in the three forms. This has become easier as books which were once limited to restricted groups of scholars are now read by every sort of people.

If he were writing today, the great Henry Adams might use all these departments for his *History of the United States*. Sixty years ago, however, he knew the sale must be restricted. Knowing this, he wrote C.S. in 1888, drawing a subtly ironic comparison between authorship and business.

> *"First, I wish you to understand my position as you would regard it in a business point of view. If I were offering this book for sale, I should, on publishers' estimates, capitalize twelve years of unbroken labor, at (say) $5000 a year, and $20,000 in money spent in travelling, collecting materials, copying, printing, &c; in all, $80,000, without charging that additional interest, insurance, or security per-centage which every business-man has to exact. This book, therefore, costs me $80,000; and on business principles I should make a very bad affair if I did not expect to get ten per cent per annum from it for ever. If I bargained according to publishers' rules, I should demand eight thousand dollars a year secured to me; and if I get it, I should still get less than I could probably have acquired in any other successful business.*
>
> *"As I am not a publisher, but an author, and the most unpractical kind of an author, a historian, this business view is mere imagination. In truth the historian gives his work to the public and publisher; he means to give it; and he*

wishes to give it. History has always been, for this reason, the most aristocratic of all literary pursuits, because it obliges the historian to be rich as well as educated. I should be sorry to think that you could give me eight thousand a year for my investment, because I should feel sure that whenever such a rate of profit could be realised on history, history would soon become as popular a pursuit as magazine-writing, and the luxury of its social distinction would vanish."

Such a modern historian as the unrelated James Truslow Adams finds before him a far more open and financially rewarding field than Henry's. He came into an era in which history had become popular — made so partly by himself and by H. G. Wells, whose "Outline" was a sudden smash hit in 1920.* The change was due both to a widening of public interest after World War I and to a new approach of authors which threw the "social distinctions," dignity and whatnot of which Henry Adams had written in semi-irony, out of the window, and tried, admittedly, to make past events interesting. Following these radical leads, even college curricula took a cathartic and presently the somnolent students woke to the pleasant surprise that such sepulchres as the Middle Ages, for instance, in Europe, contained vivid, lively, amusing spirits, not unlike themselves.

Even in the late 1880's, the unique Henry, however, was reaching in that direction and straining at the straitjacket of tradition.

"In regard to the battle of New Orleans," he wrote Charles Scribner in 1890, "I have been profuse of maps. This course is not due to the importance of the battle, which was really of little importance, military or political; but for some reason, probably sectional, the Battle of New Orleans has al-

*The Outline of History by H. G. Wells. New York: Macmillan, 1920.

ways held an undue place in popular interest. I regard any concession to popular illusions as a blemish; but just as I abandoned so large a space to Burr — a mere Jeremy Diddler — because the public felt an undue interest in him, so I think it best to give the public a full dose of General Jackson."

One of the largest enterprises in American commercial publishing was the *Dictionary of American Biography,* which was distributed both by subscription and by the retail trade. The Scribners published this for the American Council of Learned Societies. The "DAB" ignored the stuffy formula of such books by including American heroes of varied fields not always noble. Thus Jesse James, Jay Gould, Jim Fisk, John L. Sullivan, Carrie Nation, and other celebrated crooks, prize-fighters, saloon smashers, and so on, sat with the élite of statesmen and scholars. Along with the Adams presidents was Alvin, the Adams expressman, and soon after came "Pop" Anson, the ball-player, "Billy the Kid" Bonney, Walter Camp, football coach, and Buffalo Bill, the Wild West showman. Here was a book then which not only became a library "must" but got on the shelves of hundreds of private citizens. Following it, Coleman, who had managed its sales, became managing editor of the *Dictionary of American History* done in the new manner without ever sacrificing authenticity or documentation. But unscholarly folk found the dictionary so entertaining that they could read it for hours continuously, for its articles include Baseball, Rum, Poker, Barbed Wire, Prize Fights and Soda Fountains, with the roles these things played in the nation's history and social growth.

Books like this seem to breed and give birth to other books. To Coleman, when the DAH was finished, it appeared incomplete without maps, so he built an *Atlas of American History* to follow it along. He looked at all the maps he could find on which plodding students had tried to follow the Revolution, the westward trek of Daniel Boone or the intricacies of Fredericksburg, and he found many of them far less graphic than a Socony road map and some of them highly confusing. So he got into his car and drove to the historic places, saw for himself how the land lay, erased the confusion and got new maps drawn without it.

Such books are all backlog and they make not only a publisher's steadily income-yielding capital but much of the romance and excitement of the business. Of this, however, the public which is supposed to be interested only in the current best-seller and the millionaire novelist seldom if ever hears.

Sensational sellers like *In His Steps,** *The Robe†* and others suggest the presence of a public eager for religious books. Yet the sales of these novels, running into the millions as they do, give no index of that public's actual size. For each person who buys one of these from a religious impulse there are probably a dozen whose reading includes tracts, sermons, Sunday School manuals, pamphlets, lives of the saints, books of prayer and ritual. The Bible, hymnals and official prayer books have, of course, a still much larger public. Then there is the body of theology: endless Scriptural commentary, scholarly analysis of doctrine and dogma — necessary textbooks to students and, finally, the church and sect reference books, the biographies and histories which must be in the pastor's library. When the business of making and distributing such books — and the business is as old in America as the country itself — was in an earlier stage its immense success was supposed to be due to the religious temper of the whole people now lost, according to popular report, in a morass of materialism. Statistics do not back this

In His Steps by Charles Monroe Sheldon (Defective copyright), 1897.
†*The Robe* by Lloyd C. Douglas, Houghton Mifflin, 1942.

belief. Volume of sales has grown as evenly and about as fully as in any other backlog branch.

It was C.S.'s custom to appoint laymen to manage religious literature.

"You know a good book when you see one, don't you?" he asked William Savage when Savage was chosen for the job and protested his unfamiliarity with theology. "That's what people want first whether they're ministers or professors or the general reading public."

C.S. himself, certainly not a theologian, once surprised an author who had sent in the manuscript of a religious book out of the blue.

> *"It seems to me only yesterday," wrote William Adams Brown in his memoirs,* A Teacher and His Times, *published in 1940, "when, an unknown author, I submitted my first manuscript to the firm which has been my publisher ever since. Mr. Charles Scribner, the senior member of the firm, not only read the manuscript himself, but sent for me to talk over the details of the generous contract he offered me. Thus began a friendship which continued uninterrupted until his death."*

The choice of Savage to succeed the head of this department who had lately died shows that the backlog divisions of a publishing house are allied; that a person skilled as an executive in one branch may move into another providing he knows the great bases of publishing; what constitutes a good book, how it is made and how it is sold. For years before taking over religious literature, William Savage had worked in the department of "Importations."

Books brought from England provided, of course, the first intellectual nourishment for Americans. They were brought in the *Susan Constant* and the *Goodspeed* to Virginia and in the *Mayflower* and *Fortune* to Massachusetts, though not in much variety, the Bible predominating. In 1647, the importation of books became a business in Boston. Printing was restricted by law in the colonies — it was forbidden entirely in Virginia until 1730, and William Bradford was imprisoned for it in Philadelphia in the 1690's — so British books held sway. Even after the Revolution, American books were scarce and, according to Harry R. Werfel, writing of Book Publishing in the *Dictionary of American History*, "after Scott's success in 1814 with *Waverley*, British books crowded American shelves, and publishers vied in securing sheets and flooding the market with the writings of Scott, Bulwer Lytton, Dickens, Thackeray and others."

The first Charles Scribner began business in the midst of this flood, but from the start he was determined to keep his publishing American. He encouraged American authors more, probably, than any other publisher. For the importation of books from England, therefore, he started a separate company. As partner he got Charles Welford, an Englishman who operated a bookstore in New York, and "Scribner and Welford" functioned for some forty years — until Welford's death, when it was absorbed into Charles Scribner's Sons. Welford established an office in London where he kept a close watch on English publishing and was soon intimate with every publisher. Through them he came to know authors as well. He acted as a guide to London when C.S. or A.H. went over, made all the arrangements for them. He had a quick intuition about people; knew their frailties and prejudices and could tell a visiting American precisely how to cajole and how not to irritate some of the great and formidable men who ruled London publishing houses. He had, as Burlingame wrote C.S. in 1883, "the power . . . of putting men's characteristics before you in a sentence or two." He dined regularly with the celebrated Murray, introduced C.S. to stern Thomas Clarke of old T. & T. Clarke, religious book publishers, who became C.S.'s fast friend and is said to have relaxed one night to the point of going with C.S. to Drury Lane to meet a famous actress in her green room after the play.

The difference between importing and publishing is marked by a vital legal factor. Our curious copyright law, even since it has been called "international," allows protection only when a book is printed in America. As importations are printed abroad and brought over in sheets to be bound here with the importer's imprint, they become legally free here to anyone who cares to "pirate" them. The better publishers do not engage in this practice, but there is still an occasional freebooter on the high seas of the book business. So the books which are imported are usually those for which a large demand here is unlikely — of which piracy would be unprofitable. If a sale of more than one or two thousand is probable, an American publisher makes a separate, independent contract with the British author and his book comes out as a regular American publication, printed here. In late years, the use of photo-offset by which a British book is photographed and then printed by the offset process in America, has changed this, giving the book protection, yet not involving the cost of setting up and printing small lots on a regular press.

From his beginning as simply a buyer and importer of British books, Charles Welford became the House's representative in all its affairs abroad. He interested British publishers in publishing American Scribner authors in England. Through them, too, he was able to turn their authors toward his House when they came to publish in America.

"There were few books," The London Publishers' Circular wrote, *"ancient or modern, especially those of a literary*

or historical character, about which he could not tell you something as to their value in the market, and, if pressed, he was seldom at a loss to give you a fair account of their character and contents. . . . Knowing as he did so much about books, and mixing so much amongst publishers, he formed a sort of connecting link between them, and was the purveyor of literary gossip from one to another. He was shrewd at a bargain, and could, on occasion, be pretty stiff in maintaining his own ground, but he was a man with whom it was quite impossible to quarrel, nay, it was impossible for anyone who came in contact with him not to love him."

Welford died in 1885 from the first illness of his life. He was succeeded by his assistant — one of the most picturesque characters in the history of publishing.

Lemuel W. Bangs was thoroughly American by birth and taste. At Scribner's he was known as "Bangsy"; the British called him "The Senator" and loved him. He had large mustaches which, as he faced you, seemed to stand out several inches from the sides of his thin face. As far as anyone can remember, they were always gray.

"He wore," wrote Gerald Duckworth, "a peculiar frock-coat made to his own design by Poole, the celebrated tailor of Savile Row, and he had never had the cut altered since he first arrived in London. He had a pretty taste in ties and wore some choice flower in his buttonhole. 'The Senator' had many good stories to tell his friends, and used to present them with cigarettes the size of a cigar."

Duckworth, one of Bangsy's most intimate publisher friends, did not, however, give a complete account of his wardrobe. As "The Senator" died alone in the world, his clothing was sold at auction and the auctioneer's catalog is in the Scribner archives. There were, among hundreds of other items: 16 coats (11 morning, 5 frock), 25 pairs of trousers, 26 lined fancy waistcoats, 17 other suits, 188 ties, 18 pairs of spats, 20 pairs of boots and shoes, 80 silk and cotton handkerchiefs; 9 soft felt, 2 Panama, 1 opera, 1 bowler, hats and 2 caps, 14 overcoats and 31 dozen collars, all in excellent condition.

Every night at the Garrick Club he could be seen at his special table with a pint of champagne. He never varied the vintage until it gave out; then, with infinite care, he would pick another and the club laid in a special stock for him. It was served at an exact temperature.

By Bangs's time, London was full of literary agents. Bangs knew them all and got along with them better than C.S. did. He wrote C.S. soothing letters about them. When the Magazine came along, it was Bangs who interested Frederick Warne in publishing its English edition and it was Bangs, too, who calmed Warne when the Magazine printed in its very first issue an article on American coast defense against a hypothetical war with England.

Bangs's work was prodigious. His letters fill ten box files in the archives and through them one can trace a quarter century of British politics, social history, and literature.

Bangs was followed by Charles Kingsley, collaterally descended from the author of *Westward Ho!* Under Kingsley, the English house of Charles Scribner's Sons, Ltd., was founded in London.

Kingsley lived in Richmond in part of a house once lived in by Queen Elizabeth. The palace had been subdivided into a number of dwellings but Bess's bedroom was in his and his daughter slept in it. Kingsley was passionately American and so was his daughter in spite of her accent learned in English schools. She had taught her dog — a fox-terrier named Mr. Patterson — to play baseball. The diamond was a square rug and Mr. Patterson stood in one corner while she called the strikes and hits. At the third strike, he would slink away, but when she said "Home run," he would tear around the edge of the rug, back to home base.

Kingsley welcomed and entertained American Scribner authors when they went to London. He would take them to his Richmond home where they spent, with his family, an evening or so, so warm and friendly that they would forget the fog. One rainy night Scott Fitzgerald turned up there having driven all the way from London in a taxi. "He says," Kingsley wrote to Maxwell Perkins, "he has quite made up his mind to settle on this side, but I have my doubts." Perkins also had his doubts, having just received a picture post-card from Scott on which, in large letters, was scrawled, "What an overestimated place Europe is!" Both doubts were justified. A few days after came a second letter from Kingsley. Scott had appeared suddenly in the hall with his suitcase.

"Where are you going?" Kingsley asked, startled.

Scott answered with his most charming smile, thanking Kingsley for his hospitality. "But I'm going to New York," he said, "as fast as I can get there."

Importation bears a relation to the Retail Department which, in a sense, is backlog, too. The Scribner Book Store, which has existed in one form or another since the Brick Chapel days, always formed an immediate and profitable outlet for imported books. The bookstore — for more than fifty years on Fifth Avenue — has been proud of a special kind of clientele; they like books which are not run-of-the-mill; books hard to find; some of them come looking for esoteric and exotic publications in many languages.

In 1886, when Bangs was sending over books he had picked up in London in small random lots for retail sale, C.S. wrote him a letter which suggested an apparent difference in tolerances in England and the United States.

"In connection with this retail business I will take occasion to write here that you had better 'let up' on the nasty books. When they are ordered we must of course supply them but one came in last week that was really too steep. I don't think we ought to ask our retail salesmen to sell such stuff although we may fill orders given to us.

The retail store has always handled the books of all publishers indiscriminately. An occasional Scribner author, not fully realizing this, will look in the window and seeing his book less prominently displayed than, for instance, some Macmillan publication, will rush up to the fifth floor to tell his editor that "even a book by another publisher is given more space *in your own window* than mine, published by you!" And the editor must tactfully explain the divorce which exists between the store and the rest of the House; that the store leans over backward lest Scribner books seem to dominate it.

In the back of the bookstore down some steps or on a balcony there has always been a quiet space set apart from the bustle of the store for that strange, devoted, persistent and insatiable group of the book-buying public, the collectors. Here are the rare books: "incunabula," illuminated manuscripts, Americana; the first editions, English and American and foreign; original manuscripts of famous books — every literary curiosity that the detective-like experts who conduct this department are able to find in the attics and cellars of the world. Here for many years worked Henry L. Smith, whose name was familiar to the collectors of two continents. Today, rare books are handled by David Randall, who can run down a "first," a manuscript or some long-forgotten volume of poems with the ingenuity and persistence of an FBI investigator.

The romance of the rare-book business would make a long book by itself, as thrilling as any mystery story. It has, too, its comic moments. All sorts and many conditions of men become book collectors: cowboys, farmers, bartenders, prize-fighters. There is a Connecticut farmer, for instance, who collects rare editions of the French romanticist poets though he can't read a word of the language. Randall tells a story of a timid and very respectable middle-aged woman who came in to tell him with much hesitancy that her husband, a distinguished university professor, had died leaving a library of some five thousand volumes. Randall asked what the professor's subject had been and his widow told him he had held the chair of political science.

"I'd like to see it," said Randall. "There's a demand for books on political science."

"Yes," said the widow nervously, "that was his subject. But — well — you see," and she looked over her shoulder and lowered her voice, "the library is entirely pornography."

So backlog, which has so prosaic a sound to those who know of it only vaguely, has, to the insider, exciting and high-colored intervals. And to authors who rise to the point of having their works published by the subscription department in beautiful collected editions, it brings a gladdening renewal of the first pleasure of publication. This was especially true of authors like Barrie, Galsworthy, Henry James, who wrote new prefaces for the collected volumes, or Kipling, whose celebrated "Outward Bound" edition was illustrated by his father. And backlog, too, is appreciated by an author when it leads him, through educational or subscription editions, into new paths of royalty which he did not believe existed.

XI

LOYALTIES

In the last year of his life, Thomas Wolfe changed his publisher. In that year, he gave a million-word manuscript to Harper's, who published it after his death as two novels: *The Web and The Rock* in 1939 and *You Can't Go Home Again* in 1940.

The change occasioned talk in that most talkative of groups, the literary circle. Here was an author, they said, who had been "made" by one publisher and who, after his great success, had abandoned him and gone to another. It was a strange business.

It was not strange to those who knew Tom Wolfe. His friends knew that he had left Scribner's for the precise reason that the literary circle said that a Scribner editor had helped him write his books. When this gossip spread out in concentric circles from the malicious folk who had invented it and finally reached Wolfe himself, life became intolerable to him.

Such an accusation would be intolerable for any artist who took it seriously. You can tell him that his style is mannered, his substance thin, his characters "flat"; you can charge him with dullness, monotony, repetition, verbosity, inaccuracy, if you admit that the work with all its deficiency is his and he will accept or reject it in his stride. But once convince him you believe his published writing is even partly the work of someone else and you have poisoned his soul.

The surprising thing is that Wolfe should have taken this fantastic gossip seriously. Anyone remotely informed about writing knows that important work simply is not done that way. And no one denied the importance of Wolfe's books. They were, indeed, so important, so widely recognized for the truth and depth of their emotion, the universality of their human currents, the richness of their thought and the power of their presentation, that these jealous members of the literary circle were induced to seek a belittling alibi for their creator.

More urbane writers would have ignored this charge or laughed at it. More worldly writers knew what the literary circle was and always is. They knew that it centers in New York — having shifted there from Boston early in the century — and is a highly articulate group. In it are many persons who wanted to write but have decided to talk instead; they are aided in this amiable exercise by cocktail parties where it would be hard to write anyway, as there is no place to sit down and anyone who brought a portable typewriter would be looked at in surprise. Writing is not social or sociable; not done in chorus or in groups, even in its early stages. Painters often begin by sitting in a life class where they work on the same model and a teacher moves about to watch their efforts and there is some interchange between easels, but if writers tried to do this they would be in each other's hair before you could say James Joyce and the teacher booted, presently, from the room. So earnest writers do not go regularly to literary cocktail parties at least until they are all through writing for a while, which means that there will be one or two real writers, many frustrated ones, several columnists, many who merely "appreciate" literature.

But Wolfe was not an urbane writer. He was a child in the face of this kind of society. He was a stranger to New York and to the "literary world." He knew evil in its hungry and primitive forms in his own Catawba, but the complexities of "cultured," well-fed malice frightened him and filled him with suspicions of its vague but formidable power.

So the thing ate him, threatened to consume him. He saw the gossips not as occasional picayune vermin, as they appeared to sound critics and his more metropolitan fellow writers, but as enemies powerfully deployed against the integrity of his written word. He must prove that they were wrong. Looking back from this distance, he seems like a boy setting out to prove, because some teasing kid had accused him of having red hair, that it was, actually, black. But to him in that tormented moment it was a crusade.

The effort tore him apart. He was, by nature, deeply loyal. To go back on a friend, on one who had helped him through all the early travail of his gigantic production, threw his whole normal impulse into reverse. Yet as an artist he must be loyal first to himself and to his art — which was the same thing. The obvious truth that the editor had been but a kind midwife, cutting the tough cord that held Wolfe's books to him so close that they could never reach the world, did not balance the obvious lie which eventually seems to have cast a doubt upon his own belief in himself.

The record shows the tension of the conflict.

"The very truth of the matter is that, so far from ever having been unsure of purpose and direction, in the last five years at any rate I have been almost too sure. My sense of purpose and direction is definite and overwhelming. I think, I feel and know what I want to do, the direction in which, if I live and if I am allowed to go on working and fulfill myself, I want to go, is with me more clear and certain than with anyone that I have ever known. My difficulty has never been one of purpose or direction. Nothing is more certain than this fact, that I know what I want to do and where I want to go. Nothing is more certain than the fact that I shall finish any book I set out to write if life and health hold out. My difficulty from the outset, as you know, has never been one of direction, it has only been one of means. As I have

already said and written, in language that seems to be so clear and unmistakable that no one could misunderstand it, I have been faced with the problem of discovering for myself my own language, my own pattern, my own structure, my own design, my own universe and creation. That, as I have said before, is a problem that is, I think, by no means unique, by no means special to myself. I believe it may have been the problem of every artist that ever lived. In my own case, however, I believe the difficulties of the problem may have been increased and complicated by the denseness of the fabric, the dimensions of the structure, the variety of the plan. For that reason, I have, as you know, at times found myself almost hopelessly enmeshed in my own web.

"In one sense, my whole effort for years might be described as an effort to fathom my own design, to explore my own channels, to discover my own ways. In these respects, in an effort to help me to discover, to better use, these means I was striving to apprehend and make my own, you gave me the most generous, the most painstaking, the most valuable help. But that kind of help might have been given me by many other skilful people — and of course there are other skilful people in the world who could give such help — although none that I know of who could give it so skilfully as you.

"But what you gave me, what in my acknowledgement I tried to give expression to, was so much more than this technical assistance — an aid of spiritual sustenance, of personal faith, of high purpose, of profound and sensitive understanding, of utter loyalty and staunch support, at a time when many people had no belief at all in me, or when what little belief they had was colored by serious doubt that I would ever be able to continue or achieve my purpose, fulfill my 'promise' — all of this was a help of such priceless and incal-

culable value, of such spiritual magnitude, that it made any other kind of help seem paltry by comparison. And for that reason mainly I have resented the contemptible insinuations of my enemies that I have you 'to help me write my books.' As you know, I don't have to have you or any other man alive to help me with my books. I do not even have to have technical help or advice, although I need it badly, and have been so immensely grateful for it. But if the worst came to the worst — and of course the worst does and will come to the worst — all this I could and will and do learn for myself, as all hard things are learned, with blood-sweat, anguish and despair."

The violence of this defense suggests that the doubt of himself had already begun to set in. It is easy to believe that while he was writing the letter or, after he had written it, he asked himself: Suppose it were true? Suppose all the advice, the help I've had has, actually, made my books what they are? If such a question existed, he must, therefore, answer to himself as well as to his enemies.

The conflict lasted a year while he worked at top violence on his new book. Some of the conflict showed in his manuscript; its manifestations are too complex to be fully analyzed or understood. One was an impulse to satirize publishers, his in particular; to show them as malicious interferers, materialists, ignorant of the deeper values of the writing art. In his story he burlesqued with unreasonable cruelty and unmistakable identification several innocent members of the Scribner staff who had never shown him anything but kindness. Undoubtedly all this drew its color from his bitterness at his enemies' charge. But perhaps, too, by writing what it would have been impossible for the Scribners to print, he thought it would make the break easier, more final. It was, of course, unpublishable by anyone and was eventually cut, but if Wolfe had lived its writing might have been useful to him as a cathartic.

In any case, when the manuscript was finished, Wolfe made the break, took it to a new publisher and proclaimed, in his preface, that the new book "marked not only a turning away from the books I have written in the past, but a genuine spiritual and artistic change. It is the most objective novel I have ever written." Whether this foreword was partly a defense against his own darkening doubts of his work under the old regime or whether the words were written wholly without thought of his abandonment of the earlier editorial aid, it did not impress the more discerning critics when they read *The Web and The Rock*.

"Presumably," wrote John Chamberlain in the scrupulously independent review columns of Harper's Magazine, "the words were meant also to apply to the second of the two posthumous works which will eventually be published under the title of You Can't Go Home Again. *But whatever the intention of the foreword, it probably represents more of a hope than a reality. Thomas Wolfe could be 'objective': the great death scenes in his first novels (that of Ben in* Look, Homeward, Angel, *or of old Gant, the stonecutter, in* Of Time and the River) *are as sharply delineated, as effective in a word-by-word way, as anything in* Madame Bovary *or* Anna Karenina. *Wolfe was a major writer, and he will be remembered in American literature along with* Melville, Hawthorne, *and* Twain. *But unlike the Melville of* Moby Dick *or the Twain of* Huckleberry Finn, *Thomas Wolfe could never put a classical distance between himself and his work throughout an entire novel. . . . Huck Finn was obviously just as much Mark Twain as Eugene Gant (in* Look Homeward, Angel *and* Of Time and the River) *or George Webber*

(The Web and the Rock) *are Thomas Wolfe. But Mark Twain managed to stand a little apart from Huck, the better to set him in his place on the raft on the surface of a great river. Tom Wolfe could never get off the raft: and the raft frequently became the universe, not merely a moving point on a vaster surface of the water. . . ."*

In other words, many of the merits of *The Web and The Rock* were those of his other books and its defects were those of the others too.

"The albatross of Wolfe's own past," commented Claude Simpson in The Southwest Review, *April, 1940, "hangs over* The Web and The Rock. . . . *Wolfe does not succeed in impressing his readers with 'the genuine spiritual and artistic change' which the novel has revealed. In spite of promising* volte face *in its opening sections, the book must be judged largely as a continuation of the story he began in 1929."*

"It is," wrote Alfred Kazin in Books of the New York Herald Tribune, *"the same Gant career . . . and always the same Wolfe."*

If Wolfe could have lived to read these reviews and many others like them, he might have been disappointed that he had not yet been recognized as fulfilling the promise he had set for himself, but he would, perhaps, have been relieved of the obsession that the collaboration of his publisher had either made or broken the intrinsic integrity of his work. In any case the world now knows (including that small portion which once pretended to doubt it) that whatever truth there is in Chamberlain's description of Wolfe as "the most prodigious writer — and probably the only authentic genius of his generation —" his claim to those titles was not altered by his change of publishers.

And this is likely a useful outcome to this whole turbulent

incident in a publisher's history. For its effect is to confirm a conviction of the loneliness and integrity of writing. With all the effort of the most brilliant editor — spending, as Perkins spent with Wolfe a year of successive wakeful nights — the aid a publisher can give an author is forever limited. He can explain what the boundaries of a book must be: that even the endless outpouring of words which may be at once the work and the life of a genius must have divisions. As a whole this life story has an architecture — recognized when it is seen as a whole — but to satisfy an author who is rightly avid for print by giving the public a piece at a time, a containing, a boxing, so to speak, is necessary. To do this, there must be cutting, trimming and packing which does no hurt to the basic quality of the material.

But a publisher cannot give an artist ideas or mold the way of his expression. He can simply take what is there and, somehow, make it available. This was worth doing in Wolfe's case — indeed, the pressure of Wolfe's genius toward the light made it necessary.

The story cannot be closed, however, without giving, in his own words, the publisher's view. On January 16, 1937, Maxwell Perkins replied to Wolfe's long letter of December, 1936, from which quotation has already been made.

"I think," Perkins said, "that a writer should, of course, be the one to make his book what he wants it to be, and that if because of the laws of space it must be cut, he should be the one to cut it; — and especially with you, I think the labour and discipline that would come from doing that without help or interference would further the pretty terrible task of mastering the material. But my impression was that you asked my help, that you wanted it. And it is my impression too, that changes were not forced on you (You're not very force-

able, Tom, nor I very forceful) but were argued over, often for hours. But I agree with you about this, too, fully, and unless you want help it will certainly not be thrust upon you. It would be better if you could fight it out alone, — better for your work, in the end certainly; — and what's more, I believe you are now in a position to publish with less regard to any conventions of bookmaking. . . . I believe the writer, anyway, should always be the final judge, and I meant you to be so . . . 'The book belongs to the author.'"

To the end he cherished the personal friendship of Perkins, whom he appointed his literary executor.

Another writer of wholly different temper and province from Wolfe, acknowledged throughout his writing career a deep debt to his publishers for editorial encouragement. This was James Gibbons Huneker, prodigious in his production, an incessant worker whose effort finally wore him out, and of a dark and stormy mind. But Huneker was predominantly a critical writer — his one novel, *Painted Veils*, was experimental satiric fantasy — and his criticism embraced every phase of art: music, drama, painting, architecture, choreography, cinema, even magic — and literature. It was a wonder to his friends that he could read, see and hear so much; that he could live so richly in the big world he knew, yet write in such volume.

He came to all this from a humble start (professionally) teaching the piano. At twenty-seven, just as he seemed on the verge of becoming a concert pianist, he began to write musical criticism, and from that his work moved soon into all the arts, and at the same time into the intense grind of daily journalism — his columns were done for New York and Philadelphia papers. The originality of his approach, the violence of his attack, but more the perennial freshness and robust beauty of

his prose drew praise from all the world. His writing went into
French, German and Italian; it stirred and disturbed the traditional critics of Europe. And Huneker himself went to these
countries and was warmly met by their artists; men like Ibsen,
Shaw and even the shy Conrad craved and long remembered
an hour of his company.

*"He worked at white heat," said William J. Henderson
in the* Dictionary of American Biography, *"and wrote with
incredible rapidity. When his working hour was over he could
relax delightfully and became as easily a captivating con-
versationalist. But his talk flashed from subject to subject;
his mind travelled too quickly for his speech. . . ."*

People who saw him thus, did not know the shadows of his
mind which were occasionally reflected to his publishers. He
consistently undervalued his own prose; or rather, perhaps,
applied to it the same high standard of criticism that he used
to judge everything that came under his scrutiny. To his publishers he confessed this, and only their constant heartening
could dispel his misgivings. For this he was grateful until his
death.

*"I'm positively afraid," he wrote Brownell in 1915, "to
thank you as warmly as I should like to do simply because
you may suspect me of lip-service. But I shall not be afraid
of my thought of you and all you have been to me, now, as
well as the years before I met you ('Ecce the result,' do I
hear you say! Alas! you would be right in surveying my stuff
with ironical eyes). So take my words on their face value —
thank you from the bottom of my heart. The book [Ivory
Apes and Peacocks] is disgusting — and let it go at that. I'll
go back to piano-teaching. I really would only I've met with
a loss — the death of my dearest friend, a man of genius*

as pianist-artist, Rafael Josef̄y; we were working on a new Chopin *edition, an edition definitive when he died a few weeks ago. The world is grey to me. Even my beloved Chopin is dead — for the time. All this has nothing to do with your kind words — except that they came at a period which found me in the dumps. I've cut them off the galley for my wife and as my private treasure."*

Also to Brownell, in similar dumps:

"Oddly enough the 'Iconoclasts' remains the 'best seller' in my little collection of clotted nonsenses; and it's the worst I have thus far perpetrated! The hunger for propaganda in America is ferocious - and grotesque. I really believe if I went in for the solemn mystic twaddle I might have more fame, more money (I have neither, as a matter of fact). Consider the case of Elbert Hubbard!"

And of *Iconoclasts, a Book of Dramatists,* at the time of its publication in 1905, he wrote to Edwin W. Morse of the editorial staff:

". . . I know of several places where editorial copies might have been profitably sent; . . . However I suppose you feel the book is not worth while — as a seller, I mean — (of course you loathe it) — and therefore the publicity machinery has not been set running. Certainly there has been a paucity of criticisms, notices &c. throughout the country. . . ."

In the following year, Morse wrote Huneker a letter which is interesting, illustrating the service a publisher may sometimes do by negative advice.

"We have given very careful consideration, after a thorough reading, to the question of the publication of the book

which you left with me some time ago, with the general result that our advice to you would be not to publish it. There are papers in the collection which are as good as anything you have ever done, and perhaps the initial article . . . is the best thing you have ever done. Taken as a whole, however, we do not see how it would be possible for you to publish this book without a distinct loss of prestige in view of the fact that so considerable a percentage of it falls a long way below the critical standard which you have set yourself and which you have attained. . . . Our advice which . . . is offered . . . with the sole desire to advance your interests, would be to lay aside the papers in this collection which have solid merits and to wait until enough others of the same quality have been published to make a book."

This was a strong letter from a publisher who had already printed some half dozen of an author's books — and an author of Huneker's standing. It shows a consideration for the whole of his career, a thing which Huneker later appreciated. In 1920 he wrote to Arthur Scribner when *Bedouins* had just come from the press.

"It's not often that a man lives to enjoy such a gift as the one I received yesterday from Scribners; not even if he has worked 21 years under the fostering wing of your house. A beautifully made book, a frame for a mediocre picture! I am keenly sensible of the many favors and courtesies I've had from your hands and I hope you won't find me ungrateful. As I wrote Vance Thompson the other day: 'Now that I've written and published 16 books to get my hand in I hope to be able to write that novel which William Dean Howells told me that I should write!' Of course I shan't. One never does write what he expected to when young; but there is no doubt about 'getting my hand in,' and if I have practised

my scales in public it is only because Charles Scribner's Sons made it possible. Again let me say — I thank you!"

The novel, incidentally, that Huneker did write in that same year was, certainly, not one suggested by Howells. It was *Painted Veils* — Scribners did not publish it; no one did. It was privately printed and it was not till many years later, after Lawrence, Joyce, and others had accustomed the public to shocks, that the Modern Library thought it ready for the ribaldry of *Painted Veils*.

In 1919, Maxwell Perkins showed an odd perversity by asking Huneker to write an advertisement to go on the jacket of one of his own books. Poor Huneker went into a quick tail-spin — he was probably one of the few authors then writing who would have been pitched into vertigo by such a request — but he did it.

"Here is the blurb . . ." he wrote. "A rotten job. If I don't set forth the 'incomparable' merits of this 'unique' book, then the blurb no longer blurbs; if I told the brutal truth you wouldn't print it. And if I say nice sweet Dr. van Dyke phrases then — that way egotism lies. So did what most people do when they must face the music of facts; I dodged."

Huneker's warmest associations were with Brownell, whom he admired as an important critic of literature and the fine arts, though Brownell's enthusiasms and rages were less violent than his. Brownell, in addition to his letters, used to make extended and cogent comments on Huneker's galleys and Huneker would answer them at length — all on the proof margins. They saw each other rarely, as Huneker, when he was not buried in a newspaper building on Park Row (close to the bridge) moved between Brooklyn where he lived and Europe, and upper New York seemed inaccessible to him. As for

Brownell, he never went anywhere; had he traveled at all Singapore would have seemed nearer than Brooklyn.

"Dear W. C.," wrote Huneker in 1915, "are we never to meet and know the real men who so often correspond? I assure you I'm not in the least like my egregious criticisms."

From Europe, as the galleries overwhelmed him, Huneker would write Brownell long letters peppered with exclamation points.

"We loitered in rainy Rotterdam, Amsterdam, moss-grown Delft, La Haye and Haarlem. Again I threw up my hands in despair: Hals! Rembrandt! Vermeer! . . . I need hardly tell you that the Flemish Primitives enthralled me as ever, at Brussels and Antwerp. For me they are thrice as emotional as the Italians of the same period."

Then as if the descent were unbearable:

"In January I hope to begin that infernal new book — and I also hope you will like it. Only about 90,000 words, straight narrative and not a trace of mucilage in a single chapter. For 10 years I dreamed of it and now it seems thin, insipid, stale — like the fumes of a far off carouse. So go the dreams of a too heady youth. Are you feeling well, my dear friend? We are not — homesick!"

When *Ivory Apes and Peacocks* was finished, he thought:

". . . it could sell at $1.50, for at least it touches on human topics from rum to the harbors of New Cosmopolis, from art to the purlieus of the East Side — sheer, shallow impressionism, journalism and of the popular brand (I suspect). That I loathe the book need not blind you to its possible selling capacity. . . . I've written my first preface for the blithering

stuff — a few hundred words, yet a genuine preface to go at the head, not the tail, of the opus. Pardon my prolixity — and read this [manuscript] in sections. . . . Shylock! The Bible! Oh, what a case of prolapsus memoriae, *with no hope of a curative pessary!"*

But if Huneker was forever unsatisfied with the quality of his expression; if he had gnawing doubts about its capacity to interest, its style — and no doubt it was his worry about all these things that made them so good — he did not apologize for his opinions. And if, in these intervals of self-criticism, he seemed unduly hard on himself, it was nothing to the attacks he hurled at some of his favorite hates among other writers.

"Zola," he wrote in Steeplejack, *"was not a realist merely because he dealt with certain unpleasant facts. He was a myopic romanticist writing in a style both violent and tumefied, the history of his soul in the latrines of life. . . . If in the Court of Realism, Flaubert is King, then Zola ranks only as an excavator."*

Huneker died, plainly from overwork and after great suffering, in 1921. In his sixty-one years he had become a unique phenomenon in the world of critical writing.

"We are very proud," the Scribners wrote his widow, "to have been his publishers."

Charles Scribner's expression of his loyalties, inside and out of the House, were little known to the world but they were deeply felt by those to whom they were directed. It distressed him that an author or an employee should suffer; he provided, silently, for his faithful workers in their old age or illness. If these kindnesses became known, it was because they were told by the beneficiaries, never by C.S. himself, who kept the anonymity of his charities so strictly that he was sometimes called "hard" or "ungenerous." In some of the letters which never, in his lifetime, got out of his files, these charges are strictly annulled.

"May I venture," wrote Margaret Deland in 1906, "to bring to your attention the story of Miss —— whose book . . . is, I think, on your publishing list? I do not know just how many years ago you issued this book, but I think it must be at least eight or ten. . . . I do not personally know Miss ——, but her tragic story has come to me through a mutual friend, and it seemed to me that her publisher would feel the same concern and sympathy that I do, and that is the reason I am writing about it. It appears that Miss ——, who has been the only support of a widowed mother, has gradually been getting poorer and poorer. Their little home . . . has, by degrees, been stripped of almost every salable thing, and yet . . . Miss —— has kept the stiffest kind of upper lip, and never admitted, even to close friends, that the wolf was not only at the door, but had actually crossed the threshold. A little while ago Miss —— discovered that she had a hopeless malignant disease, which will, in a comparatively short time, end her life. With this knowledge came the appalling consciousness that when she died her mother would be left absolutely unprovided for, with nothing before her but the poor-house. To this silent and proud woman this thought of the poor-house for her mother was absolutely intolerable; and I suppose that her mind began to be a little shaken by this overpowering sense of dismay. At all events, it seemed to her that she could not meet it; and so, one day, a few months ago, she scraped together what money she could from the actual needs of bread and butter, and she went out to an apothecary's shop and bought as large a bottle of

chloroform as her money would purchase. She saved a little over, however, to go to a cutlery store and get a knife with a sharp blade. Then she came home and told her mother what she had done. 'The chloroform,' she said, 'is for you. I will give it to you. If there is any left over, I can have it for myself; but I am afraid there isn't enough for two, — and so I have this knife. I will finish with the knife for myself.' The terror of the trembling old woman as she heard these words, you can easily fancy. . . . As soon as she could do so without arousing her daughter's suspicion, the old lady fled out of the miserable cold little house, to the house of her neighbor, and there told this dreadful story . . . the friend . . . telephoned at once to a friend of mine, the wife of a physician, through whom the incident has come to my ears. Of course immediate steps were taken to relieve the misery and want; but they had to be taken with the greatest delicacy, for the moment any offer of help was made Miss —— said, with quiet astonishment and dignity, that she 'did not understand' why people should offer her any money; that she and her mother did not need anything. However, the money was forced upon them; — one or two pieces of old furniture still remaining were purchased at perfectly exorbitant prices. . . . They are still being carried along; but of course the daughter's only awaiting death, and that her mother should be an object of charity . . . is more than Miss —— can bear. . . . I am, of course, aware that you have a great many demands upon your help, and if you feel that Messrs. Scribner could not consider this particular case, I shall entirely understand and acquiesce in your decision. If, however, her publishers should feel inclined to help Miss —— in any way, might I say that it could only be done by the fiction of a royalty? She is so sensitive that a gift from strangers would be instantly returned. I regret to have to suggest deceit, but really there is no other way in which she could be helped, and for my own part I believe very thoroughly that truth must frequently be governed by the law of benefit."

This grim story, read after forty years during which some twenty million people met death in war and as many others acute war-inflicted suffering, sounds over-dramatized to our calloused ears; it has, too, much of the quality which made the New England plays of Eugene O'Neill seem incredibly special to many modern realistic readers and audiences. That, in 1906, it was important, real and inspiring of sympathy is evident from the concern expressed by a so-called "hard-boiled" publisher and one of the most prominent authors of the day, who, at the time, was published elsewhere.

"Your letter . . ." answered C.S., "makes clear a most distressing situation and I should be very glad to be of any service that you can suggest. Miss ——'s book was selected by us from one of the manuscripts without any previous introduction or knowledge of the author — a rather rare case and an impossible one as I am sometimes informed by letters to the newspapers. Unfortunately the book did not do as well as we hoped for. It was a quiet story, lacking accent, and was not much noticed among the crowd of new publications. We have sent the royalty reports to Miss —— regularly and it would be difficult to account for any such large increase in the sale as to justify a large payment. I have had the account made up and find that we have sold 80 copies yielding at 10% $9.60 and I have sent a check for $29.60. It seems insignificant but you will see how difficult it would be for us to explain a large amount. I should be glad to send a larger check if you can find any way of using it to Miss ——'s advantage. . . ."

He suggested further trying to find a new publisher for another of the unhappy lady's manuscripts who might do better with it and offered, if one were found, to turn over the plates of the unsuccessful book free, so that it might be reissued.

"The distressing situation of Miss ——," he concluded, "has been on my mind almost constantly since the receipt of your letter and I wish to help."

Nearly a year later Mrs. Deland wrote again:

"I think you will be pleased, and perhaps a little amused, to know the effect produced upon poor old Miss —— by your kindness. . . . I wrote you of the case, and you very delicately and kindly sent your contribution to her in the form of royalties which, of course, never existed in point of fact; but I have just learned that these 'royalties' produced the most extraordinary change in Miss ——. Of course the malignant disease remains; but, astonishing to relate, dating from the time the Scribners' check was received, it seems to have been held in check! With that check came an extraordinary revulsion of feeling. The suicidal mania entirely disappeared; she became very interested in life, and very hopeful about her work; she immediately began to write, and wrote with positive enthusiasm. I do not know the quality of her work as that has not been sent to me, but the moral fact remains; instead of despondency, misery and suffering there has come cheerfulness, courage and real happiness."

This picture from another world may not be creditable to the strange pride of the "respectable" in the unbridled heyday of capitalistic America or to the absence in that society of social security benefits but it shows a harassed businessman coping with these things in his office with a delicacy of detail for which even publishers have little time in 1946.

C.S. tried to know at least by sight and name most of the men and women who worked for him. As some three hundred were employed in the various departments, he left more intimate acquaintance to his brother, but he had a way of prowling about and picking up conversations. He would sit surprisingly at a man's desk and talk for several minutes. This occasionally frightened guilty persons. Once he sat down by the desk of the head of the Department of Religious Literature whose name had been in the papers in connection with some stage-door scandal having little to do with religion. The man sweated, trembled, and was speechless. C.S. stared at him with his most ferocious look and silence. Finally, quite undone, the man opened his mouth to protest his innocence, the falseness of the newspaper story, but C.S. stopped him, holding out his hand.

"I came to congratulate you," he said. "I didn't know you had it in you."

R. V. Coleman, now high in the councils, tells of C.S.'s first visit to his desk.

"I was a boy from the Prairies where I drove about in a horse and buggy selling books. When I was hired to come and sell them in New York, I had a little office in the Scribner building at 153 Fifth Avenue. I wasn't much impressed by Fifth Avenue but I was awfully impressed by C.S. One day, according to my habit in the Dakotas, I pulled out a plug of tobacco and bit off a good chew. Soon after, just as I was drawing the waste-basket toward me, I felt a presence. I just felt it — before I saw anything. Then I realized that the presence had drawn up a chair and was talking to me, cordially, casually, as if I'd been his vice-president. It was C.S.

" 'Do you like New York?' he said. 'Are you comfortable here? Is your office, your desk all right?'

"I looked at him and knew I had to make a decision. There was a waste-basket between my knees. But there, too, was C.S., in his fine suit, his beautifully polished shoes, his wing collar, talking to me like an equal.

"Well, I made the wrong decision — I know that now. And so C.S. in my eyes suddenly turned green and was upside down and the desk rocked and out the window the buildings along Fifth Avenue rolled and pitched. It was the last chew of my life!"

C.S.'s effort to know his people by name was not wholly successful. Once when he was prowling in the cellar — the place where disgruntled authors say publishers hide their books — with a guide, he got talking to a man pushing a truck. When the man left C.S. said to the guide:

"Who is that man?"

The guide told him. "He's been here twenty-six years."

"My God!" said C.S. "Longer than I."

But as they got on the elevator, the man tugged at the guide's sleeve.

"Who is that?" he said. "Has he been here long?"

"Quite a while," the guide whispered. "His name is Charles Scribner."

Loyalties in a publishing house are long, personal and sometimes conflict with business.

"I blame myself," C.S. wrote to John Fox, Jr., in 1905, "for not discussing financial questions more clearly with you but I don't find it easy to talk such details with friends — strange as it may sound from a publisher."

But probably the strangest letter ever written by an author to his publisher came from Henry van Dyke in 1920 to Arthur Scribner.

"What you suggest in terms of royalty, 20% is more than all right, and your proposal about an advance payment of

$5000 is more than generous. But please do not do it. We didn't use to have 'advances' in the old days of our lusty youth. Why should I have them now in the sere and yellow leaf? No, my dear Arthur, I did not expect, and do not want any advance. It is kind of you to propose it; but in these hard times I prefer to share the risk with you, and to wait with you until the book has earned its way.

"This leads to another thing I want to say,—about the Avalon edition. You have put a lot of money into it. It is beautifully made. But you can't conceal from me the fact that it goes very slowly. Now, it isn't fair to you to increase the expense. Why sixteen volumes? Why not stop where you are now? . . . A prospectus is more to be taken au pied de la lettre *than a political platform. It represents a pious wish, subject to the decrees of providence. Please consider this seriously. . . . I shall be entirely satisfied and content.*

"One more 'please.' . . . Please don't think that there is any need for paying the August royalty account in December this year. February or March or a later month will suit me just as well. You have a lot of small accounts to settle. You can keep the money for me just as safely as a trust company. So do."

This is not suggested as a model for authors' letters. The complaining kind is much healthier. If all authors were as self-effacing as this good Doctor of Divinity, publishers would be down off their toes in no time; they would become spoiled, domineering, intolerable, and practitioners of the lonely art would lose their happiest alibi. It is not likely to happen. In the first place all authors don't get offered twenty per cent royalties or five-thousand-dollar advances or have their works in gilded Avalon editions.

XII

MAGAZINES

American magazines began before American books. In the 1840's they were the bulk of the country's reading matter. Women, especially, once they had finished the immense drudgery of the home, read hungrily at the periodicals dedimated to love, romance and self-improvement. If wealth got them out of the drudgery, they were expected to give the time to "culture of the mind" with the sterner poetry, and of the spirit with ponderous or sentimental religion. In any case, magazines then (as now) leaned heavily on feminine support.

For nearly twenty years, the Scribners scorned magazines. When, as the Civil War ended, they were finally beguiled into one, it made little concession to popular entertainment. As we read it today, we are surprised that it found any audience. for it combined heavy literary material with theological dialectics and was shadowed by a dark moral asceticism; most of it was hard reading with the only lyrical relief coming from verses which sobbed over the death of someone (usually a child). Yet this sedate monthly with its incredible title *Hours at Home* seems, in the six years of its career, to have built up a large and loyal circulation.

To J. M. Sherwood, its editor, *Hours at Home* was only one of a chain of papers he edited. He is a shadowy figure today, but he must have been a busy, vigorous person, hopping from magazine to magazine and interviewing whole coveys of the clergy at the same time. He knew more reverends and doctors of divinity (all Protestants) than you could have shaken a stick at; incidentally, however, he had scraped together some explorers, scientists and disapproving readers of immoral books from whom he extracted articles. He processed the articles carefully in his chain bath with the result that nothing ever appeared in *Hours at Home* (or, presumably, in the rest of his string) which could not be read, without defilement, even on the Sabbath.

Hours at Home, according to the blurb which covered its launching, was "designed to stand among our monthly magazines as the representative of the religious element of American Literature. Besides articles on purely religious subjects, it will contain Reviews of Books; Biographical and Historical Sketches; Poetry; Notes of Travel; Moral Tales; Papers on Popular Science; and Essays on Miscellaneous topics. Discarding the Frivolous, the irreligious and corrupting, it will aim to furnish a pure, healthful and instructive literature; it will be animated also by a thoroughly Catholic [not Roman] spirit so that it may belong to the entire American church."

In a paragraph by itself:

"A limited number of unexceptionable Advertisements will be inserted in each number, at a fair price."

Scanning the unexceptionable advertisements in the first number we find a page devoted to "Health Tracts" with, among others, these titles: *Burying Alive; Cancer; Cute Things; Charms; Clergymen; Clothing Changed; Deranged; Dying Easily; Feet, Cold; Growing Beautiful; Hydrophobia; Insanity; Inverted Toe-Nail; Law of Love; Loose Bowels; Perspiration Checked; Private Things; Urination; Vices of Genius;* and *Women's Beauty.*

The text of the first issue, however, suggests less variety. There is a piece on Saint Elizabeth of Hungary; one on Christ, "The Model Man"; one on German painters (religious); "The Marys; or Silent Faith the Mother of Great Lives"; an astronomical article with religious color, added, perhaps by Mr.

Sherwood; a piece contrasting the drunken playwright, Sheridan, with the "Christian Statesman," William Wilberforce; one on the rivers of the Holy Land; one on Lyman Beecher and Martin Luther; an attack on the Mormons; an unsuccessful effort to show that the King of the Sandwich Islands was induced by Protestant missionaries to give up drinking; two stories, one a fictionized argument against atheism and the other a concession to humor but weighted with morals; seven poems, four of which are about death, though in one the dying child turns into an angel.

The modern reader of *Hours at Home,* if he can persuade himself to read much of it, must, however, admit a curious mesmeric effect. The hypnotism derives partly, perhaps, from the long-stride rhythm of the prose in which, indeed, there is too a kind of stately melody like the tune of a funeral march; partly from the insistence of the theme upon the ethereal spirit, the song of the angels, the effulgent light of heaven, the entrancing and sublime melodies of the golden harps, the soul's flinging off its earthy stain "as the bird from its wing the summer rain." One is suddenly in a dusty room with one fly buzzing; the street outside is silent in the awful Sabbath; not the passing of a single hoop-skirt inflames the flesh, not a whiff of enticing lager drifts over from the corner saloon.

Beginning in the spring of 1865, it was natural that this magazine should give space to Lincoln and the generals of the War. These articles try to emphasize the Christian character of the heroes, their modesty and their temperance. Lincoln, it seems, was always on the point of making a public profession of his faith, "but the very tenderness and humility of his nature would not permit the exposure of his inmost convictions, except upon the rarest occasions, and to his most intimate friends." The author of the article on Grant had a still more difficult time with Grant's indulgence in liquor. One article on the

American Sabbath states that "the names of Big Bethel, Bull Run, Ball's Bluff, Mill Spring and Pittsburgh Landing confirm the experience that, as a *rule,* Sunday battles turn out disastrously to the aggressive party."

In its later years, *Hours at Home* branched into more secular subjects. In 1869, the department of Books and Reading, reaching out beyond purely religious literature, discovered Walt Whitman.

> *"A generation cannot be entirely pure," wrote the editor, "which tolerates writers who, like Walt Whitman, commit in writing an offence like that indictable at common law of walking naked through the streets, and excuse it under the pretext that 'Nature is Always Modest.'"*

And he went on to warn his readers that

> *"that literary catholicity must be too broad for those who 'afford to keep a conscience,' which excuses or applauds such lecherous priests of Venus as Algernon Swinburne. . . . Let the imagination of such writers be ever so brilliant, and their diction be ever so enchanting, the altar at which they serve is that of harlotry and pollution."*

By this time certain members of the Scribner staff became restive under the cool, humid shadow of *Hours at Home.* This was symptomatic of the changing times. Darwin and Spencer, partly interpreted to Americans by John Fiske, along with the new knowledge of science and technology, were making inroads upon the old-time revealed religion. So Edward Seymour, later a partner of Scribner, Armstrong & Co., tried to freshen *Hours at Home* by getting a young newspaperman, Richard Watson Gilder, to edit it.

> *"My editing . . . being anonymous," wrote Gilder, "I naturally was pleased and encouraged to come upon a notice*

*of the magazine in the 'Tribune' expressing surprise at its marked improvement."**

But Charles Scribner (senior), though he believed in Gilder, wanted an impressive name attached to the magazine. He thought the immense prestige of Dr. Josiah Gilbert Holland would bring it into new life and success and he invited Holland to take charge.

Holland was on the top shelf of Scribner authors. His *Timothy Titcomb,* a book of fictional letters giving advice to youth, would hardly impress our generation. But its success in the sixties was tremendous. He was the Henry van Dyke of the age: deeply religious but called "tolerant" and by the extreme Jonah-whale diehards "heretical." He was, indeed, so unorthodox, as it turned out, that he refused to salvage *Hours at Home* on the ground (as he later expressed it) that it was "moribund."

Nevertheless the offer sowed a seed in the vigorous promoter field of his mind. As it sprouted, he got a friend — a real, all-out promoter and a capitalist to boot — named Roswell Smith to help him work out an idea. They discussed it, according to Holland, on a bridge in Geneva where both men were on vacation. When they had it all wrapped up, they presented it to Charles Scribner, not as a gift but as a subject for his good will and investment.

That is why the celebrated magazine *Scribner's Monthly* (which became the still more famous *Century*) must always be considered a Scribner stepchild. Holland and Smith wanted to start a brand-new magazine. But this was a big venture. If they could have a name like Scribner to attach to it — so that it could compete with "Harper's" or "Lippincott's," "Putnam's"

*Letters of Richard Watson Gilder, edited by his daughter Rosamond Gilder. Boston, Houghton Mifflin Co., 1916, p. 43.

or "Appleton's," in name at least — its start would be secure. So they offered Charles Scribner four-tenths of the stock for his name and favor and what other assistance he cared to give. Yet to avoid identifying it too definitely with the book house of Charles Scribner & Co., why not start a new joint-stock company for the purpose and call it "Scribner & Co.," minus the Charles?

If Mr. Scribner had had the astuteness of his son, he might have seen trouble ahead. He would have understood that Holland's insistence on the new company came from his refusal, as he later expressed it, "to have anything to do with a magazine that should be floated as the flag of a book-house, or as tributary or subordinate to a book-house," and that such a situation was inherently absurd. And he would have understood too that "we [Holland and Smith] who held the majority interest regarded the Scribner connection as something that should inure solely to the benefit of the magazine-house, in which the book-house was interested to the amount of its stock, and not to the benefit of the book-house, in which we have no interest whatever." And finally, C.S. would have realized that Holland and Smith intended, too, if they felt like it, to have Scribner & Co. publish books as well as magazines!

But Charles Scribner, Sr., was much governed by his affections. He loved Holland and Gilder (who was to be part of the new set-up), and he took it for granted that his firm and the magazine were all to play along happily and without friction together.

The only reason to recall all this dusty history is that it led to one of the most important and healthiest divorces in the whole of publishing history in America; that out of it came not one but three of the greatest American magazines and two vigorous book-houses in an era when all of them were urgently needed.

In October, 1870, then, came the requiem of *Hours at Home:*

> *"With this last number . . . there are no farewell words to say. To be sure, by the old pleasant name Maga will be known no longer; but it will be baptized into a new life; it will come to the familiar firesides — where so long and warmly it has been welcomed — and to many others, in cheerier, more attractive form than ever."*

The public, presumably, was set agog by this mysterious notice, but its suspense was short-lived, for in November *Scribner's Monthly* came in its glory.

> *"HOURS AT HOME,"* announced the first issue, *"whose unpretending dress and suggestive title had grown familiar to the eyes of many thousands of American families, died in October — died not of disease, not of decay — died simply that SCRIBNER'S MONTHLY might live."*

The initial number certainly offered the contrast the changing times demanded. "Illustrations" replaced "embellishments," — interspersed in the text now, not dignified by lonely special pages. To show that "the frivolous" was no longer discarded, the magazine opens with a humorous narrative poem seventeen and a half pages long. This is followed by a scientific piece, "The Bottom of the Sea," in which God is not mentioned as the author of submarine phenomena, and two pieces of fiction in serial form. In later issues, humor replaces child-mortality in the verse and an 1870's version of a comic strip became a regular feature. There is strong emphasis upon science; and politics, international relations, travel, the fine arts and literature are objectively, entertainingly treated.

Indeed, *Scribner's Monthly,* however much it became overshadowed in later years by the famous *Scribner's Magazine,* seems, as we read the old volumes even in 1946, to stand pretty solidly on its own feet as a faithful reflection of a world that was becoming wide, exciting and understood. In its pages we see America liberating itself from Calvinism and, in spite of the still dominant influence of Europe upon its intelligent top-crust, an awareness that the nation is acquiring a culture of its own. To students of manners, thought, morale, in the growing New World the volumes of its ten-year life are an invaluable record. It might have horrified the founders of *Scribner's Magazine* to say that the *Monthly* served it as model, but, looking back over the sweep of American literature, it seems to have been a sound archetype in form and variety of substance of American magazines in general, at least up to the "slick" era.

It took about six years, however, for it to revise *Hours at Home's* estimate of Whitman. Edmund Clarence Stedman's appraisal in 1881 shows the still strong influence of European opinion.

> *"Whatever we may think of his [Whitman's] chantings, the time has gone by when it was possible to ignore him; whatever his ground may be, he has set his feet squarely and audaciously upon it, and is no light weight. . . . As for public opinion of the professional kind, no American poet, save Longfellow, has attracted so much notice as he in England, France and Germany. . . ."*

Finding him impossible to ignore without showing himself to be boorishly callous to refined European judgment, Stedman goes on in this and other articles to the point of calling Whitman a "man of genius." He covers himself by explaining that he, Stedman (also a poet), can't go all the way with Whitman. Nature itself hides with lovely vines and flowers the dung which Whitman leaves exposed. But Whitman's qualities apart from this are important: his verse form, his resonance, his understanding of democracy, the deep feeling shown in such masterpieces as "O Captain, My Captain" and "When Lilacs Last in the Dooryard Bloomed." In some respects Stedman's articles are fine and even profound appreciations; they are weakened a little and indicative of the hangover of prejudice even at the start of the 1880's by his suggestion that an expurgated edition would be welcomed in American homes.

Somewhat earlier than this, Dr. Holland struck from the manuscript of "The Ascent of Mount Hayden" by N. P. Langford the following words on the ground that the *Monthly* was a family magazine: "He indeed must have been of a most susceptible nature, and, I would fain believe, long a solitary dweller in these mountains, who could discover in these cold and barren peaks, any resemblance to the gentle bosom of a woman."

Soon after the launching of *Scribner's Monthly*, Scribner & Co. issued another magazine which, from the sheer genius of its editor, seems, as we look back on it, to outshine anything in the field. This was "St. Nicholas, Scribner's Illustrated Magazine," conducted by Mary Mapes Dodge. To say that Mrs. Dodge "conducted" this brilliant performance was an understatement; she dictated it, she was its absolute queen, and she endowed it with a personality which endeared it to three generations of hard-to-please growing Americans. It was the first of the truly personal magazines; it was warm, tangible flesh, blood and heart — companionable, responsive, amusing, amused and loyal. You sat in its lap, it buttoned your shoes, it said what you, inarticulate, wanted to say; it took you where you wanted to go and it never preached or scolded. It strained your eyes in the gaslight until the sandman shut them, it spent the night under your pillow, regaled you in hungry hours of early daylight. *St. Nicholas* was "for boys and girls" and nothing before or since has ever been so wholly theirs.

*"Dear Girl and Boy," ran the first number's greeting.
"— No, there are more! Here they come! There they come!
Near by, far off, everywhere, we can see them, — coming by
dozens, hundreds, thousands, troops upon troops, and all
pressing closer and closer. . . . Glad to see us? Thank you.
The same to you and many happy returns. . . . Hurrah for
dear St. Nicholas. He has made us friends in a moment."*

The list of Mrs. Dodge's contributors was even more impressive than that of *Scribner's Monthly.* There was scarcely a famous name of the era which did not appear between its covers. Louisa M. Alcott, Thomas Bailey Aldrich, Noah Brooks, William Cullen Bryant, Hezekiah Butterworth, Rebecca Harding Davis, Lucretia Hale, Bret Harte, Sarah Orne Jewett, Lucy Larcom, Frank Stockton and Celia Thaxter all came in the first year. There was, of course, a certain attraction in writing for *St. Nicholas.* It was easier, there was relief from solemnity. There was novelty in Mrs. Dodge's break with the didacticism, the morbid approach to the child's conscience, the sentimentality which had formed the pattern of juvenile publications.

But Mary Mapes had been trained for this from her own infancy. Her father, a scientist, inventor by avocation, an original man with humorous, creative tastes, free from religious oppression, had brought her up with wide freedom of mind. His house was a rendezvous for writers and journalists, for scientific experimenters in that terrific age of technological gestation. After Mary's brief marriage to William Dodge, who died in 1858, she went back to him with her two boys. The boys helped train her mind for her life profession. In 1865 she wrote *Hans Brinker, or The Silver Skates,* one of the juvenile classics of the century and one of the first Scribner juveniles.

But the Scribners could not hold the *Scribner's Monthly-St. Nicholas* combination, attached, as it was, by a tenuous thread. Gilder, Mary Dodge, Roswell Smith were ambitious, enterprising folk and old Dr. Holland wanted to retire and sell his stock to Smith and Gilder in whom he had great faith. At the same time, the Scribners had been going through reorganizations. Charles, the founder, had died in 1871; his son Blair had reconstructed the firm with Armstrong and Seymour into Scribner, Armstrong and Company, and by 1878 Blair and C.S. were deeply engrossed in a new revolution which should concentrate all the control in the family's hands. Judging by the flood of congratulatory letters which greeted the new "Charles Scribner's Sons" which emerged, it is evident that this had been a troublous affair. But parallel with it, came a series of headaches with the more and more ambitious and independent "Scribner & Co.," and C.S. had reached the conclusion that "our views in regard to the management of the company seem to be so widely different that we could not all go on pleasantly together"— contrary to the fond hopes of his father.

Beyond all this, there was, as the decade of the 1870's came to a close, a bursting forth of new enterprises through the nation. Currency had become stabilized, capital was fluid, the great artery of the Transcontinental Railway had brought the gold from the Nevada bonanzas eastward and every kind of goods west to the settling children of the pioneers. With all this traffic, the refinements of civilization were circulating, too, and there were new markets everywhere for the produce of "culture." It was no wonder that publishing should expand in the eastern centers. There was room for plenty of book houses.

Gilder and Smith had been led by their periodical ventures to think more and more about books. Round the nucleus of the magazines, they wanted a book-house of their own. They would, of course, take certain Scribner authors with them. But that was in the cards. Such things are inevitable in an expanding age.

So when the thread snapped there was no loud explosion. It was the Scribners, perhaps, who in the end made the greatest concessions. The name of Scribner must, of course, be removed from company and magazine — though on the magazine *Scribner's Monthly* could be kept in parenthesis under *The Century* for one year only. But, on the other hand, the Scribners agreed that for five years they would publish no magazine for general circulation. So *The Century* began life with all the breaks and no threat of competition from its stepfather. For his stock in Scribner & Co., Roswell Smith paid C.S. two hundred thousand dollars.

Thus, in 1881, C.S. was left with a clean slate with no marks upon it by even semi-outsiders. He was relieved, freed of loose strings and encumbrances; yet it is equally clear that the magazine idea had taken firm root in his mind. For five years later, almost to the day, when the contract with Century expired, his own new venture proclaimed its triumphant umbilical connection with his own renovated house.

St. Nicholas, inevitably, went along with *Century.* This was real loss, real gain to the Century book-house. By this time it had added to its list, Longfellow, Christina Rossetti, Lewis Carroll, Tennyson, Whittier, Marion Harland. The English Press was proclaiming it "the King of all publications for the young on either side of the Atlantic," and "we wish we could point out its equal in our own periodical literature." While it left the celebrated Mrs. Burnett, Frank Stockton, Edward Eggleston and other favorite juvenile writers with the Scribners, it nevertheless built up a backlog of children's books for the Century Company with which, for many years, no publisher could fully compete.

The longest-lived periodical the Scribners published was a little affair called *The Book Buyer,* which began and ended its life as a house organ. It started in 1867, aiming, frankly, as its first issue announced, "to draw the attention of the reading public generally to the works imported by Scribner, Welford & Co., and to those issued by Charles Scribner & Co., and it will do this partly by printing extracts from the books rather than by tedious descriptions of them." The snobbery of putting the importations first was characteristic of the period. In 1916, when *The Book Buyer* had gone back to its original status, the flippant young man then in charge of the House's publicity got so bored with it that he let it die on the very eve of its fiftieth birthday.

But in its middle years *The Book Buyer* blossomed out into a literary magazine comparable to the later *Bookman* or today's *Saturday Review of Literature*. It reviewed impartially the books of all publishers, carried their advertising, had a paid subscription list, and was illustrated with magnificence. When it reached the peak of its career, it published signed articles by E. S. Martin, Lawrence Hutton, Bliss Perry, Henri P. du Bois, Royal Cortissoz, Harriet Prescott Spofford, Gerald Stanley Lee, Russell Sturgis, John C. Van Dyke, Hamilton Mabie, and other distinguished writers of the nineties. Departments were conducted by Rossiter Johnson and Mark Antony De Wolfe Howe — Howe's column being *Book News* from Boston, whose prestige as the country's literary center was still independent of collaboration by its police department. In its Christmas number, 1896, *The Book Buyer* contained 118 pages of text and carried 91 pages of non-Scribner advertising.

At one point *The Book Buyer* became so highbrow that it changed its name to *The Lamp* — an affectation which may have been adopted to remove from it all commercial taint and one which should have aroused the indignation of authors to whom the frank and open buying of books must always appear as one of the noblest of human exercises.

With all this history behind it, the house of Scribner was, by 1886, no tyro in the craft of magazine production. Also, the times were propitious for more, newer, bigger and more beautiful effort in this direction.

The United States was on the verge of adding to its other virtues that of being the world's most articulate nation. It had invented (or thought it had) the telegraph, and had spread that instrument widely over civilization. It had produced the finest and fastest of presses and it had made strides in photo-engraving. It had established a working cable service with Europe. And it had a lot to say, not only to Europe, which was watching it with eagerness, amusement and sometimes jealousy, but to its own people, many of whom had settled their physical problems and were avid for cultural nourishment.

It was an era of world peace. Men and women everywhere had time to read. Up to this, the readers had expected to pay for their reading, but with the growing commerce and indus-trial prosperity of the 'eighties, it began to look as if the adver-tisers were going to help on a new, enlarged scale.

This, in turn, meant better times for authors. Hitherto, those who bought the magazines had supplied the main source of the author's pay and it had been little enough.

"The brightest author in America," J. G. Holland had written in 1873, in *Scribner's Monthly*, ". . . can never get rich; and hardly one author in one hundred can realize enough from his labor . . . to rear a family in comfort," and again in 1874, "the great lack of reward to literary labor is in the matter of money. Not one author in twenty can live on his authorial earnings."

But if, now, more of the burden were to be shared by those who wanted to get commercial products before the eyes of magazine readers — supposed, in general, to be well-off folk — then magazines could be sold cheaper and at the same time authors would be better paid. That was the way it looked as the 1880's came in. *Scribner's Monthly* had already jacked advertising up to the unheard-of rate of $1.75 per agate line and it carried, for those days, a lot of advertising pages.

So, by 1886, the horizon was brighter on all sides. It was true that two great illustrated magazines were already strong in the field. But with education increasing, with the general level of taste and understanding going up; with the population expanding, prospering and showing new interest in American culture there was room for another — one that would become an integral part of the country's growth.

XIII

THE MAGAZINE

"We have decided," Edward L. Burlingame wrote, in March, 1886, to James Russell Lowell, "to begin about the end of the year the publication of a magazine, somewhat different in character from those now in the field. . . ."

He asked Lowell, who would have been — had our Republic bestowed such a title — America's poet laureate, to keep the confidence. It was necessary for Lowell to be in on the secret, for he was helping edit the Thackeray Letters, literary *pièce de résistance* of the Magazine's first year.

When summer brought its stupefying humidity to New York making the cab horses steam in the streets and wilting the boiled shirts with which the respectable male population persisted in meeting the tropic heat, rumors buzzed along with the flies. To quiet them, Charles Scribner issued, on July 9, a damp release and immediately fled into vacation.

"Yesterday in conversation with an Associated Press reporter"—read the solemn paper —"Mr. Charles Scribner, of the publishing house of Charles Scribner's Sons, 743 Broadway, New York, authorized the statement that it is the purpose of his firm to publish an illustrated monthly magazine to be known as Scribner's Magazine. *. . . He thought it possible the initial number might be printed about the end of 1886 or the beginning of 1887 but this will depend upon the completion of the preparations, which will in no case be hurried. . . .*

"Mr. Scribner desired it to be understood that the pro-

*posed magazine was an entirely new enterprise, and in no
way an outgrowth or revival of the old* Scribner's Monthly,
to which the Century *is now the successor."*

Whatever Mr. Scribner desired, however, the press continued
to understand what it pleased.

"It is reported," the *World* went on whispering, despite the
official communiqué, "that *Scribner's Monthly* will be re-estab-
lished."

"A New *Scribner's Monthly,*" heralded the *Times* headlines.

"There is to be a *Scribner's Monthly* again," echoed the
Springfield Republican.

Burlingame communicated these absurdities — so characteristic of the naïve suspicions of the era — to C.S. and spent a
sultry week-end trying to straighten out the press.

"On Saturday," he wrote the following week, "the reporters
came in on us in a swarm; and sporadic ones have come in ever
since, and burden our lives."

It was, we may guess, not too oppressive a burden. In the
letters the editor was writing of his plans, of the manuscripts
already bought —"among the most important purely literary
material that could be thought of" . . . "very important
articles" . . . "a very large amount of what I think we can
boast is unusually good fiction" . . . "we are going to make
our illustrations to all this the very best"— and to C.S., "I have
never been so absolutely absorbed in my work": in these letters
written in longhand, his stub pen seems to buckle under his
enthusiasm, and, considering the vista stretching before him,
with good reason.

There he was, thirty-eight years old, of a sudden finding himself with a big, new enterprise in his hands, a staff under him and
carte-blanche to exploit all the varied store of his cosmopolitan
experience and with a backing which would open for him the

doors of literature on two continents. The future seemed both adventurous and secure; he would live and raise his family in a brownstone house in his beloved adopted city, yet make voyages, too, where the need arose, in a limitless field of exploration.

"Ned" Burlingame, as his intimates (but only his intimates) called him, was a very different person from Doctor Holland. He was without religious prejudices or even connections. He never went to church and his opinions of the clergy were based on extra-clerical performance. His ethics were simple and definite but not codified into intolerance. He despised men who, as he called it, "sinned against the light"—who talked with tongue in cheek words they knew to be false—but he forgave and even defended others whose private waywardness led them into public scandal. He hated cheapness and pretense, he was bored by preaching, and his judgment was more by taste than by conventional morality. He was opposed to laws which he called "police codes against custom," and this included prohibition, blue laws and all legislative invasion of private behavior. So it was unlikely that much theology or didacticism would encumber the new *Scribner's*.

Burlingame was the son of a Massachusetts congressman who became a diplomat under Lincoln. Anson Burlingame had made the House ring with abolitionist oratory as a result of which, in the tense pre-war days, he had accepted challenge to a duel. His speeches seem flowery reading today but they made him a hero in the late 1850's. Lincoln sent him to China as Minister and, in 1865, he took his seventeen-year-old son out of Harvard to be his secretary at Peking. When the Chinese offered him plenipotentiary powers as head of a mission to represent China's hope for an Open Door to America and the pompous courts of Europe, Edward went part way on these travels and was dropped off to finish his education in Heidelberg, where he triumphed, surprisingly, in economics. In the spaces which American education dedicated to sport he read (or so it seemed, later, to his awed children) every book that ever was written. After his father's (still youthful) death in a St. Petersburg winter he returned to America with gifts from the dowager Empress of China and Louis Napoleon and a hideous vase (abolished in 1914) presented him by Frederick William of Prussia. At twenty-three, he married in San Francisco and came with his bride to New York, where, by 1879, he was at work on the large history of the United States edited by William Cullen Bryant and Sidney Howard Gay. As the Scribners had invested some $70,000 in this project, the transition to the regular Scribner staff was easy.

Beneath a formidable exterior, Burlingame had a gentle temper.

> "*There seemed to me*," wrote Barrie, "*to be a sort of frozen geniality about him, as if he could never quite let himself go, never quite burst some troublesome bond, never quite let you see how warm his nature was. That certainly did not rebuff me, it made him more like a figure in some book one was writing, a figure that did not easily yield to my treatment, as if I had got hold of a good thing and yet did not get inside him. He seemed to say 'you must find out how lovable I am, I want you to find it out but I can't as easily as some people show you the way.'*"

Burlingame had an immense, very bushy black beard, high forehead and bald head, severe eyes under large eyebrows, and the erectness of a general. Many an uncertain author must have taken a sidelong look at him through the door of his office and changed his mind about going in. There is a legend that once when Paul du Chaillu was with him a timid feminine visitor approached his office. Chaillu, an explorer who was in

the habit of acting out his yarns, had been telling Burlingame
a tale of digging a frozen Viking body out of the Arctic ice,
and, to show how the corpse looked, had stretched out supine
on the office floor. The visitor coming suddenly upon this scene
was convinced, not only that Paul du Chaillu was dead, but
that Burlingame, in an editorial rage of which he looked fully
capable, had killed him.

Anyone who conquered his first fright, however, was surprised that he had ever felt it, once he got across the threshold.
The austerity dissolved quickly in friendly welcome. It dis-
armed even the tyro authors, haunted always by the big, dark
shadow of themselves. For Burlingame had a trick of quickly
separating a manuscript from its author, putting it on another
plane as a job of work which both he and the author could
view impersonally. Then it seemed that he and the author
discovered its defects at the same time and were both delighted
to find them. Many a beginner discovered too, from the revealing light this editor threw upon it, that his work was hopeless.
He was not told this in words; he found it out for himself, so
there was no room for hurt feelings. The only known case of
a writer leaving Burlingame with a sense of injustice was that
of a crank in pre-magazine days who, having his large book
manuscript politely declined, threatened to kill the editor and,
a few days later, killed President Garfield instead.

But for anyone who showed a "spark," Burlingame would
take endless trouble.

*"Please don't imagine," James Huneker once wrote him,
"that I consider the editorial department of Scribner's as a
school wherein I may seek instruction; but because of your
altogether undeserved interest it has actually proved such
to me."*

In its literary material, the new *Scribner's* made a radical break with the past. In the 1880's, the snobbery with which higher-browed Americans looked to Europe for cultural caviar was sharply reflected in the book market. "The general condition of the book business," C.S. wrote Noah Brooks in 1887, "respecting all American fiction and especially short stories . . . seems to be in a hopeless state." *Scribner's Magazine* ignored this book trend. From the start, the emphasis was American. It sought out the growing indigenous culture and exploited it. Its stories by H. C. Bunner; by Harold Frederic (who is said to have flashed the first light of realism into American fiction in the Victorian era); by Joel Chandler Harris, "J. S. of Dale" Stimson, Margaret Crosby, Sarah Orne Jewett, Thomas Nelson Page were not only American in authorship, they were American in scene and substance and feeling. Where the articles centered on foreign scenes they were written from the American point of view — those of Washburne and Gouverneur Morris being officially so. In the first issue there was but a single British author, Austin Dobson.

The soundness of this policy was presently shown by the interest British authors began to take in the Magazine. Stevenson came in the first year appearing amid a galaxy of Americans, and so did Jane Brookfield with her never-before-printed Thackeray letters and, in the long heyday of *Scribner's*, Meredith, Barrie, Kipling, Kenneth Grahame, Quiller-Couch, E. W. Hornung, and Galsworthy were all to be introduced to the American public in its pages, always surrounded by American authors.

It was true, of course, that in its early career English authors were often dazzled by the rewards the Magazine offered them to appear in this company. These prices were no higher — other things being equal — than those paid the Americans (and on which American writers could not live). But American writers were not garret workers; they were not brought up — as Barrie was, for instance — on cold oatmeal; they were still nonprofessionals, economically speaking, and, having other sources of income, were expected to play some part in a glittering "society." To the modest Stevenson, however, most of whose meager earnings had been spent fighting disease and who, in 1887, crossed the Atlantic on a cattle steamer, the American magazine prices seemed a fortune.

"When I got to N. Y.," he wrote his friend W. E. Henley, "a paper offered me £2000 a year to do critical weekly articles for them; the sum was so enormous that I tottered; however, Scribner at once offered me the same scale to give him a monthly paper in his magazine; indeed it is rather higher, £720 for the twelve papers. . . . A prophet has certainly a devil of a lot of honour (and much coins) in another country, whatever he has in his own."

Again to Burlingame in the same year, he wrote:

"Well, you pay high; it is fit that I should have to work hard: it somewhat quiets my conscience."

Yet Stevenson himself, a few years later, was called to order by the editor of *Scribner's* when he fell into the popular English attitude toward the United States and its "Yankees." In England, in the early 1890's, it was common to regard American manners and standards of honor with ironic contempt and the not always playful scorn of British writers was accepted with sad head-shakings by the literary snobs here. It was not accepted by *Scribner's*.

"To put a general impression briefly," Burlingame wrote Stevenson about The Wrecker *in 1890, ". . . there was in some places a little bad after-taste left for me by the needlessly aggressive anti-Americanism of many passages. I should*

probably have some difficulty in convincing you that this didn't come from a sensitive and suffering patriotism. But I assure you that it doesn't, and that I am thinking of the artistic side first. The American types are capital, and you shall find me getting out of them all the fun there is. But what I mean is comment which I think will sometimes have the air of having been brought in, and which not only has a little an insistent note but to many people will seem like having a grievance. . . ."

With this introduction Burlingame then quotes from Chapter VII of *The Wrecker* manuscript.

" '*You seem to think honesty as simple as Blind Man's Buff,' said I. 'It's a more delicate affair than that.'*

" '*Oh well!' he exclaimed, 'that is casuistry; and are you perfectly sure that it is quite American?'*

" '*I am certain of one thing: That what you propose is dishonest,' I returned."*

"*There's a quotation, for instance," Burlingame explained, "which seems to me to overshoot your mark in all respects, and to get out of the key of the book. This quotation is an extreme case, being by no means typical; but there are several passages where it seems to me you are in danger of forcing the note in similar fashion. I have spoken very frankly about this; but won't you think of it?"*

Stevenson's answer came with the corrected proofs. "It is trusted," he wrote, "all animosity is all removed," and the quoted dialog in the printed serial and book omits all suggestion that honesty is not an American habit.

After the launching on December 15, 1886, of the first (January) number with 128 pages of text and 55 pages of advertising (grossing $7404.47) and the subsequent sale of 140,000 copies, the editor's first enthusiasm was battered by the practical limitations, compromises and conflicts which soon appeared. These were as old as magazines but they were new to Burlingame.

The thing had to be out each month — on the nose, as we say — and it would only hold so much. To lop off words from too long a piece which was, as it stood, an architectural entity was anathema. To decline a fine performance because the year ahead was packed, and it was unfair to the author to hold it for the next, could be heart-breaking. To accept a good piece and the next day to be offered a far better one on the same subject was a hard sequence to get used to.

This sort of impasse reached its apex when space boundaries shut out Joseph Conrad. Conrad was one of Burlingame's heroes. In the long hours of his night reading when, to compose his mind for sleep, he went back over the favorites, there was always a volume of Conrad on the green baize tablecloth. He must have known *Youth, Typhoon, The End of the Tether* almost by heart. Yet when *Typhoon* was offered to *Scribner's* he had to decline it because it would not go in one number.

"An account of a single storm," he wrote Conrad's agent, "written with such tenseness as this, cannot make its adequate impression if cut into two or three parts with a month between readings." Several years later he wrote again to Conrad's English publisher nostalgically about *Typhoon,* "artistically it would be nearly ruined by division, for it was of all things one that should have been read in a breath."

The long short story has always been a trial to every kind of publisher — too long for a magazine, too short for a book. Yet some of the finest productions of the literature of all languages have been cast in this inconvenient mold. Chekhov, Turgeniev and Tolstoi used it in the Russian; Balzac, Dumas in French; in English it is found all the way from Swift to

Hemingway. In late days the big magazines have handled it, calling it by the abominable name of "novelette," and in these it must be good to carry the reader through the fascinating parallel columns which tell of Grinnell Automatic Sprinklers and General Electric refrigeration.

In the nonfiction in *Scribner's* much was always topical. In the first number came a plea from an army officer to fortify our coasts which makes pleasantly archaic reading in the era of the atomic bomb. There was, too, a plea for tolerance toward socialism in a day when this theoretical philosophy still glowed with romance, and was popular among newly liberal thinkers with secure investments. There came a series on the American Railway, published while transcontinental spans were still abuilding, another on ocean steamers, and another on the mysteries of electricity. All these and others reflected the excitement which bubbled through America and, indeed, most of the western world as the century turned. Everywhere one looked, there was a new miracle. Mystic juices lighted the streets and houses, streetcars moved without visible means of traction, and the falls of Niagara — whose main function had been a stimulus to honeymoon couples — had been hitched to giant generators. Some of these crept into *Scribner's* fiction, too, in such stories as ".007" and "The Ship That Found Herself," in which Rudyard Kipling made locomotives and steamships tell their own yarns.

In the Spanish so-called War, *Scribner's* became on-the-nose topical. Richard Harding Davis, romantic in his sun-helmet, reported from ships and Cuban bivouacs, and the turnover in New York was so fast that his stuff outdistanced even the incredible rapidity with which the war was over. By the time the dash of Theodore Roosevelt and his Rough Riders up San Juan Hill was in the Magazine, Davis was in South Africa discovering a bright new British correspondent there.

"I should say," he wrote in November, 1899, "that an article from Winston Churchill would be the thing to get for this [Boer] war. I can send you Lady Randolph's address and if you write him I would suggest that you mention the fact that Lee and I did articles on the last war for you. I know him quite well and I think he would be interested to write for the same magazine."

Lee was Captain Arthur Lee, British Military Attaché in the United States during the war with Spain. So the Magazine was watching the little battles which held the whole people in a frenzy of excitement from many points of view. Later it followed the graver fights in South Africa and the Russo-Japanese affair found John Fox, Jr., in the saddle, hating the Japanese and getting little sympathy from a pro-Japanese public in America.

As the century closed, there was little to worry about on the business end.

". . . Our own magazine is still booming," C.S. wrote the English office in 1898, adding that he had raised the advertising rates. "This is justified by the increased circulation which may go to 200,000 in January [1899]."

Even then, however, there was writing on the wall. Edward Bok, who had started with *Scribner's*, had left to take charge of a fast-growing giant called *The Ladies' Home Journal,* which sold for the incredible price of ten cents and was approaching the equally incredible circulation of a million copies. S. S. McClure and Frank Munsey were already secure in the cheap magazine field. The vague threat was not, however, simply a matter of price. Big circulation by itself offered no dangerous competition. But, as Fred Lewis Pattee expressed it in *The New*

American Literature,* "literature plus advertising had become a 'big business' matter, and writings of all varieties, but predominantly fiction, were now demanded for it in amazing quantity."

So it was obvious that these new giants would get their material by the simple expedient of paying for it. At first there was resistance to the cheap magazines by the more sensitive authors, who did not like to see their best work in the company of so much trash. There was talk in literary circles about writers "selling their souls" or "prostituting their talents."

"The new magazines . . ." wrote James Barrie in 1893, "strike me as mournful signs of the times, without even an appeal to intelligence in them."

By 1899, they had invaded England too.

> *"Its success," Barrie wrote C.S. of* Scribner's *in that year, "is well deserved for you are most happy in striking the mean between the heavy and the frivolous, which none on this side seems to manage. It is doleful to see the cheap stuff published as magazines here, all photographs and snippets, knocking out the good old magazines but it is largely because the latter have stood still. I suppose a magazine is like a man, there must be either growth or decay."*

Other English first-rank writers were, however, less fastidious, especially about American publication. The prices offered by the big, new American periodicals were hard to resist, and after all what did it matter? Everything in America was more or less big and new and many things were cheap too. And the English public would never know. When, therefore, men like Kipling and Conan Doyle appeared in the ten-cent American magazines, the more squeamish American authors felt better

*New York: The Century Co., 1930; p. 56.

about seeing themselves there. The result was that publications like *Scribner's* had to raise their prices to certain authors.

These prices (except in a few cases like Kipling's) were still under the big magazine scale — the margin being "prestige"— but it was inevitable that as long as circulation and advertising remained constant and authors' rates rose, profits would decline.

All these things happened between 1900 and the First World War, and *Scribner's* held its own. This was, perhaps, its heyday. In it came Kipling's "Wireless" and "They"; Edith Wharton's triumphs, "The House of Mirth" and "The Fruit of the Tree"; Barrie's Peter Pan in "The Little White Bird"; Davis's "Gallagher" and "The Bar Sinister"; the animal stories of Ernest Thompson Seton, and the beginning of Galsworthy; articles by Edwin Arnold, Henry Norman, Theodore Roosevelt and Woodrow Wilson; the classic critical writing of William C. Brownell and essays by Howells, Augustine Birrell, Joseph Chamberlain, Austin Dobson, Andrew Lang and James Huneker. But by 1916, it is evident from the record that the threat had materialized; that from here on both the publisher and the author must think more of the "imponderables" than of ledger gains.

"I have never said so to any other author," C.S. confided to John Fox in that year, "but you rather force me to admit that there has been no profit of the Magazine for a year or two."

It is true that the Magazine's first editor had retired in 1914, but the least objective biographer of Burlingame could not attribute to this the failure to break even. The standard, under Robert Bridges, his successor, had not lapsed. The circulation had not dropped. It was simply a case, at that moment, of rising costs and of the new advertisers moving into the bigger circulation so that the revenue did not rise to meet them.

Yet the imponderables were tremendous. For the publisher

the Magazine was what Dr. Holland had called a "flag," bright and widely flown. It carried the publisher's name into every home where books were read. It attracted new authors to the house.

For the authors it was an introduction to the most thoughtful minds of the reading public. Readers of *Scribner's* (and this was true of the other first-line monthlies: *Harper's*, the *Century*, the *Atlantic*) were a solid group, almost a club. They treasured their copies, filed them, often bound them and ranged them on shelves along with their most precious books. They took the trouble to write careful, praising, critical or controversial letters to editor and authors every month. The magazines became required reading in schools and colleges. They were traditions in thousands of homes. The copy on the drawing-room or library table was a mark of distinction for the family. The file became a topical history of national culture.

These things: the certainty of eager expectation, of careful reading, and of the comment and criticism which proved it, gave an author something he could never get elsewhere. From an article in *Scribner's* there would come, for instance, press comment from the entire nation. It would attract the attention of all book publishers — and publishing "ethics" never reached the point where publication in a house's magazine was thought to bind an author irrevocably to the house. And articles published here occasionally even led to diplomatic, governmental or academic appointments for nonprofessional writers.

So, in the later Magazine days, loyal authors suffered conflicts and temptations.

"I hoped," wrote Don Marquis to Bridges in 1927, "you would like the . . . story and I so particularly want it in Scribner's *that you can have it for the price mentioned by you. I didn't offer it, even within my mind, anywhere else —*

as soon as I got the idea for it I said: 'Scribner's of course.'
For you have the sort of readers who get that atmosphere."

Two months later, however, when he sent in another story
and received a *Scribner's* offer, he weakened a little.

"I wonder if you will let me send that Flea story a few
places before I close for $750. . . .

"I particularly would like to have it in Scribner's *because*
it has such an intelligent audience.

"At the same time, I'd like to try it out on Liberty *and*
Collier's *and the* American Magazine, *before I cut my price*
on it. . . . I do need the money.

"What I would like to do would be to send this story
around to three or four places that habitually pay me a
higher rate, with the assurance from you that if they turn
it down you are still in the market for it. If this is a fair
proposition let me know."

Bridges agreed. A week later the manuscript came back to
him.

"I sent this story to Collier's," *wrote Marquis, "who usually*
pay me 30¢ a word and grab up anything that I send them,
but they sent it back with the notice that while they liked it
themselves they thought it was over the heads of their readers
—in which I entirely agree with them.

"I am not going to send it anywhere else, but am going
to take the $750. which you offered for it, as after all I really
do want it to get to a public which has some brains in its
skull."

Robert Bridges, taking charge as war closed in on Europe,
had been Burlingame's assistant since the Magazine started.
Before that he had been through a strenuous newspaper train-

ing which made him more tolerant than Burlingame of the journalistic rather than the literary approach to writing. He was a bachelor without family ties. Genial, gregarious, his acquaintance stretched out into every profession. As he walked down Fifth Avenue to lunch at his beloved Coffee House, he seemed to know everyone he passed, greeting them all with a generous wave of his hand. At the Coffee House Club, a silver plaque was inlaid into the long table at his place, dedicated to "The Squire" and no one else was permitted to sit there even when the Squire was away on vacation. Along the trek from *Scribner's* to the University Club where he lived, the policemen would salute him and the men in the windows of the Union Club would smile as he passed. As he crossed the Avenue where, as it multiplied, the traffic greatly alarmed him, a policeman would hold up his hand against the cars and beckon him over.

Bridges' loyalties were remarkable and sometimes conflicting. How, for instance, he continued an equal devotion toward Theodore Roosevelt and his old Princeton roommate, "Tommy" Woodrow Wilson — at a time when T. R. sizzled at the bare mention of his successor's name, used to puzzle Bridges' more politics-minded colleagues. But he would listen to no evil of either. This, indeed, was Bridges' most endearing trait; he would admit no gossip, no whispering attack directed at any friend.

His friendships were an asset to the Magazine because of the variety of specialists they included. There were scientists like George Ellery Hale and Robert A. Millikan, men possessed of that rare capacity among those who think in symbols, of expressing themselves in clear English to a lay public. Through the Magazine, he led into the House the great engineer Michael Pupin, whose *From Immigrant to Inventor* was an Americanization story as popular as the autobiographies of Bok and

Jacob Riis. He brought, too, William Lyon Phelps, beloved Yale professor of literature for the "As I Like It" department of the Magazine, and Royal Cortissoz for "The Field of Art."

In the detail of magazine work Bridges was meticulous to a point which sometimes worried the more rapid workers of a later day. If he smelled an error in a proof, nothing would stop him till he had personally run it down, checking and cross-checking his authorities. In this he was a little like his beloved T. R., who, even in the busiest White House hours, had a corner of his mind forever awake to the details of his literary work.

"In the bear chapter," the President wrote Bridges about the wild-animal reminiscences being published in the Magazine, "I now remember that in my correction or addition where I make Stewart speak of the 'doily' bear I used the word 'solemnly' as describing how he spoke. Did I not also use it as describing how Alf answered Alec Lambert about the hundred-thousand-year-old horse? If so, will you substitute some such word as 'earnestly' in one place or the other?"

This was back in 1905 while Bridges was still assistant editor. Even then, Bridges' friendship with Roosevelt was so close that no one in the house dared impinge on it. Bridges even handled the Roosevelt books when they were in hand, spending countless hours at Oyster Bay going over proofs and pictures while the President barricaded himself against telephone calls about the state of the nation. Roosevelt's capacity to isolate himself at will is suggested by his writing the letter about the bear just as Elihu Root was stepping into the vacancy left by the death of John Hay, Secretary of State; on the verge of an agreement with Japan affecting the future status of the Philippines and Korea; and in the midst of the insurance investigation which was one of the vital events of the second term.

To 1928, under Bridges' control, the Magazine continued in

its old form. By that time, however, some of the younger, restive folk in the House seemed to feel that *Scribner's* was "in a rut." This came partly, no doubt, from the hard pressure of competition and the fear that the general expansion of articulate media in the country would force it out unless something pretty drastic were done.

As we look back now on 1928 — which, at the time, seemed so prosperous and dynamic — it shows up as a bad year. After a decade of isolationist extravagance — an orgy of speculative folly, rackets, dishonest prohibition — we were living in a fool's paradise, our eyes following starward the spiral of the phony "boom." It was a year in which any sober analysis of popular thought or public trend was impossible. But all this is hindsight.

The promoters of a new *Scribner's* saw — or thought they saw — a public lying midway between the old *Scribner's* and the improved *Saturday Evening Post*. They wanted this public *in addition to* the old, solid reader group they already had. So they decided to keep the contents on the top level, even bettering it if possible and making it touch every immediate aspect of the exciting, changing world — but to alter the dress. They would enlarge the format, putting on a new gay cover each month — a cover which would compete with the bright colors of the *Post* or *Collier's*, yet be dignified enough to look slightly down its nose at its all-out companions on the newsstands. And text was run through the advertising pages; illustration became decorative rather than pictorial.

During its years in this dress, under the alert, original editorship of Alfred Dashiell, the Magazine ran some of the best material in its history. Hemingway, Fitzgerald, Ring Lardner, Don Marquis, Zona Gale, Tom and James Boyd gave it their best stories. The new format admitted longer pieces; *Typhoon*, for instance, could have run complete in one number. The "long short story" form was indeed a special feature, stimulated by a $5000 prize contest won by John Peale Bishop. There was, too, a series of 20,000-word biographies, each complete in one issue. A distinguished book review department called "Literary Signposts" was conducted by Robert Sherwood.

"I have read Scribner's *for forty years," Don Marquis wrote soon after the change came; "it has always kept up to a high standard, and I do not recall a period in which it has been more alive, or more sensitive to a contemporaneous life than at present."*

Yet the change did not bring the prosperity for which its promoters had hoped. Perhaps the gay new dress scared away the more conservative readers. Perhaps they found the larger job harder to file and bind. Perhaps some of the new public, lured by the smart costume, found the inside too highbrow for its taste. But beyond all this, the balloon burst in 1929 and the country spent four or five years in dark repentance. During those years, even twenty-five cents was a lot for a magazine — unless you were sure before you paid it that it would fill your bill.

It is easy to say, today, that the change was a mistake. We may say, for instance, that there is more room in 1946 for a magazine on the old *Scribner's* pattern than ever before. But we are dealing, in 1946, with a people made grave by years of war; a people infinitely more mature, engrossed no longer in national but in world culture.

Robert Bridges retired in 1930 from the active editorship. Seven years later, illness forced him to leave the House after a career with it of more than half a century. Alfred Dashiell carried on until, in 1937, the Magazine came to an end (as a Scribner publication) in its fifty-first year.

A magazine, as Barrie said, "is like a man"; it remembers and it forgets, it matures, has weaknesses and strengths, makes mistakes, and is forgiven. To its subscribers, it is a trusted friend —one that keeps appointments and seldom fails to entertain. Readers scold it if it falls below the mark and have a sense of personal injury if it offends. The files of every magazine contain plenty of angrily cancelled subscriptions. Such letters in the *Scribner's* record have the hurt, sorry tone of a man who tells his old friend he must stop speaking to him. But they are balanced by pæans of praise. And when a reader takes the pains to write in congratulation, the editor may well be proud.

XIV

PICTURES

"It must often be a shock to him [the author] to see the people he has in his mind so clearly and distinctly, appear on paper as something wholly different and outrageous."

In 1885, when Arthur Burdett Frost wrote this to Charles Scribner, it was believed essential to the printing of fiction to illustrate it. This curious prejudice held not only for magazines; a bound novel, too, must have at least a frontispiece of some striking scene in the story and usually other pictures scattered through the volume. The epoch in which the public grew up to the point of no longer needing this aid to the understanding of the more serious fiction may be spotted roughly by running through the volumes of Edith Wharton's novels. *The Fruit of the Tree* in 1907 had a dramatic frontispiece; but opposite the title page of *The Custom of the Country* in 1913, there is a dignified blank and the modern reader arriving at this point gives a deep sigh of relief.

His sigh does not reflect upon the art of Alonzo Kimball. The reader is relieved because he can now make his own pictures. Unless words can impel him to this, then words are no good. Authors knew this long before publishers were willing to admit that the reading public knew it too. Even the more sensitive illustrators themselves, as Frost's letter shows, had begun to squirm a little as far back as the middle eighties.

The influence of illustration in the history of literature cannot, to be sure, be passed off so lightly. Here it is hardly fair to recall the juveniles — the John Tenniel Alice, which is an integral part of the Carroll books, or Reginald Birch's creation of Fauntleroy — for juveniles must always be illustrated, as the child learns to read through pictures. But the images of the Dickens people which stick in our minds are Cruikshank's and the caricatures with which Thackeray himself adorned his writings are difficult to divorce from the comic characters. Anyone who has seen Gustave Doré's *Inferno* will have a hard time if he tries (though he probably should try) to remember Dante without it, and, however much we struggle, Doré's albatross will hang forever round the neck of the Ancient Mariner. And, if we attempt to lay down rules, we are confronted with du Maurier's own Trilby, with Beardsley's Salome and, in the highest brackets, with William Blake's Job or Botticelli's *Divine Comedy;* so the most we may safely say is that a time arrived when illustration no longer became *necessary* to current books of fiction or poetry and that every one except the illustrators felt better about it.

Even in the heydey of illustration in the 1880's and 1890's, when reproduction processes were improving rapidly, there were conflicts between authors and illustrators because of differences of concept. When, in 1894, Kipling's poem, "McAndrew's Hymn," was taken by *Scribner's Magazine,* Howard Pyle, one of the country's best and most popular illustrators, was chosen to do the illustrations for it. Kipling was celebrated for his scrupulous accuracy, especially in mechanical details. He did not trust even the great Pyle and wrote, fearfully, before he saw the pictures:

> *"I confess I should like to have seen the illustrator before he went to work — more for the sake of an initial L — out of the piston, cylinder & crank of a l.p. engine — than to suggest pictures. I have never yet seen a really good foreshortening of a tandem triple-expansion that was not a mechanical drawing so I hope that Mr. Pyle will put a machinery back-*

ground to his full length of McAndrew. An American artist is, naturally, very apt to draw the American type and a Scotch engineer is a type by himself altogether. Would it be too much to ask for early proofs of the illustrations."

Kipling evidently followed this letter to the editor by letters direct to Pyle which seem to have confused the plan already worked out by Burlingame and Pyle together. Their approach had focused on the human and dramatic values of the poem with less regard to the mechanical details. When the picture came in, Burlingame's letter to the artist shows the effect of this confusion.

"I think it is both a finely thought and admirably executed picture; but I feel as though in the attempt to carry out what Mr. Kipling must have written in his letters, the first strong impression made by the poem had been necessarily obscured. My own personal feeling is only that of one who had formed a different conception of the poem; and of course as far as that goes each of us is entitled to his own. But the whole spirit of it seemed to me one of force and action. Here is the engine room of a steamer thrashing along at night in the English channel under full head of steam (McAndrew says 'her gauge shows 125') everything about the engine straining (for he calls to the oiler to know if he finds the bearings hard) and the eye of the engineer, while he talks continually alert, as is shown by what he says about the safety of the people in his charge. Ferguson is shovelling coal into the fires at a furious rate below, and everything speaks of plunge and strain in the midst of a channel sea. The picture has taken an altogether different conception; perfectly level and quiet, the engine might be at rest, while the engineer seated with his back to it has a book in his hand and a spirit of thought and devotion in his face which, though very finely rendered,

has subdued for the time entirely the man of action handling his valves, shouting to his oilers and firemen, and facing his engine keenly alert. *The book especially did not enter into my conception; McAndrew's first statement being that his engine gives him his poetry and his material for meditation.*

"*So you see from what widely different points of view we approached the poem. I do not mean to argue for the correctness of mine; but I have a feeling that you will really like better to know just how it seemed to me, and then you will know too whether my interpretation approaches any closer to the one you originally had before Mr. Kipling's letters interfered with it.*"

Still tormented, however, by Kipling's fears of the detail, Burlingame wrote again, a few days later:

"*In redrawing could not the engine be so treated (perhaps taken in profile so that only one or two rods and valve handles would project into one side of the picture) that there would be no necessity for carrying out Mr. Kipling's idea of the minute representation of it?*"

An attempt to explain to A. B. Frost the kind of picture he wanted appeared in a letter by H. C. Bunner to his editor in 1893:

"*If this happens to please your fancy, how would it do to have Frost make a nice half-page picture of a grizzled, grim, burgundy-nosed old veteran lying on his pallet waiting for death? Something such an old boy, I mean, as Lord Herbert of Cherbury, the soldier brother of the sainted George. The type I had in mind when I wrote the verses was that of Henry IV. of France, as shown in his death mask in Hutton's collection. But, of course, the man himself must have been a follower of Henry V. of England.*"

With all the care it was possible to give, however; with authors and editors and artists trying to co-operate and spare one another's feelings, crises were inevitable. A violent one occurred when Richard Harding Davis, whose dynamic charm occasionally became dramatic in a flash of temper, suddenly recognized himself in a drawing by Howard Chandler Christy illustrating a Davis short story in the August Fiction Number of *Scribner's,* 1899. Davis was in London at the moment and he sent Charles Scribner a hot cable:

"CHRISTY'S PORTRAIT MYSELF MUST NOT APPEAR IN MY BOOK ITS USE IN BAD TASTE IMPERTINENT AND MOST UNKIND."

C.S. was amazed at this outburst, sent for the picture, studied it a long time and called in some of his colleagues who were friends of Davis.

"Does this," he asked, "look like anyone you know?"

They all shook their heads and remarked that it seemed to them merely a typical, dashing young man. The answer was, of course, that that was precisely what Dick Davis looked like. He was, indeed, the type itself and most of the dashing young men of the era tried their best to model themselves upon it. And as Davis had written, as he so often did, a story about a typical, dashing young man not unlike himself, Christy had caught the spirit and picked a model who as nearly as possible had measured up to the ideal.

But Davis, oblivious to all this and stewing in London under the merciless kidding of his detached British friends, refused to be mollified. He became, indeed, so angry that all of poor Christy's drawings came under his attack.

"This is the most obvious attempt," he wrote, *"to make the hero look like me that I have come across. Everyone who*

has seen it has spoken of it to me. It is a most offensive piece of bad taste on the part of the artist and a liberty and an impertinence. I can forgive his drawing one of the characters who is described as one of 'Congreve's gallants' and who is also an actor with a moustache — Imagine a man of Congreve's time with a moustache imagine any actor of any time with a moustache. I might also overlook the picture of the girl who is described in the text as having a face lit with excitement and with tears running down her face. I only ask you to look at her face — If the artist cannot follow the text let him draw pictures and publish them in a book by themselves as Gibson does — But I think it is most unfair to the author to have his story 'queered' by imaginings of the artist. As for the picture of myself that is simply a piece of unwarranted impertinence and should have been stopped by Mr. Chapin or one of the editors. . . . It may have struck Christy as amusing, it strikes me as most unworkmanlike, flippant and a liberty with you, with the readers of the magazine, and with me."

Stevenson, in 1892, was distressed by W. L. Metcalf's illustrations for *The Wrecker:*

"All the points in the story are missed. The series of little pictures of chance interviews in rooms might have illustrated any story (or nearly any story) that ever was written. The different appearances (all wrong) that he has given to my Captain Wicks would make the head of any reader spin. . . . And I will take for a test case the picture you have chosen for frontispiece. Consider the attitude of the tonsured priest who is sitting on the cabin table. If (in such a position) the rev. gentleman shall be able to drive his knife through his hand, or even through a Swedish match box, I will give Mr. W. L. Metcalf two and sixpence and a new umbrella. And

who is the lean elderly moustached gentleman seated beside the priest? No Dodd that I have seen. And again, page 340, where's the 'oldish oratorical fellow in the smart tropical array of the British man o' war's man' I see a lad of about eighteen perched sure enough on a table and in a costume familiar to the nautical melodrama but not to the British navy or the tropics."

In the later days of pictures in books of fiction, E. W. Hornung wrote a vigorous protest about some illustrations for one of his Raffles collections. Hornung had written stories over a period of years through which his notorious character grew into a gray-haired middle age. In 1905, however, he lapsed back into Raffles's youth in a new series. The artist, not apparently noticing this, had depicted the familiar gray-haired Raffles. The plates had all been expensively made when Hornung's protest came. The Scribner art department, however, did some quick thinking.

"We have noted," wrote Edwin W. Morse to the author, "your criticism of the gray hair and have arranged to have the plates burnished so that Raffles's hair will be black. This can easily be done and the effect should be to take twenty years off the great Cracksman's apparent age. We hope that these illustrations, thus modified, will meet your approval."

Such letters, however, were balanced often enough by praise. In 1902, for instance, came this letter from Arthur Quiller-Couch, the English novelist:

"I thought Mr. Howard Pyle's illustrations for Sinbad delightful — but the letter I meant to write was about Mr. Parrish's illustrations for 'Phoebus on Halzaphron.' They were so exquisite that — well I thought then and still think that no short story has ever had more honour done it. In the heat

of my admiration I was for writing off to ask you if they were by any chance purchasable — that beautiful one, for instance, of the deputation crossing the sands; or another charming one of the Mount itself. But the disgusting shortness of my purse just then restrained me, & disgust so chilled me that I never sent even a word of thanks. But this I'll do now, & thank the artist for what I shall always count a great honour."

But however the public may have outgrown the illustration of current novels it insisted for a long time on the illustration of fiction in the Magazine and still insists on pictures in the special editions of standard fiction which make up so much of the Christmas trade.

It was the illustration as much as the text of *Scribner's* which made the Magazine's reputation.

A letter from J. B. Millet to C.S. in 1913, recalls an incident a quarter century before when Millet was the Scribner art director, and points a landmark in the history of illustration.

"When I wrote Hopkinson Smith the other day . . . I reminded him of one or two things that perhaps you have forgotten, — namely: The first time a half tone engraved plate was ever used in a prominent position in any magazine, was when you consented to my using it as a frontispiece to the first number of 'Scribner's Magazine.' I remember when I took it over to Trow to be printed, the manager, whose name I have forgotten, declined to put it on the press, and called in his foreman to show him that I had given him nothing but a plain piece of copper with nothing on it that anybody could see. I had to guarantee to stand all his expense myself personally, before he would run the risk of putting it on the press. At least, that was what he asked me to do, and I agreed to do it, although probably he had no other idea than to see how much confidence I had."

It was Burlingame s intent "to print good reading first and then give it all the illustrative help possible" and not "to make a picture book merely," but as the Magazine grew and the House gained access to such a wealth of picture material, there were cases in which the illustration of an article or poem seemed to outstrip its text, and there were times when a special number contained groups of pictures alone, without text, by such fine draughtsmen as A. B. Frost or Ernest Peixotto or Edward Penfield; in color by Maxfield Parrish or Jessie Willcox Smith, or photographs by Dwight Elmendorf or J. B. Carrington.

The genius behind all this was a lad from Hartford, Connecticut, who was working for S. S. McClure in 1893. Sam McClure had already lured Frank Doubleday away from the Scribners and was constantly tempting Scribner authors to write for his magazine, so perhaps it was time the Scribners took someone from him. It was not an offer of a high salary that got Joseph Hawley Chapin. It was not C.S.'s habit to attract men to him by high pay. It was rather the chance of a secure position in which he might grow; the chance, especially, of working with books where taste and ideas and technical judgment would have full scope and where he might, perhaps, build a great department which would be his own. And this was precisely what happened, and in the forty-six years which followed, Joseph Chapin became part of the very soul of the House of Scribner.

When you met Joe Chapin away from the office he seemed too genial, too boyish, too much in love with life and too concerned with its enjoyment to be an efficient or industrious worker. But when you met him thus you did not meet his skill or his conscience; the touch on his work which was sure, hardy and tender at the same time. You did not see his hand writing figures while he talked, sorting drawings or proofs or electros without even seeming to look at them, working all the time men were coming and going with their problems or their stories or the jokes they saved up for him and never missing a word. You did not see these things away from the office. You saw his energy at an all-night party in some warm tavern, but you did not see it the night after when he stayed up just as late at his lonely desk — because you were asleep yourself. So, to his casual friends, Chapin's ability to live and work with equal enthusiasm was a mystery they could hardly believe until they saw the results. Nor could they understand the clear, broad, two-way avenue of his mind; how a man could be neither an introvert nor an extrovert, or whatever they called it in the days of Chapin's prime.

Fortunately for the record, Chapin kept, in the spare time he miraculously found apart from all his activities, a running story of his life at Scribner's. It was never printed, for Chapin was not a writer, and much of the narrative is too personal to interest those who did not know him, but it is revealing to anyone who cares what makes a great art director or what a well-conducted art department means to a publisher.

He tells, for instance, that he never let himself be blinded by big names to the work of new illustrators.

"It was my aim to maintain a sympathetic attitude toward the artist and especially toward the beginner, hoping to at least make a friend for the house even if we failed to do business together. For years I made a practice of seeing all callers, because one never knew when one might find in a portfolio the makings of a future celebrity. All this took time, but I established some important contacts. . . . I purchased from Jessie Willcox Smith, out of her portfolio, some of the first drawings she brought to New York; this was also true of N. C. Wyeth, Will James and many others."

[235]

He made many friends because he insisted on playing fair with strangers who brought their work in. At the time when he first came to Scribner's new illustrators had no protection against a conscienceless art director who would demand a lot of sketches, encourage the artist, and, in the end give the job to some one else. Chapin always "had a clear understanding with the artist from the start. I made it evident to him if he was gambling his time; and on occasions I have agreed to pay for rough sketches, if I failed to please those higher up, should such a contingency arise."

There were "those higher up" in the early days, men who knew less than Chapin about art but were firm in their determination that certain things should be illustrated in a certain way. Burlingame was one of these, as we have seen from his letter to Howard Pyle about the Kipling poem. Chapin was not involved in this particular complication, but it was obviously a case of the editor having the author on his neck, and when an author is concerned some editor must always step in. That was why an editor was "higher up" than Chapin, and it was his understanding of this that made his part of the business so successful as a "service" or, as they say now, "operational" department. Eventually, however, nearly every one deferred to his judgment — editors and authors too.

In the 1890's and early 1900's, Chapin used the time not consumed by technical detail rounding up the artists. He went to their studios, even to their faraway homes, on their fishing trips; met them at lunch or dinner at the Players', the Dutch Treat, the Century and other, more obscure haunts. He was often with them while they worked. With Ernest Peixotto, for instance, who was illustrating a history of the Revolution, he made a bicycle tour of the battlefields.

Howard Pyle was one of Chapin's earliest and best friends. He went to Pyle's school in Wilmington to meet some of the most promising artists, and some of them remained Scribner artists forever after. His visit there was characteristic. Chapin's visits everywhere seem to have been accompanied by good food and drink.

> *"After a short interview with Mr. Pyle (this visit was to be with the boys) we started for the downtown center where a luncheon had been prepared in my honor. . . . It was so hot that we marched along with our coats off. . . . To me it was a great occasion and I thought that, in spite of the heat, wine would be in order, if the boys would allow me, as a representative of the house of Scribner, to play the host to that extent. Champagne was ordered and 'presto' the heat was forgotten. After a jolly party we made our way to Herman Wall's studio (once a barn) happily located in an apple orchard. In the shade of the old apple trees we lay on our backs in the grass and watched the puffy white clouds drift lazily across the ultramarine sky. Here we became better acquainted, telling stories and swapping lies. . . . I was escorted to the station by the entire company. It was a day never to be forgotten."*

This picture of Chapin (whose figure suggested a balloon) with his coat off, lying on his back after a good meal watching clouds and swapping stories with young illustrators, must bring a smile to anyone who knew him. Wherever he went, champagne was always ordered — presto! — and there was always a jolly party.

From Pyle's school came N. C. Wyeth, Stanley M. Arthurs, Frank Schoonover, W. J. Aylward, Clifford Ashley, Harvey Dunn; and Maxfield Parrish, Violet Oakley and Jessie Willcox Smith were his pupils at Drexel Institute. At the Wilmington School there was a carpenter who made wooden boxes all alike for the boys and girls to carry their canvases in, so when Chapin would see someone approaching his office with one of these boxes he knew it would be a Pyle pupil and knew too that what the box contained would be something worth buying. Students were admitted to Pyle's school only by competition.

When Pyle became art editor of *McClure's Magazine* in 1906, he wanted Chapin for his assistant and Chapin was sorely tempted by the salary. He wrote to C.S., who was abroad, not asking him to meet the McClure offer but simply to make sure that his future at Scribner's was secure. C.S.'s cable contained two words: "Please stay." No money was mentioned by either, but Chapin stayed. It was just as well, for Pyle left McClure within the year.

Chapin's first success was with the illustration of *The Story of the Revolution,* by Henry Cabot Lodge, for which he gathered a company of artists, the dramatic and popular Fred C. Yohn among them. Soon after, the House took Theodore Roosevelt's *Life of Oliver Cromwell,* to be run as a serial in the Magazine and to be a book later. This called for illustration in a big way: authentic drawings based on historical research and study of scenes on the spot. Chapin asked C.S. if it would be desirable for him to go abroad to organize the work. Chapin's private conscience told him to stay in the office and he expected C.S. to agree. But C.S. said,

"It isn't necessary for you to go to Europe. But if you don't go now, you never will. It'll be better for you to go."

With his conscience quiet, Chapin was anything but averse to the trip. With him went Fred C. Yohn, who was to be one of the chief Cromwell artists. On the ship, they soon met F. Hopkinson Smith — a somewhat celebrated draughtsman and watercolor painter in addition to being a Scribner author — De Wolf Hopper and the company of the Broadway hit of the period "The Belle of New York," which was on its way to persuade Londoners that the barbaric city across the Atlantic also had glamour.

"On the starboard deck," wrote Chapin, "Yohn and I found our deck chairs and our nearest neighbors; a lady of the 'Weber and Fields' chorus and her sister. Frankie Bailey's legs were, if not a national, at least a metropolitan institution in the 'Weber and Fields' days, and the glamor extended even to her supporters in the cast."

Chapin's conscience haunted him, however, in the midst of these attractions, "for our friend 'Hop Smith' . . . looked at us disapprovingly, or was it enviously? when he sauntered by. In any event I realize that a more diplomatic course would have been more attention to the Smith family."

In London, Chapin assembled Ernest Peixotto, who came over from his summer home in Fontainebleau, Henry McCarter, Yohn and the British illustrators Seymour Lucas, Claude Shepperson and Frank Craig, and sent them off in different directions to "cover" Oliver Cromwell. McCarter went to Ireland for the Cromwell scene there, Peixotto did English landscapes, Lucas explored costumes. He made friends with William Boulton, a photographer as well as a historian who knew the exact location of every known portrait of persons of the era and promised to get photographs of them all. Boulton had just seen "The Belle of New York" when Chapin met him, and was a great admirer of Edna May.

"Broadway," said Chapin, "teems with girls like her."

"I think," said Boulton, "I should like very much to go to America."

Chapin invited him to go back with him but Boulton said, "No. I think we may have to go down and whip old Kruger."

In that summer of 1899, the South African War looked as

easy as that to most of the Englishmen Chapin met. Notwithstanding Edna and Kruger, however, Boulton went to the
houses of the Duke of Devonshire, the Archbishop of Canter-
bury, the Duke of Richmond, Charles Wertheimer and many
others, and made his photographs which came, in time, to
embellish the "Cromwell" of Theodore Roosevelt in *Scribner's
Magazine*.

Having arranged these things, Chapin skipped across the
Channel and we find him, presently, dancing in the streets of
Paris on Bastille day. Between wonderful experiences in cafés
Chapin managed to secure Charles Huard, Marchetti, Lepère
and the celebrated Steinlen of *Le Rire* to illustrate an article
by Ida M. Tarbell; arranged for the copying, by Pierre Cor-
nillier, of the murals of Puvis de Chavanne for reproduction
in color in *Scribner's Magazine,* and called on Daniel Vierge,
who was working on the profuse illustration of the Scribner
four-volume edition of *Don Quixote*.

He describes Vierge, who, after a severe stroke of paralysis,
had continued his work with as fine results as ever.

> *"The blow had fallen upon him without warning at the
> height of his career, depriving him of memory, speech and
> action. Despaired of by his family and the celebrated Dr.
> Charcot, he still clung to life with a rare vitality and, by the
> end of two years, he had partially recovered the use of his
> limbs. Memory returned. His right hand being useless, with
> the utmost patience he regained the mastery of pen and
> brush with his left."*

He showed Chapin hundreds of his drawings including early
sketches of Paris during the Commune. But about the work for
Don Quixote, Chapin, conscious of the Victorian pall which
at the time hung over the appreciation of illustration in America, had to warn him.

"I was obliged to ask for slight changes on two of his drawings, and he was greatly amused when I requested him to delete certain bits of realism which it was thought might shock our American audience."

After this strenuous week in which some of the pictures which made *Scribner's* famous were first laid out and friendships begun which bore fruit over many years, Chapin went back to quieter London, where, with his friend, Fred Yohn, he relaxed for hours in a hansom cab.

"I was reminded," he remembered, *"of a Phil May picture in* Punch. *The fare asked, 'Cabby, do we pass any pubs?' 'Yes, sir,' said the Cabby. 'Well, don't pass any,' replied the fare."*

This, then, was the way Chapin worked. Because of it, illustrators loved him, gave him the best they had. They knew he was always accessible; never hiding behind a screen of preoccupation or dignity, never too busy to help an earnest worker. He would enter a discussion of medium or technique with the same enthusiasm he entered a party. Often he combined these interests, and many an artist got help and encouragement talking over his work in Peter Doelger's Brewery or old Henri Martin's. It gave these men a lift to feel that their editor was their friend outside of working hours; that they could talk with him freely on the subtler aspects of painting away from the cold sharp lines of office desks and partitions. Indeed, Chapin was, perhaps, the pioneer of that continuously friendly relation, unregimented by office spaces, which has become the rule between authors and their editors.

Among his warm friends when he first came to Scribner's — besides Yohn and Chapin's earliest protector and instructor Henry McCarter — were Walter Appleton Clark, who soon became famous for his "pure wash" medium; Hugh Ditzler, William Glackens, Jay Hambidge (later author of *Dynamic Symmetry*); Frederic Remington, Parrish, Albert Levering, William M. Chase, Edward W. Kemble, and Reginald Birch, many of whom became Scribner regulars. Charles Dana Gibson, Howard Chandler Christy and A. B. Frost — whose name is more closely associated with the House in its middle years than any other — were already on the list when he came, and he made sure that they remained in spite of the tremendous demand on all sides for their work.

Gibson had an incalculable influence on the society of his time. Costumes, hair-do's, manners, drew their inspiration from his drawings. In "the Gibson girl," he founded a type to which every adolescent, dressing for her first ball, tried to conform. He introduced the American girl to Europe, making her more famous there, perhaps, than she deserved. But, preoccupied always with drawings of the *grand monde*, he was scathing in his attack on the fake tinsel of "Society" in its heyday. In a *Life* cartoon in 1889, he pictured Ward McAllister leading "the 400" — a flock of geese — by the Subtreasury statue of George Washington. His influence in New York was probably as great as that of John Leech or George du Maurier in London. He illustrated much of the fiction in the Magazine and in its book form, and Scribner's published the collections of his pictures in volumes too big for any normal bookcase, but giving his concepts full scope.

Frost, the oldest stand-by of all, was at his best in fishing and hunting pictures. These survive today more definitely than the others, perhaps because costumes in these sports don't change much, and you will find Frost prints on the walls of even the newest generation of fanatic anglers or duck shooters. Otherwise his comic illustrations seem, on the whole, more appealing than the serious drawings, but in everything he did his technical soundness is evident. His letters show his eternal effort toward perfection; his dissatisfaction with much of his work. Again and again he wrote of tearing up drawings, of starting all over again.

Frost was a conservative, disliked new forms, was frantic when the Scribner Art Department tried to get him to do vignettes. He got furious at some of the "moderns" that captured the imagination of his painter son.

"Arthur," he wrote C.S. in 1907, ". . . is a follower of Cézanne and Matisse now, the craziest of the so-called 'impressionists.' It is an insult to such men as Monet, Sisley, Pizarro and Manet to call these affected daubers impressionists but that is what they are called at present."

At the end of the century, *Scribner's Magazine* decided to go in for color in its special numbers. The 1899 Christmas issue had a Christmas poem elaborately decorated and illustrated in color by Walter Clark, and some gay colored pictures by Glackens for an Arthur Colton story. Evidently the reproductions failed to satisfy fastidious critics.

"I congratulate you," wrote one, late in December, "on the absence of color from the January number.

"My daughter of five is especially pleased as she is used to coloring the cuts herself and is disappointed when you anticipate her. It may be a fond father's delusion, but I think she does it better than your printers, certainly her register is better. But joking aside, why try to rival the Herald's *colored supplements. . . ?"*

Chapin forwarded this letter to the printer with the emphasized words underscored, and the words evidently had their effect, for the color-work in later issues drew more praise than attack.

The Art Department embraced far more than magazine or current fiction illustration. It included cover design and book jackets. It included the illustration of every kind of nonfiction, and as photography and photo-engraving improved, photographic pictures became more plentiful and more important in the "serious books." It included schoolbooks and juveniles, many of which had some sort of picture on every page. And it included the especially fine pictorial work in subscription editions: the etching and engraving in the "Thistle" Stevenson, the reproductions of John Kipling's bas-reliefs in the "Outward Bound," and the pencil drawings of Thackeray in the "Kensington." In many cases, as Chapin and his staff grew more experienced, the actual selection of illustrations for nonfiction, as well as the buying from artists or photographers, was done by him rather than by the author. In later days, the author of a history, for instance, was glad to turn the whole proof over to Chapin for its illustration. And, after forty years of the department's functioning under Chapin, such a mass of material had been accumulated that sometimes such a book could be illustrated largely from cuts, plates or drawings already on hand, materially cutting its cost. Finally Chapin became the head of all manufacturing, so that the art work was only part of the vast detail which passed daily through his hands.

He was able to do this through the efficient staff he nursed into being. In the art work S. Elizabeth De Voy mastered the detail of every phase to a point where Chapin could leave her alone with that part of the machine while he thought out questions of policy or attended thrilling meetings of the Society of Illustrators without worrying. Atkinson Dymock was hardly more than a child when he came in: he was errand boy, office handy-man, everything, and so much in demand that people couldn't handle his name quickly enough, and he became Pete. But Dymock had been keenly chosen and in his earliest years he was going to life school at night and finding his way with powerful imagination to a point where he too acquired the Chapin touch.

In 1923, it was evident that times and tastes were changing in pictures as in everything else. Since the war, magazines seemed to be more definitely screened into categories: "illustrated" and "literary." Like authors, the old-time illustrators were doing big jobs for the large-size, million-circulation "slicks," and some of the more famous ones had been captured body and, perhaps, soul by the advertisers as the new era of "art in advertising" came in. The pen-and-ink illustration of nonfiction had been almost wholly replaced by photography and magazines had grown up which made a specialty of that.

It is interesting that C.S. asked advice at this point of an ex-"slick" editor.

"What value," he wrote Edward Bok in 1923, *"do you place upon magazine illustrations in our case? We have given up coated paper and the very high-priced artists, and there is no room any longer for descriptive articles. Illustrations sometimes tempt the editor into the acceptance of rather dull stuff but on the other hand there are some most desirable articles which require illustration. We cannot be an art magazine and perhaps we should settle down to using illustrations only when required, with the exception of sometimes brightening stories."*

And Bok wrote back:

". . . I do not miss the coated paper at all. Of course, where you print on regular paper it calls for more careful over-laying and better printing. But with the proper distribution of pen and ink and wash drawings I see no reason why you should present a series of page illustrations. I used them,

of course, in the Ladies' Home Journal *very liberally because I had the large page, and they could be cut out and framed, but that is hardly true of the so-called standard magazine size.*"

It must have struck C.S. that it was also hardly true that many of *Scribner's* readers would be likely to sit down with a pair of shears with a view to framing even a Maxfield Parrish. But the interesting thing as we look back on it is that neither he nor Bok quite knew what had happened to the world; that the old-school magazine illustration which had seemed so distinguished a few years before was forever dead. The slicks would go on with their lurid aids to their fiction; *New Yorkers* would come with their beautiful humorous drawings; new *Lifes* would bloom with tremendous photography, but literary magazines must either abandon pictures or forget literature. The public had become — and how Burlingame would shudder to hear his son use the depraved word! — too "sophisticated."

So good pictures settled, at last, into their more comfortable niche, as adornments of fine books, of more value of themselves, perhaps, than as illustrations of any text. And, from this setting, words came into their full, true value.

A place like Scribner's is curiously peopled by its dead. That is partly, perhaps, because nothing in the building is ever renewed. The old walls of 597 are just the same as the day, some forty years ago, the building was opened — a little peeled, a little faded. But for two small rooms on the Fifth Floor which have been berugged and low-lighted with shaded lamps — and the one truly elegant, carpeted office of Whitney Darrow — it is all the same, plain varnish and ground glass and bare plaster. Bill Weber, of the extremely high-powered publicity department, sits at a sawed-off roll-top inherited from generations of lower-powered publicity departments before him. When a pair of shears fell through the broken bottom of a drawer and speared his ankle, he sighed, but he would not dream of asking for a new desk. These are "traditions" and one hears complaint from newer employees, but the people who have known Scribner's for a long time are sure that when the new desks and paint come in something will go out. And one of the things that will go out will be the ghosts.

Some of them are certainly there now. In the Art Department — still under the vigorous command of S. Elizabeth De Voy, with Pete Dymock's hands working while he talks with automatic sureness — it is hardly credible to an old-timer that, in a moment, a fat, laughing figure won't come out from behind a pillar, one hand jabbing the point of a story, the other holding a photographic plate.

"It's five o'clock, Joe."

"So it is. What was it, I wonder, that I was going to do at five o'clock?"

XV

POETRY

To Olive Tilford Dargan, Brownell reluctantly explained in 1907, that:

". . . the real truth is 'people' do not care for poetry — at least until it has worked its way up gradually into recognition without effort *— and then probably for one reason or another not wholly associated with its merits. Just reflect on the history of the appreciation of Arnold's for instance. We don't — as a people, enjoy the* tension *of* disinterested *effort, but delight in mulling over and expanding lazily in somnolent contemplation of the already acquired."*

Whatever the attitude of the public, however, there is probably nothing which scares a publisher so much as the manuscript of a volume of verse. Unless it is certain that the poet has a public of his own, built up with infinite difficulty through the years, the printing and distribution of the book are usually undertaken from a nonprofit motive. Under the circumstances, the number of such volumes which do actually appear each year is testimony to the nobler impulses which move through the publishing business. There may, of course, be subtle reasons for publishing a book of verse. The poet may also be a novelist; perhaps a list of other books by him has justified doing it at a loss to keep him in the family.

To this dogma, there are occasional startling exceptions. The late Stephen Vincent Benét, for example, never had a success in a novel comparable to that of *John Brown's Body*. It was said that dozens of publishers turned down this tremendous narrative poem before Doubleday, Doran & Company saw the light. Whether or not this is true or a mere repetition of the legend, the success of the poem was a tribute to the surprising American public — not to mention the courage and the foresight shown by the publishers. As an exception, Benét's success was more striking, for instance, than that of the poet-laureate Bridges or John Masefield because Benét was known only to a small group most of whom were poets themselves.

An earlier exception was Kipling, whose "Departmental Ditties" and "Barrack Room Ballads" were among his earliest work. These verses were, of course, novel in subject and rhythm; they caught on surprisingly in America — being so British in substance — until Kipling's public here equaled or exceeded that in the homeland. As a result of them, American magazines jostled one another for the privilege of printing a Kipling poem. *Scribner's* in 1894 paid fifty pounds for "The Liner, She's a Lady," upped the price to sixty for "Mulholland's Contract" and offered the unheard-of sum of a hundred for "McAndrew's Hymn." Rates like these would have justified Gene Tunney's alleged remark that when he quit the prize-ring he was going to seek "economic security" in writing poetry.

As a rule, a dollar a line was considered high pay by a magazine for short poems, and the price was likely to decrease if the lines multiplied. Poems by Austin Dobson, W. E. Henley, Edith Wharton, Edith M. Thomas and Emily Dickinson were bought by *Scribner's Magazine* for fifteen and twenty dollars. The Magazine needed poetry to fill a literary complement — not for the reason given by the English poet-laureate, Robert Bridges:

"From what I have myself seen of American magazines I have sometimes thought that poems printed in them must have been chosen not so much for their merit as for their

convenient length to fill up the gap between the prose articles."

Occasionally *Scribner's* would, indeed, run a long poem taking three or more pages, which was highly inconvenient from the point of view of make-up.

"We shall be very glad," the editor wrote W. E. Henley in 1892, "to take for the Magazine the poem 'Arabian Nights' Entertainment' which you were kind enough to send to us through Mr. Bangs. — It is seldom that we are able to print a poem of this length; but this has attracted us so much that we are unwilling to let the opportunity pass — even though the length may possibly delay publication for a few numbers, with the disposition of the Magazine's space unavoidably made for a little time ahead."

A long work of this sort was usually illustrated as an inducement to the public which was not supposed to be able to take long poems straight even in a magazine as literary as *Scribner's,* and poets accepted the embellishments eagerly enough, sometimes even supplying the artist. In 1887, the first year of the Magazine, the editor, E. L. Burlingame, wrote enthusiastically to Charles Scribner of such a case.

"One thing especially has pleased me. The letter to Stevenson about the Christmas number has brought back an immediate reply, enclosing a contribution which I think is a great thing. — It is not a story, but a narrative poem — the first he has done — and to my mind it is simply a masterpiece — the best thing in the way of a ballad-story since I don't know when, and with a union of qualities that nobody else could possibly have made — the stir and force of an old border ballad and all the weird uncanniness of the 'Ancient Mariner.' Really I don't think it is much of an exaggeration; and if it

doesn't stir people up I am no prophet.—The story is founded on an old legend of Ticonderoga ('Ticonderoga' is the poem's name, by the way), but the action is largely in the Scotch Highlands, curiously enough; and Stevenson has sent an artist friend of his up to make illustrations for him, which he will send to us in ample time for their preparations. He says they will be good, & I have faith in his judgment,—certainly nothing ever gave an artist a finer chance.—I propose to lead *the Christmas number with it; and I should say, if I didn't think you would think me absurdly extravagant, that it was likely by itself to make the number rather famous some day—like that in which some ballad of Scott's might have been first printed, if he ever had printed them in Magazines.—In any event, it is a great piece of work, and if people don't see it at once they will sometime. It shows the amazing versatility of the man; I should hardly have believed it possible even for him to do this particular thing so well. And it has such an amazing simplicity, too; it takes hold of you from the start with that very thing:—*

> *'This is the tale of the man*
> *'Who heard a word in the night,*
> *'In the land of the heathery hills,*
> *'In the days of the feud and the fight'——*

"But you will think my liking for it goes too far if I fill any more of my letter with it."

A story typical of a reception given a poet who presents his work for book publication was that of Edwin Arlington Robinson. Robinson was introduced to the Scribners by no less a person than the celebrated John Hays Gardiner, professor of English at Harvard. In April, 1900, Gardiner wrote Pitts Duffield, then on the editorial staff:

"I have just sent a letter to you to my friend Robinson; and I hope he will turn up before long with some poetry to show you. I have no idea what it is, except that it is in a single piece, and a thousand lines long or more. I hope you will find it good enough to justify my trespassing on your kindness."

This was followed by another, four days later:

"It is very good of you to be so kind about Robinson: I hope I have not imposed on you too much in sending you a lame duck, and one with such extreme awkwardness and shyness in his intercourse with the world. He has something to say, however, I feel sure."

Duffield's letters have been lost, but evidently Robinson had not struck the fire necessary to warm a publisher about a book of verse.

"I have heard indirectly," Gardiner wrote in August, "that your people did not take my friend Robinson's poem. If it will not be betraying the secrets of the publishing-house, would you mind telling me frankly what you, personally, thought of it, if you saw it? I have a great deal of interest in the man, not only because he is a fellow-townsman, but because it seemed to me from his first book that he really had things to say. I am not bold in my opinion for I have little capacity for judging poetry, and especially minor poetry; but it seemed to me that there was a note of sincerity and freshness in his work which one does not often find in little poetry books. I should be grateful for your judgment."

Duffield appears to have relaxed publishers' rules to the point of giving reasons, though it may be suspected that the main one was the simple fact that a volume of verse cannot usually be counted on to sell and that the Scribners were already committed, that year, to other philanthropic ventures.

"I was very much obliged to you," Gardiner wrote in October, "for your trouble in writing to me about Robinson. I have so much interest in him that I was glad to have an expert opinion on his work, even if it is unfavorable. I had had my suspicions before that what you say would be the opinion of people who know about such things. Though his note is true, it is a small note and not of a kind that would stir the sympathies of many people. There is nothing compelling about it. Nevertheless, I hope he may find some publisher who is more in the way of printing such things than your house."

Gardiner's letter is notable in that he, too, is taking the publisher's viewpoint. He is still not convinced of any weakness in the poetry, only that it will not stir or compel "many people."

The following year, after evidently having had similar experiences elsewhere with his protégé's poem, he tried again with another Robinson manuscript.

"Can you tell me if your people would publish a volume of poems if their expenses were guaranteed? Not my own, I may say at once. But my friend Robinson has, I believe, another collection of short poems ready for publication; and some of us who have faith in him would like to give him a chance in the hands of a well-known house. I don't know whether he would agree to such an arrangement, or not, for he is, as a poet ought to be, a good deal of a crank. I don't suppose he will ever have a large audience, but I feel sure that he has a good deal to say to those who will listen to him, and a volume of short poems from an unknown man would have a good deal better chance than his long poems."

[253]

Even this suggestion, backed up by a later letter in which he mentioned several persons (including Barrett Wendell) who were willing to underwrite the volume, did not succeed. This, of course, is not surprising. Brownell, who at this point entered into direct correspondence with Robinson, wrote him the sort of explanation which any of the better publishers might have given.

"We can only take refuge in the commonplace that it is next to impossible to publish successfully volumes of poems, and we may add that, as we are not manufacturers, we generally confine ourselves to the publication of books in whose success we can feel confidence and in whose publication we can justifiably assume the whole or a large part of the risk ourselves."

Gardiner's final letter on the subject shows that his offer was declined and is interesting, too, in showing both his confidence in Robinson and his awareness of the obstacles in the poet's way.

"Many thanks," he wrote Duffield, "for your note of yesterday: you have been very kind in the whole matter. Of course I am disappointed, but I can see exactly the position of your firm. I still have faith that Robinson will 'arrive' some day, and that he will make some mark for himself; on the other hand, your diagnosis of the present situation I can recognise as sound. What you say of his philosophy and of his sophisticated simplicity strikes me as admirably true. When he finds his constituency, however, I feel very sure that these qualities will be pretty highly valued. In the mean time I assure you that both Wendell and I appreciate the kindness and consideration that you and the firm have shown.

"What you say of Robinson's being hard to know is entirely true: he is the queerest combination of the most retiring

shyness with an occasional natural readiness to come forward that I know. And when you know him he is not very easy to understand, I suspect."

According to Hermann Hagedorn, who wrote Robinson's biography, it was not until Theodore Roosevelt began working on them that the Scribners finally admitted Robinson to the Scribner fold.

"He [Roosevelt] had discovered," says Hagedorn, "that Robinson was looking for a New York publisher and invited him to Sagamore Hill with Robert Bridges, literary adviser of the Scribner firm. . . .

"Scribners', who had refused 'Captain Craig', and the collection of later poems which Hays Gardiner had sent them, meekly accepted the presidential hint that they take over from Badger* 'The Children of the Night.'"†

It is doubtful, judging by the President's usual way in these matters, if this had been more than a hint. Roosevelt was (for him) surprisingly diffident in such approaches. In 1906, for instance, when he offered the Magazine a verse by his son, he wrote:

"My boy Ted has written the enclosed, and I send it to you to see whether you think it worth while to print in Scribner's. I thought it better it should not appear under his name. You would in any event judge it strictly on its merits, and so it is unnecessary for me to request you to do so."

That the Magazine published the poem without expecting any kudos from the President's name is evident.

---

*Richard Badger, a publisher who made a practice of putting out books at the author's expense.

†*Edwin Arlington Robinson* by Hermann Hagedorn. New York: The Macmillan Company, 1938, pp. 216, 217.

"I find Ted objects very strongly," Roosevelt wrote soon after, "to having his name signed to that poem, and I shall ask you to have it signed as I originally intended, that is, 'Jacob Van Vechten.' I am happy to say that he, like my other children, has grown to have a perfect horror of seeming to pose in the newspapers, and he is convinced that if his name were published there would be a chance for a little unpleasant notoriety, for the assertion that he only got his poem published because he was my son; that he was seeking newspaper advertisement, and so forth, and so forth. Ted thinks the effect might be bad upon him in college; and much to my amusement, he also said that if he was to go into railroading, as he hoped, it might have a bad effect upon people who would employ him if they found that he was writing poetry! So I shall ask you not to publish his name."

In the case of Robinson, Hagedorn notes that the Scribners "meekly accepted the presidential hint." But Hagedorn goes on to explain that Roosevelt also intended to write an article on Robinson's book for *The Outlook*. If, in his conversation at Sagamore Hill (of which there seems to be no record), the President told Bridges of this intention, there was something far more definite for the publisher than a mere hint that it would be desirable to publish the book. While a publisher may be open to criticism if he allows a president to hold a "big stick" over him, it is a very different matter if the president also proposes an article praising a book in an independent periodical. Roosevelt was regarded at the time, not only as an able statesman, but as a literary appreciator if not a critic. An article from him would be sure of finding an immediate and perhaps substantial audience for the book.

A curious and rather paradoxical outcome of the whole affair, which naturally escaped Mr. Hagedorn because the Scribner record was not available to him, was Roosevelt's refusal (given in another chapter of this book) to allow his appraisal of *The Children of the Night* — already printed in *The Outlook* — to be quoted on the jacket of Robinson's book when it appeared!

Later, Hagedorn says, the Scribners declined a book of Robinson's plays, and he tells of his taking them to Macmillan.

> *"Brett [of Macmillan] recognized that his company would lose money and gain little* kudos *on Robinson's excursion into drama; but he had a shrewd suspicion that the poet had an economic as well as an æsthetic future. He agreed to accept a present loss for the prospect of a remote and larger gain.*
>
> *"The Scribners," Hagedorn adds, "were annoyed, first with Robinson, later with themselves."**

Mr. Hagedorn's prescience in these observations certainly transcends the Scribner record.

A book of verse by an author who has published a shelf of important books of prose is likely to be a publisher's "must" whether or not it has profitable prospects. It is necessary to an author's integrity as a member of the House's family. There are cases, however, in which such volumes have achieved success on their own. *Underwoods* and *A Child's Garden of Verses* became classics ranking with the best of Stevenson's prose. Several critics believed George Meredith's poems better than any prose he ever wrote, and readers of them have increased with the years. The Scribners published a volume of George Santayana's poetry which was declined by his English publisher with a note saying:

> *"We do not think . . . that we could sell a book of his*

Hagedorn, op. cit.

[257]

poetry, in fact, we even fear its publication might retard his popularity."

The experience of the Scribners did not justify this fear, at least with the American public. Santayana has a body of devoted disciples in the United States who would not be without his poems, even if they were not normally readers of poetry. They were part of the man. The people who loved Santayana loved him wholly and their devotion demanded everything he produced. The nucleus of his public was a personal one: students who had attended his compelling courses in philosophy. There was a demonstration of the depth of this audience's feeling at the end of his last lecture at Harvard which no one who saw it can forget. As he finished there was the kind of spontaneous applause which greets a successful football team. Boys jumped on their seats, threw their hats in the air and stamped on the floor — then the traditional expression of approval for a professor — for a full ten minutes. And this at the end of a course on modern philosophy: Descartes, Spinoza, Fichte, Hegel, Bergson! Even to those who had heard him long and knew him well it was scarcely credible that any human being could exert such magnetism over a group of ordinary hard-boiled youth — it seemed, at the end of his talks, as if they had spent the hours under a hypnotic spell. Such a public could never ignore — of all things — his poetry.

Among the incidental American poets published through the Scribner century who were greatly popular were Nathaniel Parker Willis, Henry Cuyler Bunner and Henry van Dyke. Meade Minnegerode, in *The Fabulous Forties,** groups Willis among "the ones completely forgotten today," though since 1924 students of the history of American culture — Van Wyck Brooks among them — have found him again, and there are

*G. P. Putnam's Sons, 1924, p. 115.

even poets in 1946 who think his oblivion undeserved. There are stirring stanzas, certainly, in his "Parrhasius," narrative of the Greek artist torturing a slave so that he may catch the agony on his canvas — though the long-drawn moral at the end suggests the demand of a mid-century American public.

Bunner, remembered today for his stories, many of which are still more than readable, wrote the sort of simple, musical lyric which captured a big following in the 'eighties. Perhaps his best work was in frankly light verse or the colloquial narrative of the Eugene Field order. His "Grandfather Watts's Private Fourth" had such a formidable popular appeal that he wrote to C.S. that he couldn't keep up with his mail asking for reprint permissions. Another verse got him confused with Field.

"Dear Burlingame," he wrote in 1893, "I found 'One Two Three' in the Recorder *of Jan. 26 credited to Eugene Field, so I cut out the slip and enclosed it to Field with this, which I think you may care to see:*

> *"To Eugene Field*
> *"Concerning a Ewe Lamb.*
>
> *"O You who sing so many songs*
> *"That please so many, many kids,*
> *"Whose Muse's offspring come in throngs*
> *"That Fate to my poor Muse forbids —*
> *"They give to You, (and take from Me,)*
> *"My one lone little 'One Two Three!'"*

Bunner sometimes wrote his publisher in verse. In reply to an inquiry from C.S. about a frontispiece for one of his volumes, he wrote, in 1892 (not forgetting, in the midst of that year's hot campaign, his politics):

"Hurrah for Grover Cleveland! He is honest, brave and true;

"Hurrah for the poetry business, and hurrah for Me and You!
"If you want to see Schultz's picture, the very best thing, I
*   guess,*
"Will be to pack two grip-sacks for yourself and Mrs. S.
"And come to the Bunner Homestead and under my humble
*   roof*
"Put my taste in frontispieces and rum to convincing proof.
"Put your dollars on Grover Cleveland and your faith in
*   Croker the Great;*
"And at your convenience inform me what suits you for a
*   date."*

The poems of Eugene Field were enduring Scribner classics, and some of the volumes are still in print. Such books as *With Trumpet and Drum* and *Love Songs of Childhood* lent themselves easily to illustration; they and the Maxfield Parrish edition of *Poems of Childhood* were permanent items on the juvenile list.

Robert Louis Stevenson, whose *A Child's Garden of Verses* became a classic in the middle years, wrote a number of ballads, some of them composed in intervals of his work on *The Wrecker*. He was sensitive and doubtful about his verse. "I never," he wrote once, "could fathom why verse was put in magazines: it has something to do with the making up, has it not?" When he sent poems to his editor, he always worried unless he got a quick word of approval.

"In the matter of rhyme," he wrote about his ballads, "no man can judge himself: I am at the world's end [Australia], have no one to consult, and my publisher holds his tongue. I call it unfair, and almost unmanly." Then, in the mischievous mood which often seized him, he went on to an awful threat of vengeance. "Lord," he wrote, "wait till you see the continuation of the Wrecker, when I introduce some New

York Publishers. There's to be a capital chapter about you
and one of the Harper's coming to grief at Delmonico's;
Mr. Scribner pulls Harper off — victory seems to crown 743
[Broadway]; when an injured poetaster — But I anticipate;
it's a good scene; the quantities you drink and the really
hideous language you are represented as employing, may
perhaps cause you one tithe of the pain you have inflicted
by your silence on,

Sir,

The Poetaster,

R,

L,

S."

Henry van Dyke came in for plenty of attack from critics
who had less, possibly, to occupy them than they have today.
It is, of course, the privilege of a critic to treat such verse as
the Doctor's with acrid contempt, but it is the eternal duty
of a publisher to give the public what it wants and the public
of the early twentieth century wanted van Dyke in quantity.
And it wanted verse as well as prose. Van Dyke's public was
solid, worshipful and wholly unaffected by the highbrow reviewer. The earnest critics in van Dyke's heyday may have
given him so much attention because they were arrayed in
protest against what they supposed to be a trend or a dominant
American *motif*. In the "new era" of our literature critics forgot in their zeal for scrapping tradition that certain publics are
eternal. Today, when art forms and tastes then in exciting
embryo have matured and their maturity is taken for granted,
the critics are more tolerant.

During and after the First World War, several important
poets appeared who were primarily poets — whose prose was,
in fact, incidental. Alan Seeger's popular success was undoubt-

edly due partly to the personal adventure of his "rendezvous with death." And the sonorous and rhythmic qualities of poems like "Champagne" met the fervent feeling of '17 and '18 as few other war poems could do. So Seeger's volume went on the best-seller list, a rare achievement for lyric verse.

In the post-war period, belonging to the group of writers which included Fitzgerald and Hemingway, were John Peale Bishop and Edmund C. Wilson, whose collaboration, "*The Undertaker's Garland*," roused the interest of the Scribners though they did not publish it. When it came in in manuscript it seemed impossible as a publishing proposition, being a combination of verse and short prose. But Perkins could not forget the verse part of it. Some years later, after Bishop had distinguished himself as a short-story writer and won the *Scribner's Magazine* $5000 long-short-story prize, Perkins wrote him:

> "*I am one of the few who ever read Hardy's 'Dynasts' and ever since I did I have thought what a subject the Civil War was for such a treatment, dramatic and poetic. Now Stephen Benét has tackled it, and I suspect he has done pretty well by it, and deserves all he gets for it, but he does not seem to me to have been adequate to its great element.*"

> "*I see what you mean,*" Bishop answered, "*about the possibilities of the Civil War for epic treatment in the manner of Hardy, and I agree with you that they are there. It was a fatal conflict and one which, more and more I am inclined to think, was almost as disastrous to the North as to the South. . . .*
> "*However, my present desire is to do something less heroic than the Dynasts, or even, for that matter, than* John Brown's Body . . .—*in prose.*"

Later also, still haunted by the memory of *The Undertaker's*

Garland, the Scribners welcomed and published Edmund Wilson's distinguished *Poets, Farewell!*

Among the authors who were primarily poets and only incidentally prose writers, three who stood high on the Scribner list were Sidney Lanier, Edwin Arnold and Conrad Aiken. Lanier's greatest success in point of sales came from his arrangement for boys of the songs of Roland and Oliver and the King Arthur and Froissart chronicles. But the volume of his own collected poems was long-enduring and belonged to the Scribner backlog.

Lanier was an analytical student of prosody and wrote much about the "physics of verse." His book, *Science of Verse,* so surprised one reviewer as coming from a poet rather than a scientist that he was accused of being under "obligations to Helmholtz." Furious, Lanier wrote C.S. that this "ought immediately to be disproved to *you,* as publisher of the book," and proceeded to disprove it, chapter and verse.

When *The Boy's King Arthur,* Lanier's adaptation of Malory, came out in 1880, Lanier wrote C.S.:

"I suspect there are few books in our language which lead a reader — whether young or old — on from one paragraph to another with such strong and yet quiet seduction as this. Familiar as I am with it after having digested the whole work before editing it and again reading it in proof — some parts twice over — I yet cannot open at any page of your volumes without reading on for awhile; and I have observed the same effect with other grown persons who have opened the book in my library since your package came a couple of days ago. It seems difficult to believe otherwise than that you have only to make the book well-known in order to secure it a great sale not only for the present year but for several years to come. . . . I regretted exceedingly that I could not,

with appropriateness to youthful readers, bring out in the Introduction the strange melody of Malory's sentences, by reducing their movement to musical notation. No one who has not heard it would believe the effect of some of his passages upon the ear when read by any one who has through sympathetic study learned the rhythm in which he thought his phrases."

Edwin Arnold, though he wrote a good deal of prose on the Orient, was best known for his poetry. His relations with the Scribners began through the Magazine, for which he wrote a series of articles, later published in the book *Japonica*. In 1890, Burlingame was anxious to get a poem from him.

"The concluding paragraph of your most obliging letter," Arnold answered, "in wh. you intimate your wish for something fresh from my pen, has induced me to forward to you one of the most original (perhaps) & striking poems I have ever written. It is the real oriental story of Potiphar's (ITFÎR's) Wife, as told in the Koran and the Persian Poet Jâmi. American literature is not to-day (as of old) foolishly prudish against grave and great lessons of morality taught in the strong manner of the East, and the force of the Scriptural story comes out, I think, very remarkably, in this, the accurate legend. At all events, you can read, & judge! The one or two competent persons who have read the poem entreat me to publish it, & too enthusiastically declare their admiration, for me to repeat it. Mr. Blum, who has seen it, burns to make Egyptian illustrations to each verse; & wd. begin at his earliest leisure if you wished. . . . If you desire to make use of it, you will not mind giving me 500 dollars for it, & you w. oblige me, on receipt, by telegraphing 'accepted' or 'declined' so that I might know what to do."

The record contains a telegram "Declined" in answer and a letter which suggests, without saying so, that the disappearance of prudish prejudice against "great lessons of morality, etc.," may not yet have become true of *Scribner's*. "Several reasons united," the editor wrote, making it plain that the astonishingly high price was not the only bar, "to make us feel that it would not be best for us to accept your offer of this poem for the purposes of the Magazine." It was, however, later included in a Scribner book.

Conrad Aiken was already well-known (to poets) as a poet before he came to Scribner's. But when, in 1927, he came, he brought, not poems but a novel — *Blue Voyage*. The blurb written for this book by John Hall Wheelock, an important poet in his own right and a member of the Scribner editorial staff, gave a picture of Aiken:

> "A modern of the moderns, keenly analytical, sensitive to every sensuous impression, often ironic, sometimes perverse, and always aware of the tragic beauty and predicament of life . . . Mr. Aiken achieves for us a realization of the bitter and humorous disparity between the inner ideal world of the spirit and the inexorable objective reality which is the scene of its struggles. In the process, he has created his own forms and widened the musical range as well as the scope of modern poetry."

After *Blue Voyage* came out, there was talk between Aiken and his publisher about taking over his many volumes of poems which had been put out over the years by various publishers since 1914, and putting them out in new dress and with new heralding.

> "As to the idea of some of your earlier works," Perkins wrote him in November '27, "I too have played with the

idea, but I meant to keep it a secret for a while. I do not think it ought to be attempted until you can be brought forward more popularly than has yet happened. This is one of the things I wanted to discuss with you, — whether there might be something which you have in mind or under way that we could wait for, with a view to building other plans upon it. . . .

"Blue Voyage *is truly in its fifth edition, but of course the editions were small."*

This is an example of a publisher's desire to create a public for a poet before presenting his poems "cold," so to speak — to give the chance Brownell sadly admitted was necessary for poetry to work "its way up gradually into recognition without effort." A year later, however, the Scribners evidently thought the public sufficiently softened up for a volume of Aiken's *Selected Poems,* which won the Pulitzer Prize for 1929 — one of the most effective boosts to public recognition.

But notwithstanding the business cautions which make volumes of verse by poets who write little or no prose so difficult to publish, the Scribners have managed a surprising number of them. Edith M. Thomas and Alice Meynell were leaders in their generations in America and England. There was Lady Gregory of the Irish poets and the indomitable Englishman, William Ernest Henley. Julia C. R. Dorr was an American favorite. Olive Tilford Dargan had a fervent American following and Katharine Tynan's religious poetry won a host of Catholic disciples.

There have been several poets in the Scribner inner circle — members of the staff. Josiah Gilbert Holland, an incidental poet whose *Bitter Sweet* and other long poems had a sale which might well amaze a modern American reader, and Richard Watson Gilder, whose poems were regarded for a time as American classics, were *Scribner's Monthly* editors. Robert Bridges (distinguishing himself by the pseudonym "Droch" from the British poet) collected his verse which was was frankly light into the volume *Bramble Brae*. Bernice Kenyon, at one time a Scribner editor, won quick recognition with the fine original lyrics in *Songs of Unrest*. John Hall Wheelock, for many years poetry editor of the book staff, has made, in the opinion of such papers as the New York *Times*, a permanent contribution to American literature and has had warm praise from many critics.

One of Wheelock's letters of declination contains an explicit criticism which, before his comment closes, extends broadly over the whole province of lyric poetry. It should serve well as a guide or caution to the novice and even an experienced poet may find it useful as an aiming point in the selection of his verses when he presents them for publication:

"You have asked me to give with complete frankness our feeling about these poems. It has seemed to us that they talk too much about things without affording the reader, as poetry must, a fresh experience of the things themselves. That is a fundamental flaw, for it is by talking about things, by making use of them, by becoming accustomed to them, as we say, that we lose sight of them. Most of us pass through life in a state of semi-anæsthesia. The world about us has become so familiar that we no longer experience it. Shelley declared it was the function of poetry to strip off this veil of familiarity, to give the world back to us again in all its original strangeness, the shock of its first surprise. It is not sufficient that things be apprehended, or the idea of them intellectually conveyed. If we are to get at their essence, they must be experienced."

Under Wheelock's guidance volumes of poems have been published in late years by some of the most heralded contemporaries: Harry Brown, Louise Bogan, John Peale Bishop, Edmund Wilson, Allen Tate and Rolfe Humphries. The poems of these writers are free from the obscurity which clouds the work of many of the "moderns." And in a new anthology of English and American poetry of the past fifty years, *A Little Treasury of Modern Poetry*, edited by Oscar Williams, a representative collection of short verse — clarity has been an important criterion.

Anthologies are, on the whole, more popular than individual volumes of verse. Perhaps this accords with Brownell's theory that a public scared of poetry is more amenable if someone does part of its work for it. An anthology being a work of selection, presumably by an expert, presents something on which a reader takes less of a chance, something on which time is not likely to be wasted. And it presents "poetry"— not the work of a poet, unknown and alarming. Poetry is a unit of culture. The novice would like to approach it through something that has been picked for him, something that is guaranteed to be good for him to read — as one who does his first cautious wading into music via the phonograph might like a selection of what experts promise him is classic.

So on all publishers' lists there are standard anthologies. The Scribners embellished Palgrave's *Golden Treasury* with the pictures of Howard Pyle. They put out a group of American poetry under the authority of Boynton. They made a fine set of *"Modern Poets"* with introductions, etc., which its owners would be proud to have on their shelves and into which, having it there, they might cautiously dip. This became part of backlog. Then they built a slow but steady success for the collections of light verse by Carolyn Wells: the *Nonsense, Parody, Satire* anthologies.

Collections of poems published by subscription moved more directly than trade volumes into spaces on the shelves of folk who wanted a beautiful book even if it were poetry. Such favorites as James Whitcomb Riley and Eugene Field did not of course need sugar-coating with the American public. Yet Riley himself was overcome by the beauty of the dress in which he found himself when the Scribners put him into subscription.

> *"Of the exquisite volume," he wrote Arthur Scribner on receipt of the first of the new set, "what can I say — or try to say — or need to try? It is as lovely every-way as it is novel and individual; and when, like a very 'plunger' in dreams, I glimmeringly see nine or ten or eleven more sumptuous twins of it, all in a row, my little homeopathic library here 'stretches away into stately halls,' etc. &c.; world without end!"*

Riley, being a loyal Hoosier, had to give his trade rights to an Indianapolis publisher, but if the Bowen-Merrill Company had more letters of appreciation than his subscription publisher, they must have had a bulky file.

Kipling's poems filled three volumes of the "Outward Bound" subscription edition and he took meticulous care in their arrangement. He scrapped some, corrected others.

> *"As to Departmental Ditties," he wrote his editor in 1897, "I don't think the ditties as such ever had any sale in one vol. in America. . . .*
>
> *"I want to suppress 'em because they are unusual bad, and will not be included in any English edition that I may make. . . .*
>
> *"This is my great chance for eliminating some doggerel that I am much discontented with, and I hope in a few days to send you the poems arranged as I wish.*
>
> *"The edition generally strikes me as a wonder and a delight and I am very proud of it."*

Again, in 1897, he wrote (having evidently received kicks from scientists):

> *"Anthropological poetry has its drawbacks.*
> *"Herewith a few corrections for 'In the Neolithic Age'*
> *which appears in The Seven Seas.*
>
> *"(1) For food and fame and two-toed horse's pelt*
> read *For food and fame and woolly horse's pelt*
>
> *"(2) for 'Neath a hammer grooved of dolomite he fell*
> read   *Neath a tomahawk of diorite he fell*
>
> *"These be urgent*
> *"And in The Rhyme of True Thomas*
>
> > *for Twas nodding grass and naked sky*
> > *Twas blue above and bent below*
> > *Where checked against the wastrel wind*
> > *The red deer bell to call the doe:*
>
> > read   *Twas naked sky and nodding grass,*
> > *Twas running flood and wastrel wind*
> > *Where checked against the open pass*
> > *The red deer belled to call the hind.*
>
> *"I don't like being more inaccurate than necessary."*

It is impossible for anyone who has read it to keep from harking back — in any discussion of poetry and the public — to Brownell's remarkable appraisement. Through the history of publishing, proofs of his rightness keep jumping out of the record. The fact that books *about* poetry are more popular than the poetry itself is one example. Thus Max Eastman's *Enjoyment of Poetry* has outsold almost any volume of poems on the Scribner list. Here was a chance to approach poetry, if not "without effort," at least with a lot of comfortable boosting and to satisfy the public's "delight in mulling over and expanding lazily in somnolent contemplation of the already acquired." Yet thousands of people must have been led into the pleasure of reading poetry through Eastman's book; must have felt the sudden delight Henry Adams described in his *Education* when, after sitting listlessly through hundreds of symphonies, he found that he understood one!

Editors of the Magazine had more constant experience with poets and their products than the book editors. Magazines are the first medium (or were, until radio broadcasting appeared) through which poets reach the world. Lately many original poems — especially patriotic or American-historical — such as those, for example, of Carl Carmer, have been launched over the air. But the magazine remains the dominant and, in the case of some poets, the only instrument of publication.

Editors of *Scribner's*, which was always friendly to verse, got tons of it in their mail. Some of the authors or their promoters had curious conceptions of its function and importance. "My husband," a woman once wrote Burlingame, "has always been a successful blacksmith. Now he is old and his mind is slowly weakening so he has taken to writing poems, several of which I enclose herewith." A great number of writers used verse to prove political, sociological or economic points. Quantities of verse were religious, frequently written by God or the Virgin Mary or some departed spirit who used the contributor as amanuensis. After Seeger's death, for instance, came a letter and several verses dictated from the other world. More cranks or partly demented persons turned to the verse form than to any other.

The acceptance of a poem — unless it was "occasional," celebrating Christmas, Thanksgiving, the Fourth of July or some news event — usually added a complication to an editor's already harassed life. Poems accumulated and it sometimes took years to find places for them in the Magazine.

"I was overjoyed," a poet once wrote, "to see the poem you accepted ten years ago in your last number. Since its acceptance I have bought every number, hoping to find it. I had bought 119 copies and there it was in the 120th."

The cautious lady had not subscribed (which, as it turned out, would have saved her money), evidently feeling that once the poem appeared she would have no further use for the Magazine. The record shows that $10 was originally paid for the poem and her eagerness to see it in print cost her (at the then price of 25 cents) just three times that amount! From the Magazine's point of view the deal seems to have been quite profitable.

The record shows one event of Scribner poetic history which is likely to be regarded by some students of American literature as a mistake. In 1887, the year the Magazine was launched, Brownell had not yet joined the Scribner staff. At Amherst he was friendly with the family of Emily Dickinson, who had recently died. In November he wrote Burlingame from there:

"Doubtless ere this you have heard from Mrs. Dickinson [Emily's sister-in-law]. . . . To my newspaper trained sense the notion of a broadside of Miss D's things — 3 or 4 pages say — such as could, I feel confident, be selected from the many she wrote, & printed not as a literary discovery . . . but merely as literature — which I think many of them are — seems rather a good notion. I contribute it for what it is worth, quite aware that you are probably endeavoring to steel yourself to suggestions from people who know nothing about magazine editing."

Evidently, however, Burlingame also "steeled himself" against this, as no Dickinson broadside appeared. But in the

summer of 1889, Mrs. Dickinson's letter made it apparent that
he had finally concluded to take one poem.

*"I fear that you have been importuned in the matter of
Miss Dickinson's verses through her sister's instigation up to
the point of positive annoyance. Pray do not mind her. I
understand that Renunciation was accepted for Scribner.
. . . The two or three others which I sent as illustrations of
her versatility, if not too much trouble I will ask you to
return. . . ."*

Brownell's reply to this is missing, but in February, 1890,
Burlingame wrote Mrs. Dickinson:

*"I return herewith all the poems of Miss Emily Dickin-
son except the one ["Renunciation"] which we definitely
accepted and had put into type. It was my hope, as you
know, that we might some time arrange to present a group
of them; but this was not practicable. It has been a matter
of regret to me that we have been so long in printing 'Renunciation,' but I trust soon to have the opportunity."*

Fifteen dollars was paid for the poem and it appeared in
August, 1890. It was set from longhand manuscript and an
error occurred in the second stanza:

> *"The Sun as common went abroad,*
> *"The flowers accustomed blew,*
> *"As if no sail the solstice passed*
> *"That maketh all things new."*

The word "sail" in the third line was wrong. It should have
been "soul." When the mistake was brought to the editor's
attention, he wrote Thomas W. Higginson, who was editing a
collection of Emily Dickinson's poems for a book:

"I can't account for the misprint; — the copy (in her sister's hand) seemed perfectly clear 'sail,' for it attracted my attention at the time to what seemed a bold if not obscure figure; and her sister saw a proof in which it so stood. I am bound to confess too that in spite of my doubts the notion of a sail passing a solstice did not seem to me as much among the impossible metaphors as perhaps it should have done, & therefore I followed the question no further after the proof was passed."

It is difficult, looking at the facsimile of the manuscript reproduced in *Poems: Second Series* to see how the careful Burlingame could have misread the word, but it is interesting that editors of later editions of Emily Dickinson's works should have persistently reverted to "sail"— thinking perhaps, as Burlingame had, that it was a "bold" figure in a not "impossible metaphor."

When the Higginson and Mabel Loomis Todd edition of the Dickinson poems was published Brownell wrote C.S., "Burlingame told me Roberts were to bring out a collection of Miss Dickinson's poetry — a scheme I should have liked for us rather." C.S. perhaps would have liked it, too, if he had known that the volume would sell 7,850 copies and that by 1930 over 50,000 copies of Dickinson volumes would have been bought by her admirers.

The history of poetry, then, is — in the United States at least — punctuated by heroic struggles of publishers against public inertia, prejudice, fear or whatever it may be. At one time in the robust adolescence of our Middle West, it was not done for a male to enjoy a poem unless some guaranteed he-poet like Service, Kipling or Bret Harte had written it. There is an authentic case of a guest being asked to leave one midland home because a volume of Keats was discovered in his room. In the pre-Civil War period, on the other hand, the poetry which had a large vogue and sold well even in book form was morbid, sentimental and, in general, what Kipling would call "unusual bad."

Meanwhile publishers have used (and are still using) every device to educate the people toward poetry and are making yearly sacrifices on the altars of Euterpe and Calliope.

XVI

POLITICS

"Should you be willing to write for *Scribner's Magazine* a paper on this whole question of 'isolation,' or increased international responsibility, or an 'imperial policy,' or whatever other of the current names best indicates the parting of the ways?"

This seems, at first look, to be a very up-to-date request, bringing up two questions at least which have been constant during the 1940's. Actually, the sentence is from a letter dated July 7, 1898, from the editor of *Scribner's* to Henry Adams. That is the reason for the third question of "imperial policy."

The United States had become suddenly conscious of itself as a potential empire. In 1898, when the letter to Adams was written, the Hawaiian Islands had been annexed, the Philippines had just declared their independence of Spain and it was inevitable that they be attached in some way to the United States. The American people were divided at this moment, some believing in expansion, empire, Pacific domination, others in isolation, minding our own business at home. Expansion in 1898 meant "increased international responsibility" or "entanglement" according to the point of view; so the isolationists of 1898 had some of the same slogans as those of 1940, notwithstanding the difference in the objectives at stake.

The editor's request to Henry Adams was declined, but another written two months earlier to Joseph Chamberlain, British Colonial Secretary, bore fruit.

"There has probably never been a time," Burlingame wrote, "when any expression from an English statesman upon

[276]

certain aspects of the questions confronting us would be listened to with such interest or effect: — upon the point often urged, for instance, that the undertaking of a larger responsibility is an American duty ultimately to become a necessity, and better assumed now than then; the bearing of the debated American colonial possessions upon the possibility of an English alliance — moral if not political, — etc., etc. Mr. Olney, as you know, has recently written in one of the magazines on the question of 'American isolation,' and the debate is likely to be carried on by our foremost publishers here through the same medium rather than the newspapers.

"I beg leave to ask therefore whether you would not be willing to write for Scribner's Magazine *a brief paper as a contribution to this discussion?"*

The English were watching our expansion with a naturally interested eye. Their statesmen realized fully what some of our policy-makers have since been accused of ignoring, that American expansion in the Pacific would make us more than ever dependent on the British Navy — already a factor in maintaining the Monroe Doctrine. Englishmen who favored a closer alliance with the United States saw new hope in American colonial expansion because then we too would share the "white man's burden" and we would become more like the British Empire. Chamberlain was one of these, and in his article set out to combat American isolationist sentiment.

"The Englishman believes . . ."* he wrote, "that nations, like individuals, cannot remain isolated without deterioration. The man who pleads the claims of his family as a reason for refusing all public work and repudiating all charitable obligations is not usually a better husband or a better father

*"Recent Development of Policy in the United States," by the Rt. Hon. Joseph Chamberlain, *Scribner's Magazine*, Dec., 1898, p. 681.

than the good citizen whose purse is open and whose leisure is freely given to the service of the community in which he lives; and the nation which elevates selfishness into a virtue and shirks its responsibility to the other members of the human race is wanting in one of the principal elements of greatness. The absolute devotion of any people to its domestic politics narrows the issues of public life, gives to them a partisan and personal character, and tends to a provincialism of sentiment and aspiration."

The responsibilities which Joseph Chamberlain here hoped the United States would come, more and more, to assume, were, of course, quite different from those which anti-isolationists hope it will assume in 1946. Nor did the new policy inspired by the guardianship of the Philippines become a colonial policy. It did, however, cause the State Department to watch the Asiatic people with a new care.

In 1904, war broke out between Russia and Japan. John Fox, Jr., who went to Japan as a correspondent for *Scribner's Magazine,* formed an instant opinion.

"I tell you," he wrote Charles Scribner in October, "that the first man who puts down in vigorous print what the Japanese really is —'a magpie'— will make a tremendous hit."

But C.S. sitting in New York knew otherwise. He knew that sentiment in the United States was overwhelmingly pro-Japanese. When Fox wrote for *Scribner's,* his articles were printed but they were not popular. Nor were they when they appeared in book form under the title *Following the Sun Flag.*

"The 'Sun Flag' statement," C.S. wrote him, enclosing the royalty report in July '05, "was rather tough for both of us. . . . We did all we could for the book, but . . . the Japanese hold the field at present. Millard who is out there now, has

sent us an article or two very unfavorable to the Japanese, but I am very sure they will do neither of us any good. In the one to be published in September he questions their financial strength, but the bonds are easily sold at good prices and the bankers' statements concerning the Japanese revenue are most favorable."

The articles of Thomas F. Millard, a veteran correspondent with a perspicacity which penetrated the Oriental mind and an amazing flair for prophecy, make lively reading today. In them he warns of Japanese jingoism, her immense military preparation following the victory over Russia.

"Success is a great stimulant, and the Japanese are beginning to speak of themselves as a military nation. In the absence of any probability of encroachment upon the national territory, what does a military policy seem to imply? Against whom are such prospective preparations directed? Does there loom in the background a 'The Orient for Orientals' doctrine, with Japan as the leader? Such conjectures naturally arise in any attempt to penetrate the future."

In this and another article the same year, he tells of Japan's propaganda agencies in England and America to gain popular sympathy and blind the governments — her efforts to "bamboozle the Western world as to her real intentions and their meaning, and even when discovered so use her diplomacy as to prevent concerted action to check her."

It was, however, in his private letters to the editor projecting his articles, that Millard really let himself go.

"Mr. [Theodore] Roosevelt seems to be absolutely cap-

*"The Financial Prospects of Japan," by Thomas F. Millard, *Scribner's Magazine*, Sept., 1905, p. 369.

tured by the Japs, and unless popular opinion in America is aroused, which can easily be done simply by presenting the real facts, he may repeat in regard to Manchuria the terrible blunder he has already made in Korea. To induce such action is clearly Japan's intent in advancing this school matter at this time, and I read in today's dispatches that the Jap minister at Washington, in assuring the President of Japan's pacific intentions, intimates that Japan may consent to a modified treatment of Japanese in America provided they may freely emigrate to Korea and Manchuria. See the point? The political incentive of the whole grandstand play is now perfectly plain, and it looks like Roosevelt will fall into the trap unless something is done."

Whether the editor "saw the point" does not appear in the record, but it is obvious from much of the material printed in the year following this letter (1905) that most Americans saw only the point of Japanese greatness, and *Scribner's Magazine* was one of the few periodicals which published contrary views, notwithstanding the fact that "T. R." was one of its favorite authors.

Roosevelt did not, however, write about political questions, domestic or foreign, for the Magazine. He considered it a literary vehicle and, apart from his Rough Rider series in 1899, his articles were either historical, like his *Oliver Cromwell*, or based on personal experiences in the explorations of his strenuous "leisure" intervals. He also was a promoter of his literary friends and, among others, brought the poet Edwin Arlington Robinson into the Scribner fold. He would not let this kind of thing get mixed up with the White House, however, as this letter of October 13, 1905, by his secretary, William Loeb, Jr., emphatically shows:

"The President is in receipt of the volume of Edwin Arling-

ton Robinson's poems, 'The Children of the Night.' On the paper wrapper of the cover is printed a quotation from the President. This is rather embarrassing because the President is continually asked for permission to be quoted in the advertisement of books, and the requests are invariably declined. Will you therefore discontinue the use of the President's name in any way in connection with the book, for the reason stated above?"

Off the record he would talk frankly of politics with C.S., Burlingame and his special friend Bridges, sometimes asking their advice and warmly welcoming their approval.

"I am particularly glad," he wrote Bridges during a speaking tour in his second term, "that you liked my . . . speech. I had to act on the spur of the moment, but I was not going to allow that cheap ruffian to go unrebuked on the subject of lynching, and I was bound to say what I had in a manner that would prevent any just offense being given to the southern people, who were greeting me with such generous and cordial warmth."

While he was President, he used to meet his publisher in the quiet security of his Oyster Bay home.

"Now can not you come down here with Bridges some day and take lunch or dinner? There are several things I would like to talk with you about — not books, but general political questions as to which I should like to blow off steam."

The expression, as everyone who knew Roosevelt remembers, was graphic. When he spoke, it was like the opening of a valve on some powerful engine. He hissed his sibilants and boomed out his vowels. When, after the presidency, he would come to the Scribner offices the glass of the partitions vibrated with his voice; his words filled every corner. The sense of power he radiated inspired the fear that he might make himself a dictator.

Once when Burlingame was showing the sights of Washington to his fourteen-year-old son and they were looking at the White House through the grill, the President came rushing along with his great stride, grabbed Burlingame by the arm and took him through the gate, the boy tagging breathless behind with the Secret Service men. In his private office, Roosevelt blew off steam and the boy lost the thread of the talk in his fascination at the President's diction. Suddenly, however, Roosevelt stopped and poised his finger over a row of buttons on his desk.

"Of course," he said, "if I should *presss* this ee-lec-tric BUTTON all that would be changed!"

The boy, not having followed what went before, had an alarmed sense that if the button were actually pressed there would be a certain, devastating explosion.

"But," Roosevelt went on, biting out the word and then suddenly showing all his teeth in a tremendous grin, "of course I shall *not* presss this ee-lec-tric button."

The sweat of relief rolled off young Burlingame, and he remembered the incident some forty years later when he read a letter from Roosevelt to Charles Scribner about his Cromwell history in 1899.

"I have tried," he wrote, "to show Cromwell, not only as one of the great generals of all time, but as a great statesman who on the whole did a marvellous work, and who, where he failed, failed because he lacked the power of self-repression possessed by Washington and Lincoln. . . . The more I have studied Cromwell, the more I have grown to admire him, and yet the more I have felt that his making himself

a dictator was unnecessary and destroyed the possibility of making the effects of that particular revolution permanent."

While self-repression was not, in Theodore Roosevelt's own time, considered one of his conspicuous traits, it is evident from his private correspondence, most of which has now been published, that his public expression was comparatively temperate and that the famous "big stick" was often held in check by a clear understanding of democratic process.

During his first term, he was severely criticized for his "dictatorial" handling of the Panama Canal preliminaries with the Republic of Colombia. On this, he wrote Bridges in 1913 after the publication in *Scribner's Magazine* of an article by Emory Johnson.

"There is one thing I wished to speak to you about the other day which I think you ought to tell your contributor Johnson. At the end of his article about the Panama Canal, in a paragraph in which he spoke vaguely as if we might have wronged Colombia, he said we ought to put our case fairly before Colombia and the world. Now there has been so much infamous slander preached on this subject by The New York World and The New York Evening Post and the like that it is pardonable for a man who knows nothing about it to be misled. But it is not pardonable for a man professing to write as an expert either to be misled or to try to mislead others. This is precisely what Mr. Johnson is doing. If he does not know he ought to know that exactly what he now says ought to be done, was actually done minutely and in detail within one month of the action itself. In my general Message to Congress, and again in my Special Message to Congress, immediately after we recognized Panama and made the canal treaty with her, I gave every fact minutely and in detail. John Hay, at about the same time, also

gave every fact minutely and in detail. In the debates on ratifying the treaty, everything was thrashed out at almost intolerable length. Not a fact as to our action has been or ever will be promulgated that was not then set forth, simply because all the facts were then produced. The World spent a small fortune in trying to get hold of something discreditable. The Congressional Committees have had all the papers in the Department of State before them, and Panama and parts of Colombia have been ransacked. All that mendacity and folly and dishonesty and mean suspicion can do has been done, and not one discreditable matter of any kind has been discovered, because there is nothing discreditable to discover. There is nothing of any kind to discover. As I have said before, I was absolutely frank from the beginning, and all the facts were put forth at once. If Mr. Johnson does not know this, then he has no business to write on the subject at all, and I should be glad to have you show him this letter."

C.S. was a supporter of Theodore Roosevelt and was always an ardent Republican. That, in his youth, he was not always so profoundly impressed by his party's representatives in the White House as some of his fellow disciples is suggested by the veiled irony in this letter to L. W. Bangs in August, 1885:

"Grant is to be buried on Saturday. It will be a very imposing sight I have no doubt but it is not enough to keep me here. Dingman is going to send you a photograph of the store front with the decorations to show you how badly we feel."

In 1892 H. C. Bunner, who was on the other side of the fence, wrote him shortly after the Cleveland-Harrison contest:

"I am glad there are no hard feelings between us, and I don't see why there should be. You objected to the Demo-

cratic party on account of the crowd. Well, there certainly is a crowd. You wanted to get back into the Republican party because it was more select. Well, it seems to be select enough to suit anybody. You seem to have got all you wanted, and I thundering well know that I've got all I wanted. We are all good people together, and everything goes, and it's all right. . . .

"But, it's an elegant November. There is a slight, healthy touch of frost in the air; but the sun is shining and the blue sky is smiling, and Mrs. Cleveland is putting the old man's fur over-coat in the camphor trunk. March is a very pleasant month in Washington."

C.S.'s political opinions came to be sought for and valued by the Republican Party. In 1911, Charles D. Hillis, secretary to President Taft, wrote for his advice.

"I would be very glad to have you write me your estimate of the work of the present Administration, and to have you give a frank statement as to the sentiment of the people in general, and the Republicans in particular, with respect to the course of the President. Such a letter would be treated as confidential, unless you were willing that it should later be utilized by some reputable newspaper engaged in endeavoring to sense the situation."

C.S.'s answer did not forget the demands of the publishing business.

"In reply to your letter I would write (but not for publication) that my observation is quite in accord with the generally expressed view that the Administration has gained greatly in strength during the past year and that the Reciprocity Measure in particular is winning back whatever support was lost to the President by his emphatic approval of

the Payne-Aldrich Tariff Bill. The sentiment among the Republicans whom I meet is practically unanimous for the President's renomination, as deserved by his administration and as the strongest nomination that could be made.

"What the Republican chances will be next year it is too early to venture an opinion, for a great deal can happen before then and we don't know what the Democrats may do. Certainly Governor Dix in this state has lost much of the independent vote; in New Jersey, where I vote, party lines are a good deal broken and the people are proud of Governor Wilson's national reputation.

"While I hope I can take an impartial view of the situation, I have of course been greatly disturbed personally by the rather indiscriminate attack of the Post Office Department upon magazines and the periodical press generally. I don't really think it political but it is unfortunate that the two periodicals named in your letter are two that would suffer most from an increase in rate. No doubt it is difficult to discriminate among Second Class Matter but I have never heard any good reason why the Century *or* Scribner's Magazine *should pay a higher rate of postage than say the Sunday* Herald *with its comic, fiction, and advertising sections. But this is not what you inquired about."*

At the end of Woodrow Wilson's first term, C.S., like so many Americans, incensed by German aggression in Europe, found the President's foreign policy hard to understand. In the summer of that year, his son Charles, then active in the business, led an enthusiastic Scribner contingent in the great "Preparedness Parade" which marched up Fifth Avenue as a protest against Wilson's apparent unwillingness to face the probability of our entrance into the war in Europe. After the Republican Convention, in June, 1916, C.S. wrote of it to Mrs. Humphry

Ward, who, like most men and women in England, were impatient with American foreign policy. The letter shows plainly his convictions about his author T.R. as a political leader.

"*You have seen the result of the Convention. Roosevelt was the logical candidate and would have made the most aggressive campaign. What enthusiasm there is here for preparedness has been created principally by his personal efforts but it is doubtful whether he could have secured the full Republican vote and Hughes was the natural choice for the Convention. Roosevelt will support him and he has a fair chance of election, though it must be remembered that the country is prosperous and has not yet given much evidence of the 'heroic mood' desired by Roosevelt.*"

A month later, another letter to Mrs. Ward reflects the tension of that exciting summer.

"*The excitement of the nomination is over and everything is now quiet on the Mexican border, though most of our militia is camping out there and business in New York, including our own, is suffering from the sudden departure of so many of the younger men. I am afraid to make any prophecy about the election. The general opinion seems to be that the Republicans will win but President Wilson is strong with the people in some sections of the country. You inquire whether there is any chance that T. R. would be made Secretary of State. I don't think so. There is no Constitutional objection but I can't see him in second place and I fear he would not prove a docile member of the Cabinet. It would be altogether right for him to go to Washington as a Senator or to become Governor of New York.*"

The Mexican border disturbance has long been forgotten in the procession of wars which has since marched over the world. In 1916, however, against the deepening darkness of the European sky, the call to arms of the nation's militia to defend the southern border against the alleged aggressions of the Mexican president Huerta threw the people into a paroxysm of patriotism. Bewildered militiamen, who had looked upon their National Guard units as social clubs, found themselves showered with bouquets at the railway stations and wept over by their hysterical women who never expected to see them again. Charles Scribner, like many mature businessmen, was not impressed by this hysteria, but he gave leave of abscence to his employees called to the colors and wished them Godspeed.

In September, he was concerned over Wilson's domestic policies. He wrote again to Mrs. Ward:

> *"It is difficult to write about affairs in this country or the attitude of the government. The situation seems to change almost every day and we are in the midst of a presidential campaign, the result of which no one can predict with certainty. The threatened strike on the railroads and now on the traction lines in New York City add a new complication. The President has made use of his office to strengthen the position of the strikers and that may easily be an important issue during the rest of the campaign. He has certainly lost a great deal of support from the business interests and it is doubtful whether he can make it up from the union or labor vote. Thus far in this country the labor vote has been divided between the parties."*

C.S.'s interest in the labor situation was natural and constant. In 1895, when he was publishing a book by E. Benjamin Andrews which should contain an account of the celebrated Homestead steel strike of '92, he wrote to Andrew Carnegie for his version of the strike so as to be able to put all fact and opinion in the hands of the author. Carnegie answered in a letter which is here reproduced for the first time.

"*I find yours of the 10th before me upon my return from Pittsburgh. I do not know of any photographs taken in connection with Homestead, but I hope the writer will take the trouble to get the facts in connection with that deplorable affair.*

"*First: He will find that owing to new processes and machinery, the product was increased sixty per cent per day.*

"*Secondly: that the firm offered to divide the result of this with the two-hundred and eighteen (218) tonnage men, who alone were affected, out of a force of about three-thousand. That is to say, the earnings of these men paid according to product would have been thirty per cent greater than they were under the three years scale which then expired. The leaders of the men, however, insisted upon obtaining the entire increase, viz. 60 per cent, although the firm had spent four millions of dollars upon these works to bring about improved methods.*

"*There never was a more generous proposition made to men. Their work was not increased by the new machinery; on the contrary, it was lightened, but a few leaders knowing that we had government contracts, and especially work for the Chicago Exhibition upon which we were engaged and could not be delayed, decided to take the firm by the throat and demand the entire sixty per cent increase. It was no strike against a reduction of wages; no mechanics or workmen of any kind had their wages reduced. In strict justice, the firm was entitled to the entire increase made by this improved machinery, nevertheless, it offered to divide with the men.*

"*The report of the Congressional Committee should be read by your writer. They were surprised to find that these tonnage men were making ten to thirteen dollars per day of eight hours. Thirty per cent increase upon this was what the firm offered, but they demanded sixty.*

"You will understand, that we are naturally averse to raking up this old controversy, it does no good, on the contrary, only bitterness arises, which we have been quietly at work for years endeavoring to soften, and in which we have succeeded.

"I write this to you in full confidence, and as a personal matter on account of the long connection I have had with your house, and as the coming article is to be published, I may as well give you some facts, which, of course, I expect you to regard as strictly confidential, and not to mention my name in any way with the matter."

C.S.'s personal conservatism did not, however, prejudice him against radical writers. He welcomed Max Eastman into the Scribner fold though Eastman at the time was called, by extreme right-wingers, a "dangerous" revolutionary. John Reed, at the time his first book was published, was an editor of *The Masses,* and both he and Boardman Robinson, who illustrated it, were disposed to look favorably on the Russian experiment. Another book of Reed's was declined — evidently because its pleading of the socialist cause was not good enough.

"Several of us," Maxwell Perkins wrote Reed in April 1916, "read the 'Crimes of Charity' and were naturally impressed by it, but finally decided against it. It is always difficult to exactly explain the reasons and rather superfluous in view of the fact; but one reason was that in the light of an 'exposé article' the material had little value because no case was systematically built up. It was not in this light that we cared for it but rather as what, until somebody invents a less tiresome and bromidic phrase, you still have to call a human

document; — the simple, vivid little pictures of human beings under stress seemed exceedingly effective, but the temper of the book and its exposé character, which it seemed to us would in itself rather harm the cause of the poor than help, and also perhaps the lack of organization, so far counteracted our interest on this account that we finally decided against it."

In the last year of C.S.'s life, he approved a project to publish an autobiographical book by Leon Trotsky. There was a great deal of correspondence with Trotsky personally about this book, Trotsky's letters being written in both French and German and usually in red ink! They are not interesting, being in substance, for the most part, irascible complaints of the author's treatment by foreign publishers, agents and so on, but they show his eagerness to understand the minute details of every sort of work he undertook. They reflect the meticulousness of Trotsky's curiously legal mind which makes parts of his autobiography difficult for many readers. Perhaps, too, those who have read the story of the Brest-Litovsk conference in March, 1918, will remember how Trotsky with his legalistic language, his documentation and his detailed logic kept the Germans confused.

His most irate letter to the Scribners concerned the English edition of his book. It is interesting that he should have appealed on this to his American publisher.

"One of my friends informs me," he wrote in July, 1930, " 'with indignation that the English publisher has had the audacity to add a subtitle — as if to a film — and that subtitle: The Rise and Fall of a Dictator.' *I have not seen the English edition. If the report is correct — and it is impossible for me to doubt it — I find myself obliged to demand categorically:*

[291]

"1) *That the unworthy subtitle be immediately eliminated.*

"2) *That the English publisher publicly explain that the
subtitle comes from him and that upon my protest
it is eliminated.*

"*I hope to receive word by telegram that these two conditions are accepted. If not I shall be obliged to have recourse
to other means to defend my author's rights.*"

Perkins's letter showed that his confidence was justified.

"*I am not surprised that you were offended by the subtitle
which the English publisher used on your book. Fortunately,
I saw an advance copy and cabled at once to have it
changed. Enclosed is a copy of their letter assuring me that
they have had new title pages put in all copies that had not
actually been sold. I have written again to be assured that
this has been carried out. . . . I have also instructed him
to place such a notice as you ask for in the English newspapers saying that the subtitle was theirs and that on your
protest it has been changed.*"

Scribner's Magazine, though primarily literary in its early
days, published an occasional striking political article. "Socialism," by Francis Walker, in the first issue was one of these.
The same author followed this with "What Shall We Tell
the Working-Classes," a realistic set of advices many of which
were followed in later years, but which must have shocked con-
servatives of the late 'eighties. Other articles which are worth
rereading today are Hugh McCulloch's "Problems in American
Politics," Joseph Bishop's "Law and the Ballot," and, on foreign
affairs, John H. Wigmore's "Starting a Parliament in Japan,"
and John C. Ropes's "War as We See It Now." These and
a dozen more were in the Magazine's first five years.

The editor, at that time, was anxious to get something on French politics and the operation of the Third Republic in general. His letter to C.S. from Paris on this subject in 1891 throws a light on freedom of information and expression in that country.

> *"My search for a man to do a French Republic article has been unsuccessful — which you may perhaps think just as well, as I never have fully described to you just the kind of paper I had in mind, & it may not seem so attractive as it has to me. The difficulty of a man's writing on anything like politics here & satisfying or even interesting more than one side is even greater than at home, it seems to me. Here, people actually know only one side; at home they at least understand their opponents."*

As the First World War approached, we find the American State Department more concerned with Mexico than with Europe. In the spring of 1914, Mexico, not Germany, was the potential enemy. Henry van Dyke, a consistent Scribner author, was at that time U. S. Minister at The Hague, supposed to be the peace center of the world. In a letter to Arthur Scribner in May, he says nothing about any war clouds over the European scene but goes at length into Woodrow Wilson's Mexican policy. His view of Wilson is striking because it was at variance with that of the Scribners and indeed of many Americans who worried about our foreign policy.

> *"About Mexico," van Dyke wrote, "I have long been anxious and sad. So far as I can see President Wilson has been absolutely straight in his policy and action, and what he has done from week to week has been absolutely the inevitable. Also what he has left undone. Any other course, (and the most contradictory courses have been suggested)*

*would have produced far worse results in the end. The medi-
ation of the A. B. C. powers, (for which I have long been
working here,) is the only road on which the light shines. I
hope it is going to increase and show the way of peace and
order for Mexico. I know the President intends to avoid war
if it is humanly possible. But the simple fact is we have a
bad neighbor on the south, and we have to take the consequences of that fact. We can't recognize an* abattoir *as a
constitutional government. But we must hold our hand to the
first sign of a regime that has the promise of pacifying and
reorganizing Mexico. Huerta can never do it, and he has
never really intended to. What he meant was to subjugate,
not to govern. He has shown his impotence even to do that.
If we had recognized him he might have done it? Perhaps,
— but was that our duty, to seat a usurper and dictator?
No, — hands off as long as possible, and hands out to the first
promise of real peace in Mexico, — that seems to me the
straight line. And I think Wilson has followed it."*

When the World War broke, van Dyke was still in Holland
and was evidently as surprised as everyone else.

*"Your two letters," he wrote Arthur Scribner on August
3, ". . . have come to me in the midst of dark and troublous
times. The whole sky of Europe is black with the storm-
clouds of war. The Hague is full of agitated and distressed
Americans. . . . I am working day and night to attend to
their necessities."*

But even in October, 1915, five months after the sinking of
the *Lusitania,* he clung to his belief in the President.

*"I think that Wilson's course in the matter has been very
fine and wise. I have not met one sensible man of any na-
tionality on this side of the water, who did not agree that*

it would have been a great misfortune to the cause of inter-national justice, if the United States had been drawn, or drummed, or shouted, into an active participation in the war."

Sensible men in England, however, were changing their minds about this. In 1916, the American policy so disturbed Henry James that he changed his citizenship. Kipling became bitter. Edith Wharton, Mrs. Humphry Ward and others in Europe wrote with acute impatience at our policy.

"The election," wrote Edith Wharton after the defeat of the Republicans in November, "was a bitter humiliation to all of us Americans in France."

And, in January, 1917:

"As to our own country, I prefer silence, because I really don't understand any longer."

Such was the fickleness of temper, however, of those feverish days that when, in April, 1917, war was declared, most Americans who had abused him rallied behind the President and it became treason (even in a private club) to speak ill of him. Kipling wrote an apology in verse for his previous abuse of America and even the London *Times* changed its attitude. There was, however, in the Senate, a Scribner author who was never, according to the book he later published, quite reconciled.

Henry Cabot Lodge's diary, quoted in his *The Senate and the League of Nations* (published in 1925 after his death), gives in its entry of May 18, 1917, his view of the President at that time.

"I watched and studied his face tonight as I have done often before — a curious mixture of acuteness, intelligence

[295]

and extreme underlying timidity — a shifty, furtive, sinister expression can always be detected by a good observer.

"I wonder if the future historian will find him out. He has only to read and compare the President's message and papers and follow his mistaken policy in order to discover him.

"His war message, to which he was driven by events, was a fine one, but he has not changed his spots. I wonder if some historian of the future will see the aforesaid spots. They are all there. The man is just what he has been all along, thinking of the country only in terms of Wilson, never of the country's interest alone."

Another Scribner author, however, writing in 1945, suggests that the historians of the future have not seen Wilson as Lodge saw him twenty-eight years before.

"I think," says Ray Stannard Baker in his American Chronicle, 1945, *"the deepest satisfaction of the later years of my life has been to see Woodrow Wilson come into his own, being recognized for the pre-eminent man he was, as the true inheritor and prophet of the great American tradition."*

On Wilson's Fourteen Points, given out in the President's speech in January, 1918, Lodge had a comment which, read in the light of later economic views, seems to reveal a change in public opinion.

Point Three read:

"The removal, so far as possible, of all economic barriers and the establishment of an equality of trade conditions among all nations consenting to the peace and associating themselves for its maintenance."

In his book, the Senator says of this:

"The third proposition was in essence for universal free trade. That was never, I think, seriously considered by anyone."

When, however, in President Truman's twelve-point speech of 1945, almost exactly the same proposition appeared, the public — or at least the press — accepted it as an old story.

In the summer of 1918, as the war moved toward its conclusion, Bridges asked Lodge for a magazine article on "Guarantees of Peace."

"I was very much impressed," Bridges wrote at the end of August, "with your speech the other day, and I hope you will consider the possibility of writing an article for us of about 4000 words on the dangers of a 'Peace Offensive.'

"There seems to be an apprehension among our soldiers in France that the people at home will not stand firm enough. Your position has been so admirably stated that I believe a lot of good would be done if you made a special plea particularly suited to the magazine. Part of the article might refer to the position of the Labor Party in the final settlement."

To this the Senator replied with a statement of the view he shared with Theodore Roosevelt that the Allies must be tough with Germany in the settlement.

"I shall devote myself to the necessity of a complete victory and a conclusive, dictated peace, and shall also try to find room for a little description of German propaganda, the extent and character of which are not realized at all."

Lodge's article, appearing some three weeks before the Armistice, might, but for a few specific references to the Kaiser and other matters, have been written in 1945.

A chapter of post-World-War I history written by another Scribner author and ex-employee has been largely forgotten in the disasters of the second war. In the early 'twenties, Edward W. Bok, who had retired from the editorship of the *Ladies' Home Journal* to devote himself and his fortune to public causes, received a great volume of letters from uneasy citizens in all parts of the country. Some were disturbed by the Senate's rejection of the League; others saw the nation on the chutes toward another war, were scared by the isolationist trend, the new tariff barriers, increasing materialism and public ignorance. The letter-writers were aware of Bok's zeal and his organizing capacity.

His answer was the offer of $100,000 to be awarded to the author of the best plan "by which the United States may cooperate with other nations to achieve and preserve the peace of the world." A board of judges was appointed and skimmed from the flood of manuscripts which poured in, twenty plans which showed that there was, beneath all the follies of the period, serious thinking and an awareness of catastrophe ahead. The Award was won by Charles Herbert Levermore, and his plan, together with the nineteen runners-up, was published by the Scribners in 1924 in a volume edited by Esther Everett Lape called *Ways to Peace*.

Bok's scheme, according to Lodge, made little impression on official Washington. Perhaps this was because, as historians of the period tell us, Mr. Harding, his cabinet and the legislators had other, more pressing concerns. At any rate, this is what Lodge wrote Charles Scribner in January, 1924:

"The so-called Bok world peace plan rejects all the coercive features of the League of Nations; that is, it rejects the

League as it is today and is a remarkable admission of failure on the part of the League as now constituted. The prize plan seems to me a poor thing, but here there does not seem to be much attention paid to it either by the President or Congress. It seems to be generally looked at as a vast advertising scheme."

A book-publishing house is in a somewhat different spot, politically, from the publisher of the average magazine or newspaper. With a few conspicuous exceptions, periodicals have always been committed to the political stand of their editorial boards. It is traditional for a book publisher to keep free of all *partis-pris*. He feels that the public expects him to present all views provided they are expressed in good books. His only standard is the goodness of a book as a book; if the book is political, then the author's case must be presented in the best possible way. What the case is, is not his concern. No matter how many heads may be shaken in his editorial office over the views in a book by Trotsky or Mussolini, the editor must give as careful attention to each — to its clarity, its perfection of form, its proper promotion — as if the views were his own. A general publishing house must be a forum.

There are sections of the public which do not fully understand this. Several times in the war years publishers have been "boycotted" by angry groups because of political, especially international, opinions. During a war or other period of great tension many books are called "dangerous." But as we look back on the history of political literature, we see a succession of books which at one time or another must have had a dangerous look. If the publisher keeps a vision of long range and, above all, if his balance is never upset by prejudice or hysteria, the chances are that no "boycott" will greatly harm either his reputation or the success of an individual book.

XVII

WAR

The Scribner House began its publishing in a war year. In 1846, the United States was in conflict with Mexico – a war which historians record with little ideological enthusiasm. At the time, however, the country was at a fever-pitch of patriotism.

It was not part of a publisher's job to rush to press books about a current war. Even the newspapers and news magazines had trouble getting information from what was then the very far West. Morse's new telegraph did something toward relaying war news, but it was not yet installed over long distances. But it was out of the question to assemble data fit for a book until years after the war ended.

The fervor inspired by the Mexican affair did, nevertheless, create a fertile field for books intended to make citizens proud of their country. Colorful descriptions of the Revolution, for which there had been plenty of time for research, were in demand. One of the first books the new firm of Baker and Scribner put out under its imprint was Joel T. Headley's *Washington and His Generals,* which this reverend gentleman threw together with record speed and which had an immediate and large sale. It was followed, before the war fever cooled, by the same author's *Napoleon and His Marshals,* telling of more recent if remoter battles, and that book's success shows that the American public of the mid-century had a wider international interest than is usually suspected.

The Civil War, during its four years' progress, was, of course, far better covered by the press and by such weeklies as Frank

Leslie's with lurid illustrations. But it did not get into books —
beyond abolitionist tracts and fly-by-night pamphlets. Indeed,
as long after as 1868, there is no book listed in any Scribner
catalog which deals with any phase of it. Historians still took
their time, and no doubt readers of history in those days would
have been dubious of anything given the dignity of a bound
volume which appeared sooner.

Much later, in the early 'eighties, the war was treated in
meticulous detail by two series: *Campaigns of the Civil War*
and *The Navy in the Civil War,* running into twenty volumes,
with maps and full statistics — books which are still consulted
as impeccable authorities. The Scribners also published lives
of Sherman, Sheridan and other generals in the 'eighties and
'nineties, and they are still publishing the immensely popular
work of Douglas Southall Freeman on General Lee and the
Confederate generals.

By the time of the Spanish War in '98, however, things had
changed. The public expected the work of war correspondents
to be presented them in book form before the guns had cooled.
As we look back at the little skirmishes of that conflict it is
amazing that it so engrossed the thought and business of the
country. Letters to and from editors show a hunger for print
and pictures about it almost as avid as we have today. But
with improved communications and presses it was possible to
satisfy it. Even books were in the stores in a good race against
the war's speed, and from that time what is now called a
"quickie" was a publishing possibility.

The Magazine was the feeder and the Magazine was on the
job. To Admiral George Dewey in Manila a cable was sent
on September 30, 1898:

"For your narrative of experiences in the war and since
sixty thousand words will pay you as follows ten thousand

dollars for exclusive right to publish serially in magazine ten thousand as advance on a twenty per cent royalty on book publication total twenty thousand with prospect of royalty exceeding."

To this the Admiral's Flag Secretary replied on the third of October:

"Rear Admiral Dewey desires me to confirm his cablegram to you of the 2d instant, as follows: 'Charles Scribner's New York many thanks. Lack time prevents acceptance. Dewey.'

"He desires me to say further that, it being impossible to send the cablegram 'Collect,' he paid $35.30 (Mexican) for it, and requests that you will send draft for that amount."

Still persistent, the editor wrote back on the sixth:

"While it is a matter of sincere regret to us to hear that you feel too much occupied to write at present, we can well appreciate this difficulty; but if in the future circumstances should change in this respect, we sincerely hope that you will be willing to communicate with us again and allow us to have another opportunity, perhaps at a less distance, to talk over with you some arrangement of the matter."

The Magazine was lucky in having for this war one of the most spectacular correspondents of all time. Richard Harding Davis was not only a good reporter; he was a sort of matinee idol of the period. He was handsome, dashing, picturesque; in his uniform he looked so much like a soldier that it almost seemed to his public that he had fought the war himself. More important still, he was a symbol; his character was held up to boys as an example. There had never been a whisper against his morals, his ideals were brave and pure, he seemed to be the very inventor — and certainly the most active personal promoter

— of sportsmanship. There are few American authors whose personalities were so closely woven into their writing. For the press-agent, the book or magazine or theater publicity man, he was what we should call a "natural," and publicity experts in that era were coming into their own. Davis's photograph alone — in any of his many vivid costumes — was enough, in an advertisement, to sell a lot of magazines or books.

Davis had both journalism and literature in his background. Rebecca Harding Davis had written distinguished fiction for a quarter century before Richard started his newspaper career. Her stories, says one biographer,* were "remarkable productions, distinct landmarks in the evolution of American fiction. Written when the American novel was in all its areas ultra-romantic and oversentimental, they are Russian-like in their grim and sordid realism." While her son never pursued this pattern, at least he had the stimulus of creative writing on one side.

On the other stood a journalist. His father was editor of the *Philadelphia Public Ledger*. The boy chose a newsroom as starter. He began on the *Philadelphia Record*. His first big job of reporting was the Johnstown Flood, which he covered for the Philadelphia *Press*. In 1889 he came to New York for the *Sun*, and on the side did articles and short stories for *Scribner's Magazine*. His fiction was more in tune with the times than his mother's and was instantly popular. For *Harper's Weekly* in the 'nineties he traveled; four books came out of this — *The Rulers of the Mediterranean*, *Our English Cousins*, *About Paris* and *Three Gringoes in Venezuela and Central America*. His fiction during this time took root from his journalistic activity; perhaps the most popular story he ever wrote was *Gallagher* (*Scribner's*, August, 1890), the story of a copy boy hero.

*"Rebecca Harding Davis," by Fred Lewis Pattee, in the *Dictionary of American Biography*, V, 143.

He knew a lot about the Spanish War before it began. In 1897, he tried to get behind the rebel lines in Cuba, but, failing this in a near-shipwreck, he got behind the Spanish ones and wrote about them for Hearst's *New York Journal.* The *Journal,* working overtime, then, to get the United States into war with Spain, so distorted his stories with its headlines that Davis to the end of his life would never write for Hearst again.*

By this time, the smell of powder had become so exciting to him that he could not resist a war, wherever it might be. War was the apex of romance to Davis and no matter how he might protest (and did protest) that it was "hell," the feel for it in his blood was translated, in his writing, into romance — at least up to 1914 when the German machine in Belgium changed even his writing. So when, in Cuba, a stronger smell of powder came to him across the Atlantic, he moved from the Caribbean to the Mediterranean, where Greeks and Turks, in 1897, were at each other's muzzle-ends. When the Turks won, he went to England in time for the London Jubilee and was there when the thunder of the *Maine's* explosion called him home.

The Spanish War, as we look at it now, seems almost like a Davis creation. In any case, it was a perfect Davis vehicle. It was a sailing and galloping war, fought by hunters and yachtsmen — a thoroughly sporting event. It took off, or everyone thought it did, from the pure impulse of rescuing the oppressed from a cruel tyranny. If we look into the details, many of them, like the useless disease casualties among the volunteer privates, are sordid enough. And, actually, Davis did not ignore these things. He often protested that the public did not take them seriously enough. But the public would take nothing from Davis but glamour. This was partly, no doubt, because it was a romantic public, yet a modern critic cannot wholly blame it.

Richard Harding Davis: His Day, by Fairfax Downey; New York: Scribners, 1933, p. 136.

Davis's approach to war stories as to everything else was very different, for example, from that of the late Ernie Pyle. It was a case, apparently, of the avidly reading public making certain inexorable demands and of Davis being the perfect reporter to supply them. So if, as his biographer, Fairfax Downey, explains, Davis's copy highlighted the "Volunteers who were a society page, a financial column, a sports section and a Wild West show, all rolled into and coming under the head of war news," it was not surprising if the readers passed lightly over the wounds and fevers of which he also wrote.

It was natural that Theodore Roosevelt should become a Davis hero. His Rough Riders were no less heroes in the 'nineties because they happened to be ex-college football stars or New York clubmen. Davis wrote the first account of his ride up San Juan Hill and, after it appeared in *Scribner's,* the New York State Republican Headquarters asked the editor's permission to reprint it as part of the campaign for Roosevelt for governor. And, in *Scribner's Magazine* in 1899, Roosevelt wrote his own story as a serial which later became a book.

Thus the two most conspicuous figures — in the land fighting at least — in the Spanish-American War were Scribner authors. They were fast friends. Finley Peter Dunne, also a Scribner author, alone in the midst of all the fanfare, flag-waving and patriotic sobbing of the war, saw its humor and put it in the speech of Mr. Dooley in a bit of fabricated T. R. monologue.

> *"At this time it became apparint that I was handicapped be th'presentce of th'Army an' Navy. A number of days was spent by me reconnoitring, attended only by me brave an'fluent body guard, Richard Harding Davis."*

In New York, however, Charles Scribner, under fire as he was from the guns of romantic correspondents, was not wholly captured by the glamour. Arriving from England in May, 1898, he wrote back to L. W. Bangs:

> "We arrived safely on Saturday noon after a very pleasant voyage. We met no Spanish gunboats and as we had some pleasant people on board and the sea was smooth it was an agreeable and restful week. Of course we were most anxious to hear the news on arrival but really nothing seems to have happened and the War situation is practically the same as when I last saw you. New York has not changed, and with the exception of an extra display of bunting and newspapers and the corresponding depression of business you would scarcely know that we were at war. There is however a strong patriotic spirit and a realization of the fact that this Spanish War is no picnic. I went out Wednesday afternoon to Camp Black, one of the recruiting grounds where about 9000 men are now in camp. Major Walter Schuyler (my cousin) is now the recruiting officer in charge and I saw everything to be seen. There are a good lot of young men entering the service and a good many tramps also. The worst sign thus far is the number of Colonels and other officers appointed for political and social reasons."

When the Spanish War was over R. H. D. did not rest long on his laurels. In 1899, he was in South Africa with the Boer Army where some of his copy lost him English friends. But the British at home were divided about the merits of that war.

> "We must seem to you," wrote Arthur Quiller-Couch to Charles Scribner, "to be engaged in a very silly war. I was one of the few who opposed it from the first: but this doesn't make me less anxious to see England get successfully through with the job."

Again, he wrote:

*"I tell you, sir, this war is no jest for the British author.
And when he doesn't happen to believe in it, and gets boo'ed
upon platforms for saying so the fun becomes small indeed.
However — I suppose we shall all get back to our right minds
and pay our Income Tax somehow."*

The Boer War had various effects in the United States. Some
of these are reflected in a letter from C.S. to L. W. Bangs in
December, 1899:

*"All the reports from London indicate that business is
very much interrupted by the war. The Boers are certainly
making a good showing. The newspapers here are supporting
England fairly well; among my friends there is a general
feeling that we must stand by England because she behaved
well in the Spanish War and no one likes to see the Empire
defeated, yet there is a general feeling that the Boers have
the right of it and that war should have been avoided.*

*"Business here is very good and the country is prosperous
though Wall Street is in a panicky condition."*

After the British victory, rest was imposed, for four years,
on the war correspondents and they turned to other pursuits.
In 1904, however, a new call came from the Pacific and the
Magazine found itself with three writers — Davis, John Fox,
Jr., and Thomas F. Millard in the field. But the public found
it difficult to get up much excitement about these faraway
battles, especially as the Japanese made it so difficult for the
reporters to see any of the fighting.

*"I feel much farther from the war," Fox wrote C.S. from
Yokohama in March, 1904, "here than I felt in New York.
Nobody seems to know anything. The first batch of correspondents (who have been here two months) go in three days
— destination as Palmer says — unknown even to themselves.*

The second will follow within 30 days. I am trying to get off with the first. . . ."

The following month he wrote again:

"I'm up here in the mountains for ten days just to get away from the awful smells of Tokyo.

> *"No call of the East for me*
> *Till the stink of the East be dead. . . .*

"The first column of correspondents — 5 Americans selected two weeks before I got here — has gone — nobody knows where as nobody knows when and where the second column — in which I am — will go. . . . I have concluded that no correspondent will be allowed to see a single big fight. He may be pointed out where it took place — afterwards. I believe the Japanese let the first go only because Griscom the minister pointed out that they might imperil the good-will of the American and the English Press.

(Miyanoshita, Sagami, Japan)."

By the time the war drew to its close, however, Fox had enough magazine articles for a book and C.S. wrote him cautiously:

"The last Magazine *article appears in the March number and I write now about a possible book. We have been rather afraid of war books and of course you did not see any actual fighting, but I am sure there would be a demand for your book and if you approve, we shall be glad to publish it.*

"There would be no illustrations, which in this case I think an advantage, and the book could be quickly made. . . . There would of course be some money in it for you and perhaps a considerable amount, though I hope that in this case,

as the book is not fiction, you would be satisfied with a 15%
royalty."

To Davis on the same date, January 25, 1905, he wrote:

"As you know, we were not very hot about the war articles
because the material seemed slight and the public seems to
receive the announcement of most war books with a tired
feeling. But of course there would be a market for yours and
if you finally decide to publish, you will find us ready."

John Fox, Jr.'s, first letter from Japan, quoted above, men-
tions "Palmer." This was Frederick Palmer who, in his long,
incredibly active life, has reported more major wars than any
other American correspondent. He has done eye-witness stories
on the Spanish, the Boer, the Russo-Japanese, and both World
Wars. At the age of seventy-five, he rode into Germany in a
jeep and later went to the Pacific with the Navy.

In 1913, the Scribners published a historic novel by Frederick Palmer. The following year he was called a prophet, a
clairvoyant, a mystic oracle. For, as World War I progressed,
it seemed that every detail of it had been predicted in *The
Last Shot*. The suddenness of its beginning, the methods of
invasion, the violation of treaties, the use of mammoth guns
to level the most formidable fortifications were all there. The
Scribner publicity man (a brash boy just out of college who
enjoyed pouring out the firm's money on his private literary
enthusiasms), exploited Palmer's prophetic phenomenon to the
limit, and it had a large sale at a time when other war books
were curiously hard to sell in America. ("As you know," Perkins wrote John Reed as late as 1916, "war books are not
moving rapidly.") Frederick Palmer plunged at once into the
war when it began and a number of Magazine articles and
books were the result.

In 1914, Davis's newspaper report of the German Army entering Brussels was regarded as the most serious and, generally speaking, the finest correspondent's job he ever did. "Unsensational," writes Fairfax Downey, "brilliant in its selection of telling detail, this magnificent description crowned the career of a great war correspondent. The world was stirred with its first glimpse of the grim, minute efficiency of the mighty German war machine. Davis's dispatch fired the public imagination and was quoted everywhere. Fellow correspondents and critics acclaimed it, and it ranks with the living literature of the World War."

Another Scribner author became deeply engrossed in the war as soon as it began. This was Edith Wharton, who was in France at the outbreak, and she went at once to work caring for homeless French children. In the fall of 1914, C.S. took a quick interest in her work. Her letter of thanks suggests what the war was already doing to authors' minds and work.

> *"I am very much touched by your sending me so generous a gift for the American Hostels. They have done so much good & are running so smoothly that we have been rewarded for all the hard work of starting them; but as the war lengthens we begin to wonder whether we shall be able to keep them open till the end, & a donation like yours is a great encouragement as well as a great help. . . .*
>
> *"I am beginning now to want to get back to work, & am kept back only by the steady drudgery of the charities in which like everyone else here, I am involved. At first I could not write, & it was maddening to think I could have made a little money for the charities I wanted so much to help, & yet to be absolutely pen-tied. . . ."*

But within a few months of this letter, Mrs. Wharton had turned correspondent herself. Women correspondents were so usual in the Second World War that it is an effort to remember how rare they were in the First. It not only took the kind of physical courage women were not yet expected to have but it took moral strength to overrule the traditions, and tact to persuade the military that a woman at the front was not dangerous to the security of army secrets. But Edith Wharton's zeal carried conviction.

"I was in the first line trenches," she wrote Robert Bridges in May, 1915, "in 2 bombarded towns, &c, &c — don't proclaim it too soon, for I don't want to be indiscreet; though of course I told the general in command that I wanted to write for you about what I saw, & had his consent and approval. Still, I think I was allowed by his staff officers to do even more than was in the programme, & though the tale may be told in yr. Sept. number it might be imprudent to specify too definitely now what I saw, especially as Norman Hapgood has just come back from the same quarter having failed to get into the first line trenches."

In June her letters showed that she had won the full confidence of the French staff.

"I have just had my permit from Head Quarters allowing me to make, in the north, the same kind of trip I have just made, in such exceptional conditions, in Lorraine & the Vosges. Of course one can never tell beforehand just what one's opportunities may be; but if I have anything like the good luck I had on my last expedition I can promise you an interesting article for October. I hope to send the Lorraine article in another eight days, & I shall have some good photos to send with it, taken directly in the trenches.

"I hope to get these photos off to you at the same time, but there has been a delay in getting them (they were done

for me by soldiers in the trenches), & I am writing again for them.

"I shd be glad to hear if you want the article on the North front also."

In this same month, a letter to her from Bridges contained a passage curiously relevant to an attitude which recurred, in various places, in 1945:

"I saw Norman Hapgood yesterday, just back unexpectedly from the other side. I did not of course make any inquiries about the Vosges. He was full of admiration for the way in which the French are conducting affairs. He seemed to have found some sentiment in England in favor of not being too severe with Germany in the final settlement, as in the next fifty years Germany may be a useful barrier between Russian and English interests. I do not believe there is much in it or that it is the opinion of a very important element."

Parallel with these trips to the front and a later one in Africa, Edith Wharton managed to keep her "hostels" running efficiently. In July, 1917, soon after his arrival in Paris, General Pershing wrote her:

"It would be impossible for me to express in a brief note the very high appreciation of your American friends in the army of your splendid service for the relief of destitute men, women and children of France and Belgium.

"Your work stands out pre-eminently in the long list of devoted effort that our people have voluntarily given to France. The Red Cross is now undertaking to co-ordinate these endeavors and I shall consider its mission a brilliant success if it even approximates your splendid achievement.

"May I not include my personal greetings when I say that

*you have earned the lasting gratitude of the people whom
you have served and have made Americans very proud of
the record of their fellow-countrywoman."*

The effect of war upon older authors who are unable to take part in it has always been disastrous to their thought, and the meeting of this disaster and triumphing over it is an act of high moral courage. The novelist has been especially hard hit by the two world wars — less, perhaps, because of the interruption of normal habits of work than by the sense in an artist's mind that his material was dissolving before him. With the coming of the war of 1939, all society, all the morals and customs, mental attitudes, emotional conflicts, which are a creative realist's basic material went suddenly into flux. A "novel of manners" became impossible because manners no longer seemed to exist, and how they would re-establish themselves no one knew. Overnight, normal situations and normal responses had become dated, and anything which might be written about the reversed human impulses might again become dated within the year. Some writers of fiction found their only way out in a historical story set in an era which was secure because it was far in the past.

The chaos in the years of the second war was so vast that it has made us forget the upheaval wrought by the first. But the impact of the social revolution of 1914 on sensitive interpreters of social behavior was, perhaps, even more violent. Then, moral attitudes a century or more old were — or seemed to be — suddenly abandoned. No doubt they had long been crowding the exits and the war had simply opened the doors. In their places came materialism, expediency and license of conduct in violent contrast to the long Victorian decorum. There came, too, the usual heroic war sacrifices which also upset the artists whose medium was life because they were romantic episodes. But in

1914 these things arrived without preparation whereas in 1939 they had had a quarter century of introduction.

Henry James, peculiarly a novelist of manners, recorded the impact in the third month of the First World War.

> "*It's difficult to work in face of the War monster — that is the trouble; he is so much bigger a reality than anything we can pit against him. If he ever comes to shrink again: — one can so but wonder* when! *— we shall doubtless leap astride of our own animals and set our lances in rest, performing in fact feats of gallantry beyond any in our record; but he looms too large for the moment for most of us, or for* me, *to do more than pretend just to keep in the saddle, sitting as tight as ever I can. See me please in this attitude, not unhorsed but a good deal held up; have patience with me as you have had it before, and I think I can promise you shall be justified. Those of us who shall outwear and outlast, who shall above all outlive, in the larger sense of the term, and outimagine, will be able to show for the adventure, I am convinced, a weight and quality that may be verily worth your having waited for. So, presumptuous as it may sound, those things are what I propose quite brilliantly to do — in testimony whereof I am yours, dear Mr. Scribner, very faithfully . . ."*

There is, here, the determination to keep his balance. But two months later, he had become emotionally involved along with the Englishmen among whom he lived. His letter to C.S. in December is so characteristic of his later manner, so prescient of the bitterness which at last caused the abandonment of his citizenship, so revealing of the effect of war upon a novelist's thought process that it deserves reproduction in full. It was written in answer to an assurance by C.S. that he and his friends were already strongly in line against the German aggression.

"*I think I quite understand what you tell me of American feeling in presence of our prodigious European situation. It is the feeling that I gather without exception from the letters of my relatives and friends on your side of the sea, and I couldn't ask or dream of anything better. I confess that without this impression and expression of it I should be deeply unhappy, so strong and distinguished, morally speaking, do I find the position of France and England, to say nothing of that of the inestimable Belgium, in face of the most insolent and fatuous arrogance of aggression that a group of self-restricting nations surely ever had to face. It is all very horrible, from this near view of ours — I mean the immeasurable, the unspeakably lamentable sacrifice of splendid young life and manhood is; but War even on the abominable scale on which we are being treated to it has in it this of infernally inspiring and exciting and even sustaining, that after the first horror and sickness, which are indeed unspeakable, Interest rises and rises and spreads enormous wings — resembling perhaps alas too much those of the hovering predatory vulture, and hangs sublime over the scene, as if not to lose a single aspect of its terrible human meaning. It is very dreadful, but after half dying with dismay and repugnance under the first shock of possibilities that I really believed had become extinct, I began little by little to feel them give an intensity to life (even at my time of it) which I wouldn't have passed away without knowing. Such is my monstrous state of mind, of sympathy, of participation, of devotion, let me frankly call it, in its poor way, touching all our tremendous strain and stress. The curse of these things, I admit, from the poor old discomfited artist's point of view, is that such realities play the devil even with his very best imaginations and intentions — so that he has, unless he gives everything up, to contrive some compromise between the operation of his genius (call it) and that of his immediate oppression and obsession, in which all sorts of immediate and subversive sympathies and curiosities and other damnable agitations are involved. He can fortunately say to himself that there is nothing of these even that won't be indirectly and eventually fertilising to his blest faculty — which yet for the time may so suffer from them; but he hates to be beaten if only temporarily, and — well, what I think I am saying, let alone feeling, in fine, is that I'm not beaten, not at all, but positively fighting as hard as if all the plans and proposals, all the begun things, in my head, were the arrayed and increasing Allies themselves, and the blight that presumptuously would be, but that steadily and inevitably less and less shall be, were the entirely objectionable and so far from insurmountably destructive Enemy. I have no less than three books admirably begun for you, but with one of them, for which present conditions are most favourable (or, more exactly stated, least unfavourable) stretching out his neck furthest in the race, and almost certain, I conceive, to come in first. On him I am now putting my money, and hope to let you know before long that he is within near sight of the winning-post. On this assurance believe me, dear Mr. Scribner, all faithfully yours . . ."*

In 1916, the unity of the British front was somewhat disturbed by events in Ireland. The Government in London believed not unplausibly that with conditions on the Western front as desperate as they were, it was no time for the Irish to renew agitation for an independent republic. But the means they used for repressing the uprising were repellent enough to at least one Irish Scribner author.

"I should have seen you before I left New York, but I was almost off my head with the happenings in Ireland. At one swift swoop they shot more poets than I care to count. I

knew most of them in Gaelic days better than I knew Rupert Brooke who was a dilletante compared to these stern Republicans. Or put it this way — they had chosen their cause before they began to write poetry. Brooke had finished his writing by the time his cause met him. It has been a hard war on the arts. The same St. George's day that Brooke died in Lemnos Sterling the young Oxford poet was killed in Flanders, and I met a painter the other day who could only moan that sixty winners of the Prix de Rome were slain in France. It looks as though only the pot-boilers will be left. We would all be relieved if some of the critics were killed, but apparently they are all being employed by the Censor, if I may judge from the tastelessness and ferocity with which some of my letters are treated.

"I hope my book will not shame you in England though it will grate on their war-nerves. I shall always be grateful to you for your kindness and interest in adopting it. I look upon it now as a rather misbegotten kind of elf and write in copies I give away — 'pour faire sourire les morts,' for the living are past laughter."

Shane Leslie was then working on *The Celt and the Teuton*, which seems to have caused the Scribners some concern, not because of any stand on the Irish question, but because it might look to the public, when it came out, as "another war book!" In the fall of 1916, E. L. Burlingame wrote him about this a letter which throws a light on the attitude of the American reading public toward such books less than nine months before the nation declared war.

"Mr. Scribner . . . has a feeling which I certainly share that the title is a little unfortunate for purely practical reasons because it would be almost certain to make the book classed in most people's minds as a book about the war — and

books about the war with a few natural exceptions are be-coming increasingly hard to sell. This is especially true of books of general discussion such as the announcement of 'Celt and Teuton' might seem to forecast and the impression would be an undoubted handicap to start with for a book which as a study is almost and might have been quite inde-pendent of the actual cataclysm. If the 'Teuton' could be got rid of or in some way subordinated so that from the start the really chief motif could be to the fore — the study of the Celt — the difficulty would disappear. . . ."

As the war clouds closed in upon the United States, early in 1917, a book by Mrs. Humphry Ward, *England's Effort,* was ready for the press. A letter to her from Maxwell Perkins in March reflects the jitters of the nation's press when the question of the book's syndication arose.

"The difficulty is . . ." he wrote, "that all the papers are very cautious indeed, and especially with regard to war material. Moreover, several of the more conspicuous papers in which syndication would have been particularly suitable had already made arrangement for special articles, which they thought was all that they could undertake to carry of that nature at present."

The progress of the war through that year was traced by Mrs. Ward's letters to C.S.

"I am amazed that you should say —'the situation at the front now is lacking in supreme importance.' Here we are hanging *on the news from Flanders, and feeling that it is* quite *on the cards there may be a* serious *peace offer before Christmas. The men at the front and the men coming home are extraordinarily confident.* Anything *may happen, when we have once completed the capture of the Passchendale*

*ridge, & it looks as though Haig were determined to accom-
plish it. I heard from Lord Cavan this week. He is with
General Plumer in the thick of the fighting. 'We are very
busy'— he says —'and very successful.' "*

And in December, to Perkins:

*"Alack! — the Cambrai battle has not yet given us Cam-
brai, & the withdrawals lately have been disappointing. But
after all we still have a great portion of the Hindenburg &
must have cost the enemy a terrible casualty list. . . .*

*"Do you think that a popular statement of the aims of the
Allies, as soon as they are once more re-stated, on this side
as well as on yours, would be likely to reach the American
public? General Charteris proposes to shew me the evacu-
ated districts about Ypres, & east of Bapaume — and he speaks
of 'the moral of the troops'— as being a matter on wh. it
would be useful to write. . . ."*

With America in the war, war books came into a new de-
mand here. In 1917 and 1918, Scribner's *Poems of Alan Seeger;*
Houghton Mifflin's *The First Hundred Thousand* by Ian Hay;
H. G. Wells's novel, *Mr. Britling Sees It Through* (Macmillan);
Donald Hankey's *A Student in Arms* (Dutton); James W.
Gerard's *My Four Years in Germany* (Doran); Henri Barbusse's *Under Fire* (Dutton); and Edward Streeter's *Dere
Mable* (Stokes) were on the best-seller lists along with three
"inspirational" books by Coningsby Dawson (John Lane) and
a good many "quickies." The demand lasted over to the fol-
lowing year when Blasco Ibáñez's *The Four Horsemen of the
Apocalypse* (Dutton) led the fiction list and then stopped
abruptly.

With the signing of peace, the curtain came down. The American people as a whole wanted to forget, wanted "normalcy,"

prosperity and automobiles, and its attitude was reflected by the book-buying public. Editors shook their heads as manuscripts by soldiers bursting with their experiences poured into the offices. To publish these books, thrilling and fascinating as many of them were, would have been a waste of time, money and paper. One post-mortem, Philip Gibbs's *Now It Can Be Told* (Harper), and John Maynard Keynes's dire prophecy, *Economic Consequences of the Peace* stood virtually alone on the lists of 1920, and neither of these had successes comparable with, for example, Empey's *Over the Top* in 1917.

When the curtain rose again, the glory had departed. War reappeared as unadulterated hell. The panoply was drab, the bugles played in discord. High words about making the world safe for democracy were lost in the mud; the temper of all who wrote now of the war was one of disillusion. The forerunner of the new war books was *Three Soldiers* by Dos Passos (Doran) in 1921, though the success of this novel was largely among the critics and the higher brackets of the reading public, the curtain being still down.

In 1923, Maxwell Perkins came upon a manuscript which he thought so fine that he was willing to go to the mat for it against all the prevailing prejudice. This was the novel *Through the Wheat* by Thomas Boyd. To check on his own feeling, he gave it to an editor who had spent two years in the army — including action in the Argonne. The response was immediate, the pressure of the whole editorial force became irresistible and Charles Scribner assumed the risk.

The book was not a large financial success, though it was far from a loss. But more important than this, it was hailed by the critics as a leader of the new war fiction, and so it proved. The Scribners' courage in giving it a chance to raise the curtain after a four years' intermission inspired other writers, and there came presently an epidemic of fine books, plays and movies. It was followed in 1924 by the tremendous success in the theater of "What Price Glory?" by Maxwell Anderson and Laurence Stallings, and *The Big Parade,* an international movie sensation, by Stallings in '25.

In 1925, too, came John W. Thomason's *Fix Bayonets.* Thomason was a captain of Marines, a brilliant draughtsman as well as a writer, and his book was powerfully illustrated with drawings sufficiently full of horror to fit the new war mood. Of *Fix Bayonets,* Alexander Woollcott wrote to Robert Bridges in March, 1925:

> *"I am returning herewith the galley proofs of* Fix Bayonets. *I kept them so long because I wanted to read the story twice with some interval between.*
>
> *"I think the story is magnificent and with the exception of* What Price Glory *I have run into nothing descriptive of the American soldier in the field which seemed to me so completely to re-capture the smell and flavor of the A. E. F.*
>
> *"I think this man writes magnificently and if, in the Sign Post piece I shall write for the June* Vanity Fair, *I express that feeling mildly, it will be in the conviction that he will be best served by someone merely pointing to his article, rather than by someone who shrieks his praises in advance. Thundering in the Index is no favor to anybody."*

Thomason himself acknowledged Boyd's mastery. "I think his work," he wrote Perkins in April, 1925, "is the ablest yet written on our part of the war."

In 1926, Scott Fitzgerald summed up the epidemic to date with credit to Boyd:

> *"God, what bad luck Tom Boyd had! Stallings made the killing with the play and movie; now Thomason makes a contract with Hearst for a lot, I guess, and Tom who came*

first came too early, I suppose. Yet What Price Glory? *would never have been written, I suppose, except for* Through the Wheat. *Not that Tom's novel wasn't a success in a way but to make about $6000. as an originator & see others rake it in like croupiers later — I know how bitter it must make him."*

Possibly Fitzgerald exaggerated Boyd's bitterness. It did not, certainly, stop him. He continued to write short stories of the war and, after a collection of these called *Points of Honor* had appeared, he wrote Perkins:

> *"In the mail Scribner's forwarded me came a letter from James G. Harbord, my divisional commander in France and later in charge of the S. O. S. . . . His letter has made me feel quite pleasant for a little while, and I thought you might like to know its contents:*
>
> *" 'My dear Mr. Boyd: . . . your very interesting . . . war stories — "Points of Honor" . . . are a truer picture of life as a man in the Marines must have seen it than anything else I have read. Every word of them is of special interest to me.' "*

For years, books, stories and pictures by John Thomason were features of the Magazine and he wrote regularly to Perkins from the various parts of the world to which the ships took him.

In 1926 came a letter suggesting that the movies, caught up also in the epidemic, had not kept up to the book level.

> *"You know, most of the war movies are bunk: fair-haired patriots springing to arms at their country's call, with ever a thought for home and beauty and the Dear Old Flag, and leaning up against a scared and pathetic enemy who burns futile powders, and so forth. There are a lot of things in* The Big Parade *that are fine — they showed it aboard last night — but there are a lot of other things that make me ill. I would not be a party to such a crime, if I could help it. No*

*need going into details; you know how **I** feel. (Have you ever seen anything as helpless and pitiful as German machine gunners in an American war picture?) — Oh, well——."*

From the Pacific in 1925, Thomason wrote prophetically:

"A lot of things," he told Perkins, "made me regret leaving New York. . . . But after all, this is my job. Twenty years from now, out in the Pacific, a bell is going to ring — I'll be there or the men I train will."

The bell rang four years before the twenty, and Colonel Thomason was there though he died before victory. Many of the other Scribner war writers were dead: Davis, Mrs. Wharton, Alan Seeger (who met his "Rendezvous" before his book was published), Mrs. Ward, John Reed and Tom Boyd. Of those who wrote of the First World War and survived to write of the second, the most brilliant was Ernest Hemingway.

A Farewell to Arms, published in 1929, was thought by the critics to be one of the greatest of the war novels. It gave — perhaps because it came so late — something quite new to the war story because it placed the war as a wholly abnormal — almost a romantic — episode in a setting of normality. Its last page, on which the hero looks back to his normal life and gropes for its threads, gives a sense of tragedy which sets the book apart from anything before it. In *For Whom the Bell Tolls,* set amidst the guerrilla fighters of the Spanish civil war, this same sense is present throughout the book, reached through the constant throwback of thought to the background of peace. This transition is, of course, the method of what many think the greatest war novel of all time, Tolstoi's *War and Peace.*

A reason, aside from its power as a novel, for the uninterrupted demand for *For Whom the Bell Tolls,* is its picture of the laboratory of World War II and, indeed, the pattern of underground fighting which underlay every orthodox military operation in Europe for at least five years of that war. Published in 1940, it held a place for two years on the best-seller list and has sold, in six years, nearly a million copies.

Between the wars, after Hitler had come into power in Germany, one of the most impressionable of all Scribner authors spent a time in Berlin. It was a vacation time for Tom Wolfe; he had gone abroad partly to escape from the American "literary world," which, as we have seen, had deeply embittered him. He reflected this bitterness, to some extent, upon America in general — at least momentarily. It was in this mood (in 1935) that he met the Germans, and they both refreshed and puzzled him.

"For two weeks I have done nothing but meet people of all sorts, go to parties, have interviews, get photographed by the Associated Press — and I have literally lived at the Ambassador's house. . . . It did finally get a little too much for us so yesterday Miss Dodd and I left Berlin in her car and all through a wonderful sunlit day drove . . . through this magnificent, beautiful and enchanted country. . . . We are going back to Berlin tomorrow through the wonderful Harz mountains and I have not space or power enough here to tell you how beautiful and fine and magical this trip has been. I am telling you all this because you and I have often talked about Germany and the German people whom you do not like as much as I do and about what has happened here in recent years. But I want to tell you that I do not see how anyone who comes here as I have come could possibly fail to love the country, its noble Gothic beauty and its lyrical loveliness, or to like the German people who are I think the cleanest, the kindest, the warmest-hearted, and the most honorable people I have met in Europe. I tell you this because I think a full and generous recognition must be made

of all these facts and because I have been told and felt things here which you and I can never live or stand for and which if they are true, as by every reason of intuition and faith and belief in the people with whom I have talked I must believe, are damnable.

"Now I so much want to see you and tell you what I have seen and heard, all that has been wonderful and beautiful and exciting, and about those things that are so hard to explain because one feels they are so evil and yet cannot say so justly in so many words as a hostile press and propaganda would, because this evil is so curiously and inextricably woven into a kind of wonderful hope which flourishes and inspires millions of people who are themselves, as I have told you certainly not evil, but one of the most child-like, kindly and susceptible people in the world. I shall certainly tell you about it — someday I should like to write something about it but if I now wrote even what I have heard and felt in two weeks, it might bring the greatest unhappiness and suffering upon people I have known here and who have shown me the most affectionate hospitality. But more and more I feel that we are all of us bound up and tainted by whatever guilt and evil there may be in this whole world and that we cannot accuse and condemn others without in the end coming back to an accusal of ourselves. We are all damned together, we are all tarred by the same stick and for what has happened here we are all in some degree responsible. This nation today is beyond the shadow of a vestige of a doubt full of uniforms and a stamp of marching men — I saw it with my own eyes yesterday in one hundred towns and villages across two hundred miles of the most peaceful, lovely and friendly looking country I have ever seen. A thousand groups, uncountable divisions of the people from children eight years old to men of fifty, all filled beyond a doubt with

hope, enthusiasm and inspired belief in a fatal and destruc-
tive thing — and the sun was shining all day long and the
fields the greenest, the woods the loveliest, the little towns
the cleanest and the faces and the voices of the people the
most friendly of any I have ever seen or heard so what is
there to say?"

It is important to compare this letter with a story published
two years later in the *New Republic* and afterwards incor-
porated (with changes) in the novel *You Can't Go Home
Again.* The story, "I Have a Thing to Tell You," shows the
growth in the interval of his bitterness against the "fatal and
destructive thing" he had found the people inspired to believe
in. It is the simple narrative of a train journey out of Germany
— its tragic episode the thwarted escape of a Jew. In the picture of the arresting officer, Wolfe releases his full fury.

"All of a sudden, without knowing why, I felt myself
trembling with a murderous and incomprehensible anger.
I wanted to smash that fat neck with the creases in it. I
wanted to pound that inflamed and blunted face into a jelly.
I wanted to kick square and hard, bury my foot, dead-center
in the obscene fleshiness of those clumsy buttocks. And I knew
that I was helpless. . . . I felt impotent, shackled, unable
to stir against the walls of an obscene authority."

Yet at the end of the story Wolfe distinguishes sharply between the evil thing symbolized by the officer and the people
— the "magic" land, "a geography of heart's desire." The conflict was acute.

Germany "was the dark lost Helen I had found, it was the
dark found Helen I had lost — and now I knew, as I had never
known before, the countless measure of my loss — the countless
measure of my gain — the way that would now be forever closed

to me — the way of exile and of no return — and another way that I had found. For I knew that I was 'out.' And that I had now found my way."*

If this story has escaped any of Wolfe's devoted readers, he will probably find it worth his while to look it up in its original form. Like the letter transcribed above it is essential to a full understanding of this author's mind under the impact of the threat he did not live to see fulfilled.

The Scribners had their share of the immense volume of books about, and inspired by, the Second World War. Correspondents in this war had opportunities to see action with the armed forces far greater than in the fighting of 1914–18. And the public, too, was more avid than then for books of action, of personal experience, journalistic as they might necessarily be.

It is still too soon for novels and we may only guess at their temper. Perhaps the best of the first war are still to come. *The Red Badge of Courage* appeared more than thirty years after the end of the Civil War. And, as late as 1944, a large part of the reading public was diverted from current events by Joseph Stanley Pennell's *The History of Rome Hanks*, a Civil War story. So, if literature is spared by the atomic bomb, we may look far ahead for fiction based on the late conflict to reach its apex of power and popularity.

*The *New Republic,* March 10, 17 and 24, 1937; Vol. XC, Nos. 1162, 1163, 1164.

XVIII

THE NEXT HUNDRED YEARS

The future of literature — intricately connected with the future of its midwife, the publishing business — is as dangerous and as fascinating to speculate upon as any phase of the nation's activity. The guessers, as always, are busy assembling statistics, trends of the past, and in the modern manner are working with the aid of graphs. Seasoned critics have spotted the highs and the lows, basing their spots perhaps on what might loosely be called the comparative immortality of the products. The spots become less certain as they are more recent; lately there have been curious and unexpected waves of revival which have washed some of them away. The waves are not new; after all there was a thing called the Renaissance which revived books buried under more than a millennium of oblivion. It is only that now there seem to be more waves.

A few years ago there were resurrections of the Brontës, Anthony Trollope and Jane Austen, whose novels of manners presumably belonged to an era on which the door had definitely shut. Today, after an epidemic of bare style, word economy and brutal directness, the complex and often oblique Henry James is having a new vogue. So it is never safe to say that a book or a genre is dead or fatally dated.

During a time of turbulence and war, creative writing is supposed to decline and then to have a vigorous revival in the following era. Lately students of trends have pointed to the fine period of production in the 'twenties when post-war disillusion and reflection restored the artists' equilibrium after the patriotic fever. They observe, however, that as the threat grew

[328]

of the second war, after the middle 'thirties, writers of fiction became so enmeshed in causes — political, social and economic — that they lost their detachment and their art suffered accordingly. Now these prophets are predicting a repetition of the cycle, granted a reasonably long interval of peace.

And what of publishing? What of the actual physical forms of books? There is no question that, whether the public is better informed, sager, more curious or more educated, or whether sales methods have improved, there is more actual book buying than ever before. Some promoters have found this so encouraging that they have made new plans for the quantity production of cheap books — not reprints, but new books, both fiction and the "serious" variety. If this happens, will the old-time publisher — with his special, careful, warm relations with authors; his watchfulness over the details of printing, binding and intensive selling — disappear?

There have been threats before. Schemes for cheap books have been tried and were occasionally successful. With all the new devices for articulation and entertainment: movies, broadcasting, picture magazines, television — it was supposed that people might stop reading entirely and substitute quick visual and audible impressions for the intellectual process of translating little black marks into thoughts and ideas. Other skeptics were alarmed by the avidity for "digested" books and stories and articles. Yet what actually happened under these awful menaces? The serious reading public grew by leaps and bounds. More and more fine books were put out, sales of expensive books increased, the prosperity of the old publishers and their authors grew perennially.

The answer, probably, is in the enormous reservoir of potential readers. All the devices are leading them out of the dark, inducing them to new awareness, bringing them to the point where the devices no longer satisfy. If a movie or a broadcast makes a man think who never thought before, his thinking is likely to go on of its own momentum reaching toward new fields. He may progress from a movie to an illustrated magazine; from the caption of a picture to a story or article; from a digested piece his curiosity may lead him to seek the full one; from a cheap paper book may come the desire to own and range on his shelves beautiful and substantial volumes. So, more and more people are climbing the stairs, so to speak, and every day more are arriving at the top.

It is unlikely, therefore, that the best of serious writing is likely to suffer in any predictable future. No honest graph made today can fail to show an upward line.

The chances seem to be, then, that publishing on the highest level will continue to defy competition. Publishers on that level will prosper but they will not grow rich, for a subtle demon will be forever prodding them, distracting them from the pure and simple gold. Behind the demon will stalk an author; a new, peculiar author with an odd and fascinating ware, a commodity that will glitter in the market of the few, unfit for mass production. It will be fun, says the demon, to print his book, a deep inside delight, more warming than ancient brandy, more quickening than vintage champagne. And the publisher will pass up the acres he dreamed of adding to his land, the new wing to his house, the extra car to his garage, to print a book that will sell in the currency of satisfaction. He has always done it and he always will. The weakness was born in him or he would never have become a publisher on the highest level, and if it dies in him he will fall off and somebody else will climb up to where he was.

All this does not mean, however, that in normal times of the future he will not be richer than he was a century ago. He will, and the author with him. In the past fifty years, the author-publisher coalition has gone a long way toward coming into its own. The author has progressed (with the aid of the great philanthropists of Hollywood) almost from oatmeal to caviar. In the fringe of every writer's dreams today are serials, first and second, the stage, movies, radio, television, book clubs and an alert press watching for him. Even if his book fails to meet the expense of writing it, it may plant a demand for his future work in a dozen fields. And all these things help the publisher too, for in the new world that new communications and new media of articulation have made so compact, an infection on the air spreads wide and fast.

Anyone who saw Europe in the late war or in the time just after it must have become poignantly aware of what a craving has come to the people of the interrupted civilizations for material to read. Under the Occupations, reading outside the formulas became so clandestine and difficult that a hunger grew, greater sometimes than the hunger of the body. An author-editor who went, in the early months of 1945 to France and Italy, was asked, again and again, by the spiritually starved folk: "Tell us of the books: what has come out in the world since we were cut off; what is happening to writers, what are they saying? When you go home, send us books, magazines, print — for God's sake send us books!" And in the Army, in the Nissen huts behind the line, in the outposts and the dugouts, lay the copies of the Service Books, tattered, dog-eared, stained and spattered with the print literally read out of them. When this author-editor landed for refueling in Greenland, the men of the ATC base there stormed his plane, searched under the seats for papers, magazines, books, for God's sake something to read besides the labels on the K-ration boxes!

These are the things that make us know here, flooded with print, where a book for a dime or a dollar or five means only a walk round the corner, what happens to people when the print stops.

[331]

So publishing will go on; the shy author, the distraught author, the captious author will still seek the foyer of his publisher and find warmth there, an easing of his tension, a straightening of his mood. And it is likely too that, whatever the clamor of the air outside, blaring with loud speakers and droning with propellers, he will find quiet there and a chance to think.

The House of Scribner is facing these possibilities robustly. As far as its authors can see the century has added no apparent heaviness to its shoulders. A new generation, interrupted by the war, is settling into its place. George McKay Schieffelin, C.S.'s grandson, back from the Navy, is already an experienced hand in publishing. The fourth Charles is on his way in.

The chief of the editorial staff continues as he works to doodle portraits of Napoleon which with each passing year bear a more and more convincing resemblance to Maxwell Perkins. Across from him in the old north office, beneath the portraits of his father and grandfather, sits Charlie Scribner and welcomes his visitors — authors and employees — with a mellowness of humor which it has taken, perhaps, three generations of experience and renewing youth to evolve. His modesty is conspicuous as if, indeed, the uninterrupted continuity of a business in a single family for a hundred years were the most natural thing in the world.

INDEX

Adams, Henry, *Education*, 124, 135, 140, 271; on history, 20, 140, 157, 158; *History of the United States*, 157, 158; request for magazine article, 276.

Adams, James Truslow, historical method, 140, 158; *The March of Democracy*, 139.

Adirondacks, 18, 57.

Advertising, publisher's, 28, 90, 91, 116 ff., 203, 309.

Agents, book, 147 ff.

Agents, literary, 10, 53, 54, 55, 65, 165.

Aiken, Conrad, 263, 265, 266.

Alcott, Louisa M., 200.

Aldrich, Thomas Bailey, 200.

Alice in Wonderland by Lewis Carroll, 226.

Amazing Marriage, The, by George Meredith, 46.

American Council of Learned Societies, 159.

American Magazine, 220.

American Prose Masters by William C. Brownell, 156.

Americanization of Edward Bok by Edward Bok, 141, 221.

Anderson, Maxwell, 321.

Anderson, Sherwood, letter on novel, 13; letter to Perkins, 1935, 10; on poetry, 34.

Andrews, E. Benjamin, 288.

Anthologies, 268.

Appleton's Magazine, 196.

Arabia Deserta, 14.

Arnold, Edwin, 29, 56, 218, 263, 264.

Arnold, Matthew, 248.

Arrow of Gold by Joseph Conrad, 135.

Arthurs, Stanley M., 237.

Ashley, Clifford, 237.

Atherton, Gertrude, 76, 77.

Atlantic Monthly, 134, 219.

Atlas of American History, 159, 160.

Atomic bomb, 327.

Austen, Jane, 328.

Authors, advances to, 38, 39, 190; and advertising, 29, 30; amateur, 52; creative, 1, 79; effect of war on, 313 ff., 328; financial troubles, 204; first acceptance, 42, 43, 62, 63; first meetings with publishers, 40 ff.; "getting in a rut," 29; humility of, 4; and illustrators, 226 ff.; intimacy with publisher, 15, 55, 56; loneliness of, 1 ff.; loyalty to publisher, 30, 31, 48, 52, 169 ff.; magazine's aid to, 211, 212, 219; of mystery stories, 11, 20; new, 12, 32, 53, 109 ff.; pathology of, 6, 9; professional, 52, 53; revisions by, 11, 46, 91 ff., 110; on strike, 54; tools of, 13 ff.; young, 15, 32, 62, 63, 82; violent emotions of, 6, 29, 94, 95, 122, 167.

Aylward, W. J., 237.

Backlog, 138, 144 ff.

Badger, Richard, 255, 255 n.

Bailey, Frankie, 239.

Baker & Scribner, 57, 75, 76, 78.

Baker, Isaac D., 75, 76.

Baker, Ray Stannard, 296.

Balzac, Honoré de, 9.

Bangs, Lemuel W., appearance, 164; C.S.'s letter on Boer War, 307; English representative, 1893, 54; 1911, 66, 86; and W. E. Henley, 250; and George Moore, 86; C.S.'s letter to, on Spanish War, 306; C.S.'s letter to, on U. S. Grant, 284; wardrobe, 164, 165.

Barbusse, Henri, 319.

Barrack Room Ballads by Rudyard Kipling, 249.

Barrie, James M., at Box Hill, 45, 46; on "brilliant" writing, 10; collected works, 168; and Conan Doyle, 47; early poverty, 211, 212; estimate of Burlingame, 209; and E. W. Hornung, 47; late attitude toward, 9; *The Little White Bird,* 218; on

and Howard Pyle, 227; relations with Scribner's, 29; "The Rhyme of True Thomas," 270; sales, 132, 249; and Charles Scribner, 43; and *Scribner's Magazine*, 211, 215, 249; *The Seven Seas*, 270; "The Ship that Found Herself," 215; suggests authors, 48, 49; "They," 218; and white man's burden, 49; "Wireless," 218; on World War I, 295.

Kipps by H. G. Wells, 38, 65, 86, 97, 98.

Knopf, Alfred, 127.

Korea, 222.

Ladies' Home Journal, 216, 246, 298.

Lambert, Alexander, 222.

Lamp, The, 203.

Lang, Andrew, 218.

Langford, N. P., 199.

Lanier, Sidney, 126, 156, 263, 264.

Lape, Esther Everett, 298.

Larcom, Lucy, 200.

Lardner, Ring, and Fitzgerald, 16; "Haircut," 16; short stories, 223.

Lawrence, D. H., 181.

Lawsuits, 127 ff.

Leacock, Stephen, 131.

Lee, Arthur, 216.

Lee, Gerald Stanley, 203.

Lee's Lieutenants by Douglas S. Freeman, 57, 58, 301.

Leech, John, 242.

Leslie, Shane, *The End of the Chapter*, 47; *The Celt and the Teuton*, 317, 318; on critics, 123; introduces F. S. Fitzgerald, 48; on Irish disturbances, 316 ff.

Letters to His Children by Theodore Roosevelt, 135, 136.

Levering, Albert, 242.

Levermore, Charles H., 298.

Lewis, Sinclair, *Main Street*, 136.

Libel, 96.

Liberty, 220.

Lincoln, Abraham, 193, 208.

Linn, James Weber, 154.

Lippincott's Magazine, 195.

Literary World, The, 74.

Literature, future of, 328 ff.

Little Lord Fauntleroy by Frances Hodgson Burnett, 227.

Little Treasury of Modern Poetry, A, edited by Oscar Williams, 268.

Little White Bird, The, by James M. Barrie, 218.

Locke, William J., 132.

Lodge, Henry Cabot, 238, 295 ff.

Loeb, William, Jr., 280, 281.

London *Times*, 295.

Look Homeward, Angel by T. Wolfe, 7, 16, 174.

Looking Backward by Edward Bellamy, 38, 132.

Lord, Edward T., 152 ff.

Lost generation, The, 47, 138.

Lovett, Robert Morss, 154.

Lowell, James Russell, 206.

Lucas, Seymour, 239.

Lucky Sam McCarver by S. Howard, 14.

Lusitania, 294.

Luther, Martin, 193.

Mabie, Hamilton, 203.

MacGrath, Harold, 132.

Maclaren, Ian, 132.

Macmillan Company, 118, 135, 257.

Magazines, advertising in, 217 ff.; appeal to women, 191; early American, 75, 191 ff.; as feeders to book-house, 196, 219; and morality, 82, 83; poetry in, 249 ff.; religious, 191 ff.; "slick," 245, 246.

Maid in Waiting by John Galsworthy, 138.

Main Street by Sinclair Lewis, 136.

Major, Charles, 132.

Man of Property, The, by John Galsworthy, 138.

Mann, Joseph McElroy, 104.

Manuscripts, declined, 38 f., 61 ff.; "not read," 52; preparation of, 34.

Mapes, Mary (see Dodge, Mary Mapes).

March of Democracy, The, by James Truslow Adams, 139.

Marching On by James Boyd, 93, 94, 102, 114.

Marks, Percy, 137.

Marquand, John, 17, 29.

Marquis, Don, 43, 219, 220, 223, 224.

Martin, Edward S., 203.

Martin, Henri, Restaurant, 241.